CLOSING THE CIRCLE

CLOSING THE CIRCLE

Environmental Justice
in Indian Country

James M. Grijalva

CAROLINA ACADEMIC PRESS
Durham, North Carolina

Library of Congress Cataloging-in-Publication Data

Grijalva, James M.
  Closing the circle : environmental justice in Indian country / by James M.
Grijalva.
      p. cm.
  Includes bibliographical references and index.
  ISBN-13: 978-1-59460-341-9 (alk. paper)
  ISBN-10: 1-59460-341-3 (alk. paper)
1. Indians of North America--Legal status, laws, etc. 2. Environmental law--
United States. 3. Indians of North America--Government relations. I. Title.

  KF8210.N37G75 2008
  344.7304'6--dc22

                                                                  2007044667

Carolina Academic Press
700 Kent Street
Durham, North Carolina 27701
Telephone (919) 489-7486
Fax (919) 493-5668
www.cap-press.com

Printed in the United States of America

For Theresa, Rosa, Louis and Carmen

CONTENTS

PREFACE

Though I wasn't aware of it at the time, my first exposure to the concept of Indian country environmental justice was in 1972 and, odd as it sounds, occurred because of a baseball bat. My father, soon to become a career Indian Health Service dentist, was assigned to the Colorado River Indian Tribes' reservation near Parker, Arizona for the summer. It was hot. Daytime temperatures frequently exceeded 112°. One of those days I was looking for shade along the irrigation ditch that ran near our government house and came across an old wooden baseball bat sticking out of a heap of discarded garbage. As any eight-year old American boy would, I immediately recognized the bat for the treasure it was and took it home, not realizing that I had just scavenged in an Indian country open dump.

Many years later, after spending the rest of my childhood living in and near Indian country in New Mexico, Arizona, South Dakota and Alaska, I enrolled in the environmental law program at Lewis & Clark law school in Oregon. I was fortunate to be there when Michael Blumm taught one of the nation's first Indian country environmental law courses, using materials compiled by Judy Royster, who was at that time a natural resource fellow at the school. Judy later became one of the country's leading authorities on natural resource and environmental law in Indian country, coauthoring with Mike the only casebook on those subjects. Coincidentally, as a member of the law review at Lewis & Clark, I worked on an article[1] analyzing one of the cases we studied—a federal decision out of Washington on hazardous waste management in Indian country—authored by Richard DuBey, a Seattle attorney who represented multiple Indian tribes in filing an amicus brief in the case.

Upon graduation, my spouse Theresa and I headed south to paddle our kayaks down the mighty Colorado River through Grand Canyon with a dozen friends. After 225 miles of huge whitewater rapids, dramatic canyon walls, serene beach camps, and wondrous side hikes, none of us were happy to see the commercial shuttle driver parked at the river takeout on the Peach Springs Indian Reservation. We loaded our gear, took a group photo, and the driver took us up the slow rocky road out of the canyon, stopping near the top to throw the trash and waste we generated during the eighteen-day trip into the Hualapai Tribe's unsupervised community dump. A month earlier a federal court in South Dakota had held the federal government and an Indian tribe liable for operating dumps very similar to that one. On the long ride back to Flagstaff I couldn't help thinking about the baseball bat I found seventeen years earlier in a pile of garbage on the Colorado River Tribes' reservation a few hundred miles downstream.

I began my law practice in the litigation department of a Seattle law firm that wanted to build an environmental law practice group. Six months later the firm hired an experienced environmental lawyer to chair the group, Richard DuBey, who wrote the Indian country hazardous waste article I helped edit in law school. Richard brought his client the Puyallup Tribe of Indians, and soon I was spending most of my time developing tribal environmental programs and negotiating federal claims for damages to tribal natural resources from hazardous substance releases in the Commencement Bay Superfund site near Tacoma, Washington. In 1992, the National Law Journal published a special investigation on environmental justice and focused part of its attention on the Puyallup Tribe, quoting Bill Sullivan, the Tribe's environmental director and my primary contact, as saying that the Tribe acted as the conscience for the U.S. Environmental Protection Agency (EPA) in the slow, grinding process of the Superfund cleanup. I thought those words rang true, and they have stuck with me over the years. Michael O'Connell, former general counsel to the Hopi Tribe, later joined us and we built a vibrant Indian country environmental law subcomponent to the firm's more traditional environmental law practice.

When the opportunity arose to realize my passion for teaching, I left the firm for the University of North Dakota, in the heart of Indian county on the northern plains. Silas Ironheart, environmental director of the nearby Spirit Lake Nation, soon asked if I would speak with the Tribal Council about the opportunities for tribal governmental roles within federal environmental law programs. Shortly thereafter, I started the Tribal Environmental Law Project as a component of the University's Northern Plains Indian Law Center, and my students and I helped Si and the Spirit Lake Nation prepare a successful application for treatment-as-a-state under the Clean Water Act. Since that time the Project has worked with some twenty-five tribes across the country in various capacities on multiple environmental law issues.

Those experiences have driven home for me Bill Sullivan's comment that Indian tribes can act as EPA's conscience. In a larger sense tribes also bring a measure of human humility and respect for the natural world modern American environmental law seemingly lacks but, I think, desperately needs. The presence of tribes at the table helps remind federal and state bureaucrats why environmental management programs exist in the first place, and contributes unique perspectives on the challenges of achieving the shared goals of reducing and eliminating harmful environmental pollution risks.

Of course, tribes have to be at the table for that to happen. Regrettably, too often they are not, or if present they lack the leverage necessary for garnering genuine respect from the other players. One of the main premises of this book is that tribes' absence from the national dialogue and implementation of federal environmental programs is largely responsible for creating environmental injustice in Indian country, the concept that some minority communities suffer disproportionately higher environmental risks than many white communities. The several reasons and explanations for tribes' limited influence trace their roots to an anomalous confluence of federal environmental, administrative and Indian law creating the perception if not the reality of a regulatory void in Indian country.

The overall thesis I put forward here is that the most potent available solution for realizing Indian country environmental justice derives from the same combination of factors that caused it. Courts have fairly consistently deferred to EPA's administrative discretion and expertise in reconciling environmental law and policy with Indian law and policy. The Agency has repeatedly exercised its substantial authority under the modern environmental laws to link Congress' preference for local program implementation with federal Indian law's doctrine of retained tribal sovereignty in a legal and administrative framework effectively offering tribes a coequal seat at the table. The seat comes with an unparalleled opportunity for translating tribal environmental value judgments into federally enforceable requirements constraining Indian and non-Indian polluters inside and outside Indian country. It offers a genuine chance for tribes to protect and preserve the health and welfare of their citizens, the quality of the Indian country environment, and most importantly, their land-based indigenous culture.

The book begins by describing the similarities and differences between the environmental justice issues facing Indian country and other communities, notes the generally unrecognized presence of Indian issues and indigenous peoples in the development of the environmental justice movement, and highlights the literature's more fundamental omission of the government's first programmatic environmental justice actions, taken in Indian country. The second chapter continues the foundation by examining the origins of EPA's Indian program that derived from its recognition long before the movement began that Indian people faced unacceptable disproportionate environmental risks requiring strategic federal attention. Chapters three through six identify the primary themes of the Indian program through detailed but accessible accounts of how particular media-specific regulatory programs have been or can been applied to Indian country, and the unique challenges they presented and continue to present. The book concludes with my belief that, at least for the moment, the most effective opportunity for achieving environmental justice in Indian country is the development of tribal environmental management programs within the rubric of federal environmental law, allowing tribes to reconcile for themselves the cultural dissonance between western tolerance for environmental degradation and sacred indigenous obligations to all their relations.

ACKNOWLEDGMENTS

My personal and professional associations with many people contributed greatly to the writing of this book. I simply could not have completed it without the love and support my spouse Theresa Grijalva has bestowed on me for over twenty years. My children, Rosa, Louis and Carmen, don't understand why the book has no pictures, but their smiles and encouragement and the original artwork that adorns my home office kept me going on many occasions. My mother Jane Welch-Sprague's longstanding work with non-profit charitable organizations of every sort, and my father Michael Grijalva's devotion to a career in Indian health, helped instill in me a strong social justice ethic that has found its outlet in the subject of this book.

Numerous tribal and federal environmental lawyers have generously shared their insights, advice and experience with me over the years, including Richard DuBey, Michael O'Connell, Dean Suagee, Tom Schlosser, Kayln Free, Kevin Washburn, Elizabeth Bell, Rich McAllister, and the late Leigh Price who wrote EPA's Indian Policy. Several key EPA environmental staff have also freely shared their knowledge, patiently answered my many questions, and labored to locate obscure documents, including Ella Mulford, Casey Ambutas, and Danny Gogal. I'm indebted to the many tribal council members and tribal environmental agency staff that gave me the opportunity to work with them, and wish particularly to recognize Bill Sullivan at the Puyallup Tribe and Silas Ironheart at the Spirit Lake Nation. Members of several indigenous environmental justice groups have helped me see new angles on these topics, especially Tom Goldtooth of the Indigenous Environmental Network, Lori Goodman and Anna Frazier of Diné CARE, Enei Begay of the Black Mesa Water Coalition, and Jolene Catron of the Indigenous Waters Network.

Most of the ideas presented in this book were developed, tested and refined over the course of ten years teaching in the summer environmental law program at Vermont Law School. I am grateful to two consecutive directors of the School's Environmental Law Center, Patrick Parenteau and Karin Sheldon, for continuing to invite me back year after year.

At the University of North Dakota I received significant research support from a cadre of fine law students, including Betsy Spain-Elsberry, Joe Vacek, John Hoff, Crystal Ovsak, and Tim Richards. Rhonda Schwartz and Kaaren Pupino in the Thormodsgard Law Library were relentless in their search for supporting material and never once showed dismay in the face of repeated requests for ancient congressional reports. I also benefited from institutional research support graciously provided by two law deans, Candace Zierdt and Paul LeBel.

CLOSING THE CIRCLE

CHAPTER 1

INTRODUCTION: SEEKING ENVIRONMENTAL JUSTICE IN INDIAN COUNTRY

A growing body of scholarly literature offers a fascinating diversity of opinion on the theoretical and practical underpinnings of the contours, causes and challenges of environmental justice. Most commenters agree, however, that as a socio-political phenomenon the environmental justice movement in the United States blossomed in response to the appearance of various studies and reports in the 1980s and early 1990s suggesting the world's most progressive environmental regulatory nation was overlooking its more vulnerable populations.[1] People of color and those from low-income communities rallied around impassioned allegations of environmental racism, drawing strength from a variety of earlier movements challenging systemic inequities in the administration of government—civil rights, organized labor, American Indian self-determination, grassroots and anti-toxics—and some support from the mainstream environmental movement.[2] Policy and program actions taken in the 1990s by the federal executive branch and particularly the United States Environmental Protection Agency (EPA) in response to the growing public pressure for equity are typically cited as the first official governmental efforts confronting environmental injustice.[3]

Indian people are fairly accustomed to seeing social movements and federal initiatives come last to Indian country if at all. Too often its seems Indian concerns are at best an afterthought in the political, popular and scholarly dialogue on pressing national issues like civil rights, economic empowerment, criminal justice, health care, education and environmental protection. But that was not the case for the environmental justice movement or EPA's programmatic reactions to it. Though largely overlooked in the literature, Indian issues and indigenous activists were present at every stage of the modern movement's evolution, and EPA's environmental justice program responses

3

consistently included specific strategies for seeking equitable protection of the Indian country environment.

The reason for the Agency's specific and separate attention to Indian country has been noted in a small but growing body of Indian environmental justice scholarship.[4] Indian tribes' status as sovereign governments under federal law and their strong cultural and spiritual connections with the natural environment uniquely distinguishes them from every other minority and low-income group affected by environmental injustice. To be sure, citizens of America's tribal nations often face a variety of disproportionately high health and environmental risks from multiple pollution sources just as members of other groups do. Yet, the existence of such risks may derive more from jurisdictional uncertainties hampering effective regulatory control than unfair program implementation, and their solution may lie in tribes' inherent powers over their territories.

EPA recognized both of those possibilities shortly after the first Earth Day and other significant developments in 1970 marked the beginning of the modern age of American environmental law and regulation. Tribes' homelands would simply be left out of the new federal programs being developed and implemented across the nation unless some creative action was taken. Scholarly commentary to the contrary notwithstanding, EPA's reaction to that threat some twenty years before the environmental justice movement began was the first time the federal government confronted the possibility of disproportionate environmental risks affecting minority communities

The Environmental Justice Movement

Data collected in the 1980s and early 1990s by the federal government and independent organizations demonstrated disturbing correlations between race, income and environmental threats ostensibly controlled by the modern laws. Following the 1982 arrest of 500 protesters for civil disobedience in opposing the siting of a polychlorinated biphenyl waste disposal facility in a predominantly poor African-American community in North Carolina, the U.S. General Accounting Office surveyed the racial composition of communities surrounding four existing hazardous waste landfills in the southeastern United States and found African-Americans constituted the majority population in three of them. The United Church of Christ Commission for Racial Justice, which participated in the North Carolina protests, expanded the geographic focus in 1987, reporting a statistically significant correlation nationally between race and proximity to commercial hazardous waste facilities like land-fills, lagoons and incinerators, and to closed or abandoned toxic waste sites.[5]

In early 1990, at the University of Michigan School of Natural Resources Conference on Race and the Incidence of Environmental Hazards, a coalition of social scientists, academics and civil rights activists formed and requested EPA initiate a series of actions addressing the mounting evidence of disproportionate environmental impacts on minority and low-income communities. EPA Administrator William Reilly responded by constituting within the Agency an Environmental Equity Workgroup charged with reviewing the evidence and considering how existing EPA programs, risk assessment and communication guidelines, institutional relationships and outreach might give rise to inequitable risk reduction and be adjusted to correct such instances. In 1991, Reilly announced by memorandum to his staff the Agency's first official position on the subject: "The consequences of environmental pollution should not be borne disproportionately by any segment of the population."

That same year the movement coalesced with an unprecedented First National People of Color Environmental Leadership Summit where community activists issued a set of seventeen principles under the terminology of environmental justice. The earlier term environmental racism's implicit focus on intentional discriminatory decisions arguably overlooked disproportionate impacts created inadvertently and seemed preoccupied with identifying problems rather than solutions, and EPA's term environmental equity implied a redistribution of risks among racial and economic groups rather than overall reduction and elimination of risks.

The Summit's principles and the movement they helped foment instead attacked the causes and consequences of disproportionate environmental impacts from four broad justice perspectives.[6] Distributive justice sought more equal protection through a lowering of environmental risks rather than a shifting or reallocation of existing risks. Corrective justice urged more equal governmental enforcement in minority and low-income communities, and sanctions and remedies on par with those routinely ordered in more affluent white communities. Procedural justice confronted the reality that the people most affected were often not included in the government's decision-making processes, or if they were, lacked the resources and information necessary to participate effectively. The broad concept of social justice tried to take account of both public health and economic opportunity as indispensable aspects of the quality of life in these communities; people should not be faced with choosing between an unsafe livelihood and unemployment.

The 1992 report of EPA's Workgroup retained the environmental equity term but incorporated much of the justice approach in focusing on the distribution and effects of environmental problems, the process for making environmental policy, and how environmental programs were being administered.[7] To no one's surprise, the Workgroup found a general lack of existing data on environmental health effects analyzed by race and income, and wide variation in the extent to which different Agency programs and regions accounted for environmental equity issues. Reilly responded to the Workgroup's suggestion for prioritizing those issues in a more centralized fashion by creating the Office of Environmental Equity in 1992.

Public pressure on the Agency for real action increased two months later with the publication of a special investigation by the National Law Journal that discovered significant inequities in the rates of environmental enforcement and hazardous substance cleanup in minority communities. EPA's responses to violations of several key regulatory programs and releases of hazardous substances under the Superfund program in those communities were generally slower, its cleanups less rigorous, and the enforcement sanctions levied lower or non-existent. A 1994 study updating the Church of Christ report concluded the disproportionate environmental impacts had grown to the point where people of color were forty-seven percent more likely than whites to live near a commercial hazardous waste facility, and found sixty-three of sixty-four recent empirical studies documented environmental disparities by race and income for ambient air pollution, toxic exposures and environmental health effects.[8]

That year environmental justice caught the attention of the White House. President Bill Clinton issued an executive order entitled "Federal Actions to Address Environmental Justice in Minority Populations and Low-Income Populations," which directed every federal agency make achieving environmental justice part of its mission, and develop a strategy for addressing any disproportionately high and adverse human health or environmental effects of agency programs on minority and low-income populations.[9] EPA's Office of Environmental Equity changed its name to the Office of Environmental Justice, and drawing on the recommendations of the recently created National Environmental Justice Advisory Council, an independent body comprised of stakeholders from communities, organizations, industry and government, issued the Agency's environmental justice strategy in 1995.[10]

The strategy was effectively the Agency's first official environmental justice policy, but it echoed several key themes of the 1992 environmental equity report. Both documents reported a lack of relevant data on the impacts of federal environmental programs on disenfranchised groups and urged enhanced data collection and integration within existing information management systems. The equity report and strategy both sought more significant community involvement through improved public participation procedures, increased outreach to impacted communities, and additional partnerships with local and national organizations.

The strategy also followed the equity report's approach of using goals and principles in lieu of defining the core concept. The Agency openly admitted in the 1992 report its difficulty in defining environmental equity, offering in its place Administrator Reilly's basic principle of allowing no disproportionate effects of pollution on any population segment, supplemented by the stated goals of making public health and environmental protection available to all groups, and implementing environmental programs in ways that equitably conferred benefits and risk reductions on all groups. The 1995 strategy did not acknowledge its lack of a definition for environmental justice but simply posited two goals—one a slightly refined version of Reilly's principle of no disproportionate effects, and the other ensuring those affected by environmental decisions have opportunities for participating in making them—and three guiding principles—engaging communities through a variety of communication means, helping them access pertinent information, and advocating environmental justice with other federal agencies.

Several years later the Agency folded these concepts into a definition of environmental justice that continues to guide its policy and program actions today:

> Environmental Justice is the fair treatment and meaningful involvement of all people regardless of race, color, national origin, or income with respect to the development, implementation, and enforcement of environmental laws, regulations, and policies. Fair treatment means that no group of people should bear a disproportionate share of the negative environmental consequences resulting from industrial, governmental and commercial operations or policies. Meaningful involvement means that: (1) people have an opportunity to participate in decisions about activities that may affect their environment and/or health; (2) the publics [sic] contribution can influence the regulatory agency's decision; (3) their concerns will be considered in the decision making process; and (4) the decision makers seek out and facilitate the involvement of those potentially affected.[11]

Achieving this vision of environmental justice, EPA recognized, would require new partnerships with a variety of stakeholders including grassroots organizations, local governments, business concerns and other federal agencies.

The Agency's existing relationship with state environmental agencies was the most crucial, however, because they played the primary implementation role under the main federal environmental laws. States most often issued the operating permits required for lawful pollution discharges, monitored facility operations for compliance with environmental requirements, and determined whether and to what extent regulatory violations would be enforced. EPA's environmental justice strategy thus promised increased environmental justice emphasis, training and guidance directed at state implementation of federal programs.

Indian Country Environmental Justice

Indian country was the first place EPA applied its twin environmental justice themes of seeking fair treatment and enhancing the public involvement of disaffected groups, but it did so nearly twenty years before announcing them as the Agency's environmental justice policy in the late 1990s. The stimulus for EPA's early focus on environmental justice in the Indian country context was the unique characteristic that distinguishes Indian tribes from other minority groups affected by pollution and implicates a somewhat different source of and potential solution for environmental injustice in Indian country. Long political relations with the federal government and the resulting body of federal Indian law recognize in Indian tribes a pre-existing and continuing sovereignty as governments and impose on the federal government a trust responsibility for Indian welfare. The government-to-government and fiduciary relationships between tribes and the United States alters the constitutional concept of equal protection that underlies environmental justice; while American Indian citizens of the United States are entitled to fair treatment like other people of color, their dual citizenship in Indian tribes allows for different legal treatment, a sort of "measured separatism,"[12] reflected in an entire title in the United States Code of federal laws devoted specifically and exclusively to Indians and Indian country.

EPA recognized the separateness of federal Indian law and Indian country when it first began implementing the modern environmental regulatory programs that two decades later would give rise to the environmental justice movement. Judicial decisions addressing federal power and tribal sovereignty over Indian reservations threw doubt on the comprehensiveness of federal-state partnerships emerging from the new federal environmental programs, leading the Agency to experiment with unprecedented federal-tribal partnerships and direct outreach to tribes in the 1970s.[13] Different creative approaches were necessary, the Agency announced in 1980, to address "the serious possibility" that the Indian country environment would otherwise be less effectively protected than environments elsewhere.[14] Or, in the language of the contemporary environmental justice movement, the risk that Indians might suffer disproportionate health impacts and lack meaningful involvement in environmental decision-making was unacceptable and required focused Agency attention.

EPA's efforts toward Indian country environmental protection through special relations with tribes expanded greatly in the 1980s alongside presidential policy statements favoring tribal self-determination and congressional amendments creating state-like regulatory roles for tribes in the environmental programs. So when the early studies on race and environmental risk commonly associated with the beginning of the environmental justice movement came out, parallel data for Indian country was also emerging. A 1985 survey of twenty-five Indian tribes indicated as many as 1,200 facilities generating or disposing of hazardous waste on or adjacent to their reservations.[15] A broader environmental survey of seventy-four reservations representing a combined human population of 369,500 and a landmass of forty-two million acres in 1986 reported twenty-one major sources of air pollution, fifty-two community dump sites, landfills or uncontrolled open dumps, and at least 130 sources of water pollution.[16] These and other sources contributed to a broad variety of environmental concerns expressed by tribes, including water-borne diseases, violations of drinking water standards, surface water quality impairment, uncontrolled dumping of solid waste, abandoned mine wastes, and violations of air quality standards.

The 1986 survey observed that an overall lack of comprehensive federal and tribal environmental infrastructure was contributing to the problems identified. It also noted nearly every responding tribe reported involvement in some form of broadly defined environmental management activity, lending additional credence to EPA's view that addressing environmental justice in Indian country required creative solutions utilizing tribes' governmental status. Shortly before the First People of Color Summit in 1991, EPA asserted:

> Indian tribes, for whom human welfare is tied closely to the land, see protection of the reservation environment as essential to preservation of the reservations themselves. Environmental degradation is viewed as a form of further destruction of the remaining reservation land base, and pollution prevention is viewed as an act of tribal self-preservation that cannot be entrusted to others. For these reasons, Indian

tribes have insisted that tribal governments be recognized as the proper governmental entities to determine the future quality of reservation environments.[17]

The Agency's cultural generalizations and assumptions of tribal interest were strongly endorsed just months later at the Summit. The significant but typically unreported presence of indigenous advocates there succeeded in memorializing the tribal management approach in two of the seventeen principles announced:

> 5. Environmental justice affirms the fundamental right to political, economic, cultural and environmental self-determination of all peoples.
>
> ...
>
> 11. Environmental justice must recognize a special legal and natural relationship of Native Peoples to the U.S. government through treaties, agreements, compacts, and covenants affirming sovereignty and self-determination.[18]

Tribal environmental management, however, was not merely an exercise in political science and environmental health but was in fact perceived as fundamental to cultural survival. The Summit's first Principle equated environmental justice with affirming "the sacredness of Mother Earth, ecological unity and the interdependence of all species." An Indigenous Environmental Statement of Principles prepared by the Native Lands Institute in 1995 noted the common native phrase "we are all related" reflects cultural and spiritual traditions of seeing all living things—insects, reptiles, fish, birds and mammals—as "peoples" having important relations with indigenous peoples. Professor Rebecca Tsosie more comprehensively explained in 1996 that traditional ecological knowledge is a culturally and spiritually based means by which indigenous groups relate to ecosystems built on perceptions of the earth as an animate being, land as essential to indigenous identity, human relations with other living beings, and balance and reciprocity between humans and the natural world.[19]

Recognizing such human connectedness naturally imposes special obligations of protection. Tribal environmental lawyer Dean Suagee characterizes the development of environmental programs by tribes as discharging part of a sacred trust born of cultural traditions with ancient roots in the land.[20] The ancient fundamental laws of the Diné or Navajo people, uniquely merged with contemporary tribal law in written format, embraces these views explicitly:

Diné Natural Law declares and teaches that:
A. The four sacred elements of life, air, light/fire, water and earth/pollen in all their forms must be respected, honored and protected for they sustain life; and
...
D. The Diné have a sacred obligation and duty to respect, preserve and protect all that was provided for we were designated as the steward of these relatives.[21]

Tribal management is doubly important because western environmental law as implemented by federal and state agencies is generally unable to account for Indian visions of environmental justice that include the physical, social and spiritual relations affected by various land development uses.[22] The Indigenous Environmental Statement of Principles offered as an example of that myopia western risk-based analysis that focuses primarily on acceptable rates of individual human harm and death, suggesting Indian country risk assessments must also account for the spiritual and psychological well being of the collective community as well as individuals. EPA's 1992 environmental equity report, which commendably devoted a separate section to Indian country issues, made some inroads in that vein, explicitly noting a need for incorporating cultural considerations like subsistence practices and higher than average wild food and fish consumption rates into the Agency's risk analyses.

EPA's first effort at that challenging task was a groundbreaking comparative risk project nearing completion as the equity report was issued. Between 1986 and 1992, EPA was involved in some twenty-five comparative analyses on environmental risks facing different states, regions and cities that, despite the growing concerns over environmental justice at the time, considered the entire population of the study areas without segregating data for minority groups. EPA broke new ground in 1992 with its first environmental justice comparative risk study, performed in Indian country. The study concluded the 20,000 to 30,000 American Indians constituting eleven tribes in Wisconsin faced different environmental risks than the population of the northern Midwest as a whole.[23] The risk analyses EPA employed accounted for the different pathways of environmental contamination that Indians face, and interestingly, calculated economic damages to cultural and religious values as well as subsistence lifestyles. The project concluded that the disproportionately higher risks faced by Wisconsin Indians from both on and off-reservation pollution sources could be significantly reduced by the development of effective tribal environmental management infrastructure. Tribal programs could translate traditional cultural and spiritual values into the rubric of environmental quality standards affecting the substantive requirements of pollution permits issued under the modern federal environmental programs.

EPA's 1995 strategy adopted tribal program development as one of its primary objectives for Indian country environmental justice. Like the equity report, the strategy treated the issues unique to tribes separately, emphasizing their difference from environmental justice concerns elsewhere. In other areas of the country the Agency was focused on adjusting the federal and state programs already in place so they operated more fairly and with greater transparency. In Indian country, the disproportionately high environmental risks appeared more attributable to a surprising lack of operating programs. The perception of an environmental regulatory gap in Indian country had prompted EPA's early creative approaches to tribal partnerships, and its contemporary commitment to filling that gap manifested itself in 1994 with the creation of the American Indian Environmental Office. The Office of Environmental Justice's 1995 strategy also noted the need for filling jurisdictional gaps in national environmental protection and promised coordination with the Indian Office in developing and implementing Indian country programs in a government-to-government fashion consistent with tribal sovereignty and the federal trust responsibility.

CHAPTER 2

THE LONG JOURNEY BEGINS: DEVELOPING EPA's INDIAN PROGRAM

Public concern for environmental quality is so ingrained in the national consciousness today that it is hard to imagine a time when it was not. But in 1970, when EPA was created, national awareness was undergoing a radical epiphany. The 1960s witnessed dramatic and increasing evidence that society's focus on the clear benefits of advancing technological capacities had almost completely overlooked their corollary potential for devastating negative consequences. The Cuyahoga River in Ohio literally caught fire, California beaches and shorelines were stained with spilled crude oil, fishing and swimming areas in Massachusetts were closed because of chemical contamination, and birds and food grown for human consumption across the nation showed startling levels of pesticide residues. The obvious and direct threats to human health, as well as to the quality of life, created the perception, if not the reality, of a national crisis.

Congress possessed no general public welfare authority, but it did have broad jurisdiction over interstate commerce. Congress enacted limitations on waste disposal in rivers and oceans that hindered national commerce as early as 1889. Much of the modern industrial activity resulting in environmental degradation traversed state borders or affected interstate commerce. And transboundary migration of water and air pollution threatened general national interests in public health. In the mid-1900s Congress enacted the precursors to the nation's modern environmental laws, which consisted largely of financial and technical assistance available to states for developing environmental management programs.

State governments inherently possessed "police powers" for protecting public health and welfare, and had historically exercised them through land use restrictions like zoning, housing and building codes. But more extensive environmental regulation increased the cost of doing business, and individual states were loath to erect disincentives for new and expanded economic development.

So, by most accounts, Congress' indirect approach of providing assistance did not stimulate effective state action. States utterly failed to control industrial activities contaminating land, water and air in the 1950s and 1960s.

On April 22, 1970, some twenty million Americans demonstrated in the streets on the nation's first Earth Day sending a message federal politicians dared not ignore. President Richard Nixon created EPA through a reorganization of federal responsibilities related to health and the environment, and Congress greatly expanded the federal role in environmental management. Just days after EPA was born in December 1970, Congress passed the Clean Air Act, which stamped modern federal environmental law with the main features it retains today. The Act's approach—later denominated cooperative federalism—envisioned a new federal-state partnership that acknowledged both the national interest in environmental management as well as states' historic responsibilities for public health and welfare.

Congress created federal management programs that states would implement under EPA's supervision. States were required to satisfy minimum federal standards but could set requirements more stringent than those in the federal program. If a state was unwilling or unable to meet the minimum federal expectations, EPA was authorized to run programs directly in lieu of state implementation. In this manner, cooperative federalism respected states' value judgments about the proper balance between economic development and environmental protection, but only to the extent they supported the national interest in environmental protection.

Although Congress created a strong and expanded federal role, it clearly expected local implementation of federal programs. The Clean Air Act, and every federal environmental statute adopted later, recited states' primary responsibilities in its arena. Congress believed and EPA agreed that local governments were better positioned to conform uniform federal requirements to site-specific conditions and needs.

> EPA and the states have been given joint responsibility by Congress for national environmental programs. EPA and the states must develop a workable partnership in which each performs different activities that are based on the partner's unique strengths. The resulting division of labor must be both coordinated and mutually reinforcing. States are best placed to address specific local problems as they arise on a day-to-day basis, while EPA is best able to address generic problems: long-range issues; inter-state, national, and international issues; and to strengthen and assist state agencies as components of the na-

tion's operational field network for environmental protection. Delegation [of federal program responsibility] puts the state in the role of primary implementors [sic] of environmental programs, allowing them to tailor national programs to fit local conditions and needs within bounds that ensure reasonable consistency and equity among states.[1]

Congress reproduced the 1970 Clean Air Act's cooperative federalism approach in laws regulating pollution of surface waters like rivers and lakes in 1972, pollution of underground waters in 1974, disposal of solid and hazardous wastes in 1976, and cleanup of hazardous substance spills in 1980. Congress sought by these laws comprehensive protection over every environmental medium from border to border and ocean to ocean, but apparently left a gaping geographic hole in the regulatory net: no provisions addressed Indian country.

Indian Country Environmental Regulation

"Indian country" is a federal Indian law term of art that describes the geographic areas within the United States that are primarily governed by federal Indian laws and policies rather than state legislation. The term includes but is larger than the approximately 77,000 square miles of formally designated Indian "reservations," the one kind of Indian country familiar to many Americans, and the some 56 million acres of land that American Indian tribes and tribal citizens own both within and outside formal reservations. A federal statute passed in 1948 made clear Indian country also encompassed certain former Indian lands later conveyed to non-Indians by federal patent or other means:

> [T]he term "Indian country" as used in this chapter means (a) all land within the limits of any Indian reservation under the jurisdiction of the United States Government, notwithstanding the issuance of any [non-Indian] patent, and, including rights-of-way running through the reservation, (b) all dependent Indian communities within the borders of the United States whether within the original or subsequently acquired territory thereof, and whether within or without the limits of a state, and (c) all Indian [land] allotments, the Indian titles to which have not been extinguished, including rights-of-way running through the same.[2]

As EPA's Indian program was taking form in the mid-1970s, the United States Supreme Court extended this definition of Indian country, developed by Congress for delineating federal criminal authority, to cases involving questions of civil jurisdiction.[3] The new federal environmental laws clearly created civil regulatory programs, which raised the question whether and how they might be applied in Indian country. Congress' silence on their implementation presented EPA with two important questions implicating administrative, Indian and environmental law.

First was the threshold question whether these laws applied in Indian country at all. As non-constitutional governmental entities, administrative agencies like EPA possess only that authority given to them by Congress. If Congress' silence meant the laws did not apply to Indian country, EPA lacked implementation authority there, resulting in a significant break in the national regulatory circle and frustrating Congress' intent for comprehensive coverage.

The Supreme Court has long tolerated an asserted broad congressional power over Indian affairs, and pursuant to that power, Congress has passed hundreds of Indian-specific laws. At one time the Court insisted Congress speak explicitly when it intended to pass Indian laws, but the Court seemed to reverse course in 1960, implying that federal laws of general applicability applied to Indians and Indian country unless Congress said otherwise.[4] The first reported Indian country environmental law case followed that new approach in 1972, applying a federal law requiring environmental impact statements to a proposed housing development within an Indian pueblo despite the law's silence on its application.[5] The next year, EPA interpreted the federal water pollution law as applicable to Indian reservations despite its silence.

That decision, though, raised a second and more difficult legal question: with whom would EPA partner to implement federal programs in Indian country? The local partners Congress arranged for EPA, the states, had limited governmental claims on Indian reservations.

Before and after the origin of the United States of America, governmental relations with indigenous peoples were conducted primarily at the federal or national level. Early international law treated indigenous communities as sovereign nation-states, capable of declaring war and peace, engaging in international commerce, and regulating their external affairs through treaties executed with foreign nations. The United States Constitution delegated power over Indian affairs to the federal government, which executed dozens of treaties with various North American Indian tribes and enacted hundreds of laws regulating Indian affairs. The Constitution also declared the general supremacy of federal law, implying that state actions interfering with federal-tribal relations must yield.

The classic illustration is the foundation Indian law case, *Worcester v. Georgia*,[6] decided in 1832. The United States and the Cherokee Nation executed a treaty in which the Cherokees reserved a homeland that was later completely encompassed by boundaries claimed by the newly minted State of Georgia. Ignoring the sophistication and much longer pedigree of the Cherokee government, Georgia enacted laws purportedly abolishing the Tribe's sovereignty and regulating Cherokee territory in its place. Pursuant to those laws, Georgia imprisoned Samuel Worcester, a non-Indian Christian missionary, for proselytizing in Cherokee territory without a state license. The United States Supreme Court flatly invalidated the state law and ordered Worcester released. The Court described the Cherokee Nation as "a distinct community, occupying its own territory ... in which the laws of Georgia can have no force."[7] The State's laws improperly infringed on the Cherokee's governmental sovereignty, and were also repugnant to the federal Constitution because they interfered with the federal-tribal relationship forged in the treaty. Over time the Supreme Court retreated from *Worcester's* per se rule, but continued to recite states' limited authority in Indian country.

EPA first encountered the legal question of state authority in Indian country in 1973. The impetus was a 1972 federal law requiring permits for water pollution discharges. Congress tasked EPA with initial implementation of the permit program, but directed the Agency to develop regulations for delegating that responsibility to states upon a showing of authority and capability. Congress, however, said nothing about the status of Indian country within states. Nearly 150 years of Court decisions since *Worcester* suggested Congress' silence meant states were barred from regulating Indian country activities. In 1973, the Supreme Court said broadly "[s]tate laws generally are not applicable to tribal Indians or an Indian reservation except where Congress has expressly provided that State laws shall apply."[8]

Because Congress offered states no environmental authority on Indian reservations, they could not be effective federal partners except pursuant to some other independent authority. Hence, EPA's 1973 rules governing state program delegations said EPA would directly implement the water permit program over Indian activities on Indian lands rather than delegate that responsibility to states.[9] That simple and straightforward approach was the first cornerstone of the Agency's developing Indian program.

Federal direct implementation of Indian reservation programs for Indian facilities, however, was an imperfect solution to the legal questions EPA faced. First, it did not address the regulatory status of non-Indian facilities in Indian country. Second, it left non-reservation areas of Indian country unprotected. Third, it left EPA assuming a permanent role at odds with Congress' preference for local implementation. The cooperative federalism model generally relied on direct EPA program operation as an interim measure while local institutions developed program capacity in the first instance, and afterward only if local programs fell below federal standards.

Direct federal implementation was also at odds with a new national Indian policy emerging in the early 1970s. Federal Indian law is a notoriously complex subject in part because the history of national Indian policy reflects dramatic swings between the opposite poles of endorsing and ignoring tribal sovereignty. Before European contact, indigenous communities were true nation-states with inherent governmental sovereignty. At contact, practical necessity and international law required acknowledgment of that fact, though it quickly gave way to an ethnocentric assertion of superior European powers capable of unilaterally limiting tribes' sovereign powers. Western arrogance reached its zenith during the 1800s when federal lawmakers and judges declared tribes, whose existence predated the United States by thousands of years, incapable of managing their own affairs. Chief Justice John Marshall once famously made the ethnocentric declaration that "[Indian Tribes] are in a state of pupilage. Their relation to the United States resembles that of a ward to his guardian."[10]

The genius of western society and civilization was necessary, it was asserted, for Indians to overcome the limitations of their traditional ways and become productive members of the new political community. The federal government thus wrested control from traditional tribal governments over nearly every significant aspect of Indian life, including property ownership, religion, tribal affiliation, civil and criminal justice, and basic subsistence. A central aspect of these assimilation policies was the widespread confiscation and sale of tens of millions of acres of Indian land, resulting in huge increases in the number of non-Indians living inside Indian country.

When it later became clear that the federal government failed completely in its mission to transform Indians into Europeans, federal policy dawdled in the early 1900s with a rhetorical commitment to tribal self-governance. Tribal control, though, was tolerable only when exercised by non-traditional tribal governments who looked distinctly Euro-American, and whose decisions were subject to federal veto. That ostensible tribal control failed to produce immediate results, and federal policy swung back again, this time going farther than ever before. Believing the entire system of Indian law was the root cause of the so-called Indian problem, and eager to be released from its treaty and trust obligations, Congress began "terminating" the political existence of tribes. Termination opened the door for the first time to state control of Indians and Indian country. The results were widely recognized as disastrous, and even states joined in the chorus of those calling for the end of termination.

Objections to termination policies echoed with the civil rights movement of ethnic minorities in the United States in the 1960s. In 1968 and 1970, presidents of both parties publicly rejected termination and called for a national Indian policy embracing tribal self-determination. Tribal self-determination implied dropping the historic guardian-to-ward model in favor of federal-tribal relations conducted on a government-to-government basis. Tribes were local governments more familiar with their citizens' priorities and interests than the federal trustee. Viewed as governments and not dependent wards, tribes could assist in better tailoring federal programs to tribal needs. Tribal views could be accessed through genuine consultation, but ideally tribal governments would assume operational responsibilities for federal programs, with a concomitant decline in direct federal implementation.

Tribal self-determination resonated particularly well in the environmental realm because of the popular view widely held in the early 1970s of Indians as the continent's first conservationists. The Council on Environmental Quality's first annual report, issued in the aftermath of the first Earth Day in 1970, asserted "the first [humans] upon this land, the American Indians, treated it with reverence, blended with it, used it, but left hardly a trace upon it."[11] On the second Earth Day in 1971, a powerful anti-pollution public service television announcement capitalized on that view:

> In that enduring minute-long TV spot, viewers watched an Indian paddle his canoe up a polluted and flotsam-filled river, stream past belching smokestacks, come ashore at a litter-strewn river bank, and walk to the edge of a highway, where the occupant of a passing automobile thoughtlessly tossed a bag of trash out the car window to burst open at the astonished visitor's feet. When the camera moved upwards for a close-up, a single tear was seen rolling down the Indian's face as the narrator dramatically intoned: "People start pollution; people can stop it."[12]

Then a 1972 film portrayed, inaccurately, an 1854 speech in which a famous Indian leader allegedly not espoused a native conservation land ethic, berated modern society for not respecting the Earth as "Mother," and warned its poor habits would come home to roost.[13] Suddenly Indian and environmental concern became synonymous, and public discussion turned to whether

America might somehow tap native wisdom in solving the environmental problems facing Mother Earth.

EPA's 1973 decision to implement the water pollution permit program directly in Indian country was at odds with the public discussion and the new national policy of increased tribal authority and decreased federal control. Presidential rhetoric of tribal control in lieu of federal management suggested EPA's missing local partner in Indian country was the tribal government itself. Congress had not spoken on the question in the environmental statutes, although it endorsed self-determination in 1972 and 1975 laws authorizing greater tribal control of federal Indian education and service-related programs.[14] Yet, those programs offered no tribal regulatory authority potentially affecting economic activities occurring on lands owned by non-Indians. Despite nearly two hundred years of Indian law cases frequently containing references to inherent tribal sovereignty over tribal territories implying such authority, as of the early 1970s not one case had been decided with that direct result.

Nonetheless, EPA embraced tribal self-determination in two program-specific contexts in the mid-1970s. The first was a 1974 Clean Air Act program EPA created to prevent significant deterioration of existing good air quality by imposing on certain new sources of air pollution permit conditions whose stringency depended on the affected area's air quality classification. EPA initially designated nearly all areas of the country Class II, but provided for redesignation to the more stringent Class I or the less stringent Class III. EPA recognized such classifications implicated local (and highly political) considerations, so it offered redesignation authority to states, federal land managers, and on Indian reservations, to tribes.[15] Once approved, the tribal redesignation begat federally enforceable conditions imposed by EPA via permits for air pollution sources within and adjacent to reservations.

The Agency's second self-determination action concerned local implementation of the 1972 federal pesticides law. The law prohibited commercial application of registered pesticides except by certified persons. Congress provided for state certification, but did not say whether a state certificate was required or applicable to reservation applicators. EPA's 1975 rules required applicators on Indian reservations obtain certification from tribes.[16] Commercial applications done without tribal certification violated the pesticides law, exposing the applicator to federal enforcement sanctions.

The tribal roles EPA proffered in the air and pesticide programs were identical to those played by state governments. Tribes were subject to the same eligibility and operation requirements, and once approved by EPA as meeting federal standards, carried the same potential to influence environmentally harmful activities. Significantly, the pesticide role offered tribes direct regulatory authority over non-Indian actors on reservations. The air quality role was indirect in that EPA and not the tribe translated the tribal air classification into facility-specific conditions. But it too was significant: the federally enforceable conditions derived from tribal value judgments, and could be imposed upon facilities outside tribal territories and thus clearly beyond the reach of tribal sovereignty.

Despite these potential consequences, EPA's rules generated neither adulation nor condemnation. As required by federal administrative law, EPA solicited comments from the public before adopting its rules. EPA received no praise or support for its new self-determination approach; in fact, not a single tribe or tribal organization commented. Two states did comment. They took issue with EPA's assumption that states lacked civil regulatory authority over Indian reservations, but neither directly challenged the treatment of tribal governments as appropriate EPA partners, or the assumption of tribes' inherent sovereignty over non-Indians. EPA's response disavowed any intention to alter existing jurisdictional schemes, and claimed it would partner with any state showing Indian reservation authority. EPA nonetheless made clear it saw no congressional permission for state implementation in the silent environmental laws.

Congress validated EPA's view shortly thereafter, codifying EPA's tribal air program role in 1977 amendments to the Clean Air Act and adopting EPA's tribal pesticide program role in 1978 amendments to the federal pesticides law. Congress sought no tribal or state input, nor undertook deliberative consideration of the issues presented. It simply accepted EPA's exposition of tribal self-determination in the context of environmental law's cooperative federalism: tribal program roles would resemble states' roles. This was the second cornerstone of EPA's developing Indian program, which in the mid-1980s came to be known as the tribal "treatment-as-a-state" approach.

Congress' casual adoption of the treatment-as-a-state approach was remarkable in its own right, but especially so given an impending legal battle over the first exercise of the tribal air program role EPA created in 1974. While Congress debated the 1977 Clean Air Act amendments, EPA was considering the nation's first application for redesignation to the more stringent Class I air quality, submitted by the Northern Cheyenne Tribe for its reservation in south central Montana. The State of Montana did not object, but a host of off-reservation energy and coal mining companies (as well as the neighboring coal-rich Crow Tribe) saw potential for increased compliance costs and urged EPA's disapproval.

The companies overlooked the opportunity to lobby Congress, but the Tribe did not. It proposed a tribal treatment-as-a-state provision, which the Committee on Environment and Public Works incorporated nearly verbatim into the Senate bill, describing it as giving tribes "the same powers as States."[17] The Tribe also sought protection for its pending redesignation. The Committee report specifically noted the Tribe's proposal (the only application submitted under EPA's 1974 rules), and included language in the bill preserving any redesignation approved by EPA before the Clean Air Act amendments became effective.

Congress' affirmation of EPA's 1974 tribal experiment was clear. EPA approved the Tribe's application just days before the 1977 amendments were signed into law. Several years later, after a federal court rejected the companies' and the Crow Tribe's legal challenges, the redesignation did impact off-reservation industry. EPA forced the Montana Power Company to redesign its proposed coal-fired energy facility in Colstrip, Montana in order to protect air quality on the Northern Cheyenne reservation thirteen miles away.[18] And the Crow Tribe, whose own reservation was immediately upwind of the Northern Cheyenne reservation, abandoned plans for a similar facility when feasibility studies predicted a nearly $300 million pollution control cost increase attributable to the Northern Cheyenne redesignation.[19] Illuminated by this hindsight, EPA's and Congress' treatment-as-a-state approach represented unparalleled respect for tribal value judgments on reservation environmental quality.

Not surprisingly, the national conversation suddenly saw a proliferation of tribal environmental management references. The Council on Environmental Quality called for consultations with tribes in the preparation of environmental impact statements, and the Bureau of Indian Affairs explicitly linked environmental protection in Indian country with tribal sovereignty. EPA's Office of Pesticide Programs awarded a grant to the organization Americans for Indian Opportunity for a series of regional EPA-tribe meetings to inform tribal leaders about available tribal pesticide management roles and educate EPA on tribal sovereignty, culture and needs. A portion of each regional meeting was devoted to discussions of other EPA programs, even though at this time (other than the air redesignation role) those programs contained no tribal roles. These exchanges marked the first federal outreach directed at improving meaningful tribal involvement in federal program implementation, setting another cornerstone of the Agency's Indian program.

The First Indian Policy

Increased tribal interest, expanded federal discussions on tribal environmental management, and Congress' clear affirmation of tribal roles in the air and pesticide laws helped broaden EPA's focus on Indian issues beyond program-specific contexts. An EPA Indian Work Group created in the late 1970s was tasked with developing Agency policy on program implementation on Indian reservations. From the outset, the Work Group focused on state-like program roles for tribes, and in the summer of 1980, Agency leaders reached consensus that a policy involving tribes in a more central regulatory role was warranted. The Work Group prepared a draft Indian Policy in a matter of months, and in December 1980 EPA became the first federal Agency with a formal Indian Policy officially embracing the new self-determination era.[20]

The heart of the 1980 Indian Policy was an unqualified proclamation that tribal governments should play a "key role" in the implementation of environmental programs for the reservation environment. The Policy offered several justifications for its position, notwithstanding Congress' general silence on the matter. Congress and the Executive branch had announced support for tribal self-determination, and tribes appeared eager for stronger influence over federal Indian programs. Tribes also possessed inherent sovereign responsibility for protecting their lands and citizens. States, on the other hand, had limited authority on reservations, which in the context of EPA's statutory programs meant "the environment of Indian reservations will be less effectively protected than the environment elsewhere." EPA explicitly rejected that consequence as unacceptable because it undermined national protection and violated the spirit of the federal trust responsibility over Indians and their lands, or in modern terms, constituted environmental injustice.

The federal trust doctrine was the Court's guilt-induced reaction to the indefensible assertion of federal power over the continent's indigenous peoples at contact. It theoretically softened the harshness of the legal fiction of tribes as wards in need of a guardian by positing in the federal government broad "moral obligations of the highest responsibility and trust … judged by the most exacting fiduciary standards."[21] In reality, federal actions are largely beyond judicial review except where they directly concern federal mismanagement of tribal property assets.[22] On occasion, courts have questioned otherwise legitimate and rational administrative action for consistency with the trust responsibility,[23] but the obligation remains largely an unenforceable moral one. A relevant case in point was the court's recent rejection of claims by the Gros Ventre and Assiniboine Tribes that the federal government violated the trust responsibility by permitting two cyanide heap-leach gold mines upriver from the Tribes' reservation.[24]

Legally enforceable or not, moral obligations sometimes have more profound impact than legal ones. The 1980 Indian Policy observed the federal trust responsibility in its pledge of adapting federal programs to the special circumstances and needs of Indian reservations, and promoting an enhanced role for tribal governments in the implementation of those programs. The Policy's principles iterated and extended the early program cornerstones: EPA would not delegate its programs to states, but would implement them on reservations directly, tailoring them as appropriate to tribal needs and priorities by working closely with the affected tribe until the ultimate goal of full program assumption by the tribe was realized.

> The environment is generally best protected by those who have the concern and the ability to protect it. Indian people show an acute sensitivity to their loss of great tracts of this country. Even since the establishment of the original reservations by treaty, the Indian land base has shrunk to a minor fraction of the original reservations. This historical fact, combined with a long-standing cultural respect for the earth and its environment, is reflected in tribal expressions of concern for the land, its irreplaceability, and the importance of its environmental quality.[25]

The Policy promised direct attention on existing legal barriers to tribal operation, but that promise constituted at best only a superficial acknowledgement of the legal elephant in the room. Congress' general view on program implementation for the reservation environment was unknown. Congress had not specifically authorized state roles, but neither had it prohibited them, and every major federal law recited states' primarily responsibilities for environmental management. Congress had adopted EPA's administratively created tribal roles in two fairly narrow programs, but was as yet mute on the dozens of other federal programs.

In the absence of clear congressional direction, the Supreme Court's Indian common law controlled. Cases in the late 1970s reflected the continuing viability of several key foundation principles on state and tribal power on Indian reservations, but importantly, the contexts of those cases were only partially relevant to EPA's program needs. The Court endorsed inherent tribal sovereignty when exercised by a tribal court over an adoption case where all parties were Indian.[26] It cited respect for tribes' separate sovereignty in declining review of a gender discriminatory tribal law as applied to a tribal member,[27] and allowing a subsequent federal prosecution of an Indian previously prosecuted by the tribe under tribal law.[28] The Court also barred a state tax law from reaching the on-reservation property of an Indian, despite the terms of Public Law 280, an unparalleled and unrepeated federal authorization of state court jurisdiction over certain cases arising in Indian country.[29] These Supreme Court decisions rather clearly suggested EPA could safely authorize tribal implementation of federal programs at least as they applied to Indians and Indian-owned facilities.

But the nineteenth-century assimilation policies put millions of acres of Indian country land into non-Indian ownership, and federal policies for reservation economic development in the 1950s and 1960s relied almost exclusively on non-Indian exploitation of tribal lands and natural resources. Effective environmental programs on Indian reservations, then, required a local partner capable of managing non-Indian actors and non-Indian lands. None of the contemporary Supreme Court cases directly addressed whether tribes possessed regulatory authority over non-Indians in Indian country. Scattered references in those opinions implying such authority, like the Court's oft-cited description of tribes as "unique aggregations possessing attributes of sovereignty over both their members *and their territory,*"[30] were non-binding dicta.

A red flag flew in 1978 when the Court pronounced that tribes' territorial powers did not include protecting the peace by prosecuting the criminal activities of non-Indians on reservations.[31] That case foreshadowed the modern Court's imminent departure from the foundation Indian law cases, but its result and rationale were explicitly limited to the criminal context, not directly relevant to EPA's civil regulatory schemes. And as EPA was developing its 1980 Indian Policy, the Court found a tribe's interest in a federal regulatory scheme for Indian timber harvests, coupled with a corresponding federal interest, adequate justification for barring a state tax law from reaching a non-Indian timber hauler's commercial activities on the reservation.[32]

Although tribal control over non-Indians was then and continues to be today perhaps the most contentious issue in Indian law, EPA forged ahead despite these legal uncertainties. Its 1980 policy decision in lieu of waiting for clearer guidance represented perhaps a genuine acceptance of the federal government's moral obligation toward Indians. Well-intentioned governmental policies, however, often give way to political reality and circumstance. EPA's Deputy Administrator Barbara Blum signed the Indian Policy at the tail end of Jimmy Carter's presidential administration. One month later, Ronald Reagan took office and replaced both EPA's Administrator and Deputy Administrator Blum. During the nomination process, Reagan's new EPA Administrator, Anne Gorsuch, guardedly answered congressional inquiries on the 1980 Indian Policy. Careful study of the new policy was needed, she said, before making any decision on whether and how it might be implemented.[33]

Developing a More Deliberative Approach

Gorsuch made good on her promise to Congress, but the study would take two years. In the meantime, tribal interest in assuming program roles, and tribal requests for EPA assistance, spiked around several unrelated events in 1981. Americans for Indian Opportunity issued a handbook whose objective was increasing tribal management of environmental health impacts associated with natural resource development activities.[34] The Council of Energy Resource Tribes, representing 37 resource-rich tribes, called for federal program delegations and technical assistance to tribes in the same manner as states.[35] Most significantly, a federal appeals court rejected the first major challenge to the developing Indian program by upholding EPA's first tribal delegation: the Northern Cheyenne air quality redesignation. Rejecting a veritable barrage of constitutional, statutory and procedural arguments challenging the off-reservation impacts of the Tribe's more stringent value judgment, the court deferred to the Agency's view of the silent Clean Air Act in *Nance v. EPA*.[36]

After *Nance* was issued, several tribes quickly followed Northern Cheyenne, seeking EPA approval of Class I tribal redesignations. Approximately a dozen tribes were using EPA assistance for developing inventories of reservation air and water quality, and another dozen or so were actively engaged in developing air, water and pesticide programs. These and other tribes approached EPA on all manner of environmental issues, with the result that by 1983 "virtually every program and every [EPA] Region with federally-recognized tribes has made some effort to respond to reservation problems."[37]

But, with the guiding principles of its Indian Policy in limbo, EPA's responses were inconsistent and unpredictable. For example, EPA's Region VIII responded favorably to the funding request of the Southern Ute Tribe in Colorado for an air quality inventory even though the Clean Air Act did not list tribes as eligible grantees. The grant envisioned the Southern Ute Tribe's coordination with its neighbor, the Jicarilla Apache Tribe in New Mexico, located in EPA Region VI. Grant money was available in Region VI, but the Jicarilla Tribe's request was rejected because the policy study Reagan's new Administrator had promised Congress was not yet completed.

EPA's programmatic responses were also schizophrenic. In considering potential tribal roles under the Clean Air Act and the Superfund law, EPA for the first time explicitly articulated the 1980 Policy approach as tribal "treatment-as-a-state." EPA supported that approach in the President's 1981 draft Clean Air Act amendments, but ignored tribes' sovereign governmental status in electing to treat them "as any other entity" in the Superfund program. A series of new rules on state delegations followed the 1980 Policy by iterating EPA's early decisions to retain implementation responsibility on reservations on the assumption that states lacked authority. On that basis EPA rejected the State of Washington's 1982 request for hazardous waste program responsibility on Indian reservations. Yet, in the context of the Superfund program for remediation of hazardous substance spills, EPA required states posit assurances of responsibility before EPA would devote federal cleanup money to sites on Indian lands.

These confused and inconsistent pronouncements produced frustration inside and outside the Agency. EPA's credibility in Indian country was rapidly diminishing, in part because it had attempted to take seriously tribal self-determination in a manner no other federal Agency had. EPA was the only one of some twenty-five federal agencies and three federal departments reporting an official Indian policy when surveyed by Americans for Indian Opportunity for its 1981 tribal handbook. But although that policy was on hold, the Agency was engaged in a deliberative study of the complex issues with unprecedented depth and focus. In mid-1982, the Agency's Office of Federal Activities prepared a draft report, drawing heavily on the Indian Work Group's analysis for the 1980 Indian Policy. After extensive consultations with EPA's Office of Planning and Resource Management and Office of Intergovernmental Liaison, a nearly 100-page draft "Discussion Paper" was circulated to every EPA region with Indian tribes, to every media program, and to a host of other EPA offices in December 1982.

Before any comments on the Discussion Paper arrived back at headquarters, Reagan took two public actions pertinent to EPA's study. In January 1983, Reagan charged his newly created Presidential Commission on Indian Reservation Economies with addressing existing federal legislative and regulatory obstacles to creating positive economic environments on Indian reservations.[38] One such barrier, identified in an earlier congressional study, was jurisdictional uncertainty over natural resource development.[39]

That same month Reagan also issued a public statement endorsing tribal self-determination, which he expressly linked to tribal self-government.[40] He pledged an Executive Branch commitment to federal-tribal relations on a government-to-government basis, echoing his predecessors' statements disavowing the outmoded federal government-to-tribal ward approach. But Reagan observed the hypocrisy of those statements when viewed in light of near total federal control of federal programs and the continuing practice of federal decision-making with little or no tribal input. As local governments with responsibilities for tribal citizens' health and welfare, Reagan asserted tribes were positioned better than federal agencies to adapt federal programs to tribal needs and priorities. Reagan pledged administration efforts to allow tribes "to resume control over their own affairs" and "restore tribal governments to their rightful place among the governments of this nation."

EPA's 1980 Indian Policy adumbrated Reagan's 1983 statement. The Policy's main thrust was federal retention of reservation programs rather than delegation to states, but it clearly anticipated an increased level of tribal governmental involvement in program administration. EPA envisioned tribal self-determination in the context of EPA's cooperative federalist programs as leading to eventual tribal assumption of local roles. The 1982 draft Discussion Paper, prepared before Reagan issued his self-determination statement, constituted a report on the Agency's study of Indian issues and was not intended as a policy statement itself. But its analysis and recommendations were unmistakably drawn from the core tenets of the 1980 Policy, and as such, nicely paralleled Reagan's view of the new federal Indian approach.

The Discussion Paper reported the perceived advantages and disadvantages of three possible management regimes for Indian reservation programs: implementation by EPA, by state agencies, and by tribal agencies. Its fundamental recommendation ostensibly took no position on these three alternatives; instead, it called for a flexible Indian policy allowing case-by-case decisions on the appropriate implementing party. Two of the four proposed criteria for such decisions supported the claimed neutrality of the recommendation. One simply demanded effective programs, and another, recognizing Congress' goal in creating the cooperative federalism paradigm, suggested a major objective be delegation to the local level.

The other two criteria inexorably took that neutral foundation toward a clear preference for tribal implementation. One criterion sought to avoid a confusing patchwork of interagency responsibilities by insisting the local governmental partner have jurisdiction over all reservation sources of pollution. Regulatory jurisdiction over Indian reservations was addressed in a legal appendix of the Discussion Paper. One of its primary conclusions was the nearly inarguable proposition that states lacked jurisdiction over Indian facilities unless specifically authorized by Congress. None of the environmental statutes included such authorization, and in light of the emerging national policy of tribal self-determination, EPA viewed securing state amendments as politically impracticable. So even if a state could show jurisdiction over non-Indian polluters—a debatable proposition at that time—the proposed criterion of jurisdiction over all reservation polluters effectively meant EPA would not delegate to states.

Conversely, the legal appendix concluded that tribes possessed adequate authority over all reservation pollution sources. If *self*-government meant anything, it surely included regulatory power over tribal facilities and tribal citizens. The harder question, of course, was tribal jurisdiction over non-Indian polluters in tribal territories. EPA's affirmative conclusion, which directly served its (disclaimed) predisposition favoring tribal implementation, seemed a reasonable interpretation of two contemporaneous Supreme Court cases. One allowed the application of a tribal tax law to a non-Indian mineral developer doing business on Indian lands, calling taxation a "fundamental attribute of sovereignty."[41] The other case denied tribal jurisdiction over non-Indians hunting and fishing on non-Indian reservation lands, but said nonetheless that inherent tribal sovereignty could extend to nonmembers of the tribe whose activities threatened the health or welfare of tribal citizens.[42] A health and welfare threshold naturally fit EPA's statutory mandates.

The Discussion Paper's remaining criterion and recommendations made clear EPA's intention to follow the self-determination policy laid out in the 1980 Indian Policy. The Paper proposed EPA's decisions on delegable programs "endeavor" to give tribal governments "the primary role in environmental program management and decision-making." EPA was urged to establish levels of Agency resource commitment and criteria for allocating limited resources among tribal recipients. The Discussion Paper also recommended developing an implementation strategy so as not to repeat the mistake made with the 1980 Indian Policy.

In short, almost nothing in the Discussion Paper was inconsistent with tribal self-determination. There was just one glaring omission in its development: EPA never asked tribes for their views. The irony of an unprecedented Agency statement respecting tribal governmental perspectives developed with absolutely no tribal outreach was not lost on some EPA staffers, who urged inclusion of tribal representatives in any implementation work groups formed later. As an apparent afterthought, EPA's Chief of Staff John Daniel did direct distribution of the draft Discussion Paper to two Indian organizations—the Council of Energy Resource Tribes and the Commission on State-Tribal Relations—and received favorable responses from both.

The Discussion Paper was finalized in summer 1983, over two years after Anne Gorsuch had called for the study. But Gorsuch did not see the Paper;

she had left the Agency three months earlier, amidst significant internal chaos. Her replacement was William Ruckelshaus, who had been EPA's first administrator under Richard Nixon. President Reagan asked Ruckelshaus to return to Washington D.C. and give direction to the foundering organization. Ruckelshaus arrived ready to meet "new realities, new challenges, and try different approaches."[43] The "special status and circumstances" of tribes and Indian country seemed perfectly suited to that approach.[44] He declared full support for Reagan's statement on tribal self-determination during his confirmation process. Almost exactly one year later Ruckelshaus informed Congress the Agency was nearing release of an official Indian Policy.

Again, EPA prepared the Policy without the input or involvement of tribes, but regional offices were directed to send the draft policy to tribes for reaction. EPA also remedied another shortcoming of the Discussion Paper's distribution, sending the draft Policy to a number of federal agencies with experience in Indian country. Comments received from outside the Agency, as well as from EPA offices and regions, were uniformly positive and encouraging on the Policy's general tenor of respect for tribal self-determination. But some tribes and experienced EPA staffers noted the Agency's repeating history of lofty unimplemented policy commitments. They openly expressed skepticism whether the Agency intended to go beyond rhetoric and implement real change.

Resource limitations were the proof in the pudding. Treating tribes as states would increase EPA's potential partners several fold. Some managers questioned whether real progress could be made without a substantial infusion of new resources. The water director, whose office would later house the Indian program, bluntly stated "[i]f we are to meet current Agency priorities, we simply cannot assume the additional responsibility of implementing the Indian Policy."[45] The budget process for fiscal years 1984 and 1985 was complete, so no new Indian program activities would occur until 1986 unless funds were reallocated internally. Agency directors predicted program managers would not readjust dollars without a clear showing by the Administrator and Deputy Administrator of the relative priority of the Indian Policy.

The Deputy Administrator, Alvin Alm, was perhaps more familiar with Indian issues than any of the Agency's senior management. Alm played a role in EPA's first two Indian country actions. He was involved in developing the Agency's regulations for federal implementation of the water pollution permit program on Indian reservations in 1973, and for tribal air quality redesignation in 1974. Alm supported the draft Policy's direction but he was wary of the criticisms of rhetoric leveled at the 1980 Indian Policy and Reagan's 1983 Statement. He directed the Policy language be tightened so "that we do not appear to promise more than we are likely to deliver."[46] The new Indian Policy would be institutionalized over the long term by incorporating its principles into the Agency's strategic planning, annual budget processes, and performance and evaluation reviews. In the near term, administrators and program managers were urged to reallocate existing resources to demonstrate even minor concrete implementation results.

The Second Indian Policy

EPA issued its second official Indian Policy on November 8, 1984. The format and content of its introductory text, policy statements, and principles were strikingly similar to the 1980 Indian Policy. "[T]he keynote of our efforts will be to give special consideration to tribal interests and the close involvement of tribal governments in making decisions and managing environmental programs affecting reservation lands." The introduction, updated from the 1980 Policy, linked this approach to Reagan's 1983 themes of respect for tribal self-government and federal-tribal relations on a government-to-government basis. But of course, this was essentially the treatment-as-a-state approach EPA first set out in 1974.

The 1984 Policy expanded the 1980 Policy's six principles into nine:

1. The Agency stands ready to work directly with Indian Tribal Governments on a one-to-one basis (the "government-to-government relationship"), rather than as subdivisions of other governments.

2. The Agency will recognize Tribal Governments as the primary parties for setting standards, making environmental policy decisions and managing programs for reservations, consistent with Agency standards and regulations.

3. The Agency will take affirmative steps to encourage and assist tribes in assuming regulatory and program management responsibilities for reservation lands.

4. The Agency will take appropriate steps to remove existing legal and procedural impediments to working directly and effectively with tribal governments on reservation programs.

5. The Agency, in keeping with the federal trust responsibility, will assure that tribal concerns and interests are considered whenever EPA's actions and/or decisions may affect reservation environments.

6. The Agency will encourage cooperation between tribal, state and local governments to resolve environmental problems of mutual concern.

7. The Agency will work with other federal agencies which have related responsibilities on Indian reservations to enlist their interest and support in cooperative efforts to help tribes assume environmental program responsibilities for reservations.

8. The Agency will strive to assure compliance with environmental statutes and regulations on Indian reservations.

9. The Agency will incorporate these Indian policy goals into its planning and management activities, including its budget, operating guidance, legislative initiatives, management accountability system and ongoing policy and regulation development processes.[47]

The principles described a familiar hierarchy of management options and tools for implementing them. EPA's preferred tribal role was as a full cooperative federalism partner, operating delegable programs on-reservation, just as states did off-reservation. Of course, that role was aspirational since Congress had explicitly authorized tribal roles in only two narrow programs by 1984. Still, those authorizations had come on the heels of EPA's interpretations of silent statutes and had drawn little objection. When EPA approved the first tribal program delegation no state objected. Several non-Indian companies did, but the court deferred to EPA's administrative judgment on the proper implementation of the statutory program despite the absence of clear Congressional guidance.

Several 1984 Policy principles focused on realizing the Agency's preferred full tribal role. EPA would identify and eliminate existing barriers by making regulatory changes and seeking statutory amendments. EPA would affirmatively encourage tribal participation and program assumptions through outreach and technical and financial assistance. EPA would enlist the support and assistance of other federal agencies with experience in Indian country like the Bureau of Indian Affairs and the Indian Health Service. Recognizing the potential for transboundary impacts and disputes, the Agency would also encourage cooperation between tribal and state governments. That principle envisioned comity among equals; disputes would be resolved in an atmosphere of mutual respect, and not simply by sacrificing differing tribal values.

True to the spirit of self-determination, EPA's preferred full tribal role was not mandatory. Tribes were free to elect a lesser program role, or no role at all. Where the tribe self-determined not to seek full delegation, EPA would retain implementation responsibility for that particular program. EPA would also directly implement reservation programs during the time a tribe was developing program capacity. In any case, EPA would not delegate reservation programs to states unless Congress expressly authorized state jurisdiction.

Whatever role tribes elected, EPA's work would by guided by several operating assumptions. The federal government's trust responsibility for tribal environmental interests would inform EPA decisions affecting reservations. Conflicts between neighboring states and tribes would best be resolved by early intergovernmental cooperation, with EPA playing a facilitator-type role. In matters of federal enforcement, EPA would take its usual compliance approach with non-tribal reservation violators in cooperation with the tribe. For tribal facilities, EPA would focus initially on compliance assistance, resorting to enforcement only if federal assistance failed. In more general matters like Agency operations, planning and management processes, accountability mechanisms and budgeting, the Policy entreated Agency personnel to institutionalize its goals at all levels.

Along with the 1984 Policy, EPA issued a companion Implementation Guidance for initial short-term efforts at actualizing the Policy. The Guidance designated a lead headquarters office for resolving implementation issues with the assistance of the Indian Work Group. The Work Group would facilitate overall Policy coordination, address existing legal barriers to tribal program assumption, and identify appropriate Indian programs and pilot projects. Program offices and regional offices were expected to support this work by staffing the Work Group.

Programs and regions would also conduct the on-the-ground work sorely lacking to this point. The Guidance directed they open formal lines of communication through direct, face-to-face contact with tribal governments. Improved EPA-tribe communication was a predicate to realizing the Guidance's explicit expectation that managers affirmatively seek tribes' views on EPA decisions directly or indirectly affecting tribal territories. To enable informed input and participation, the Guidance directed managers provide appropriate information and technical assistance to tribes just as EPA had done for states during the development of their programs. However, as predicted by regional administrators commenting on the draft Policy, no new resources followed these expectations. Offices were directed to reprogram previously allocated funds for Indian program activities for the upcoming two fiscal years.

Despite these practical shortcomings, the 1984 Policy articulated a clear albeit unquantifiable Agency goal of respecting tribal governments' value judgments about environmental quality and achieving a level of Indian country environmental protection equivalent to other areas of the nation. Policy goals are just goals of course. They were no more enforceable than the federal trust responsibility for general tribal interests. Yet, the Administrator's approval gave this Policy the opportunity not presented by the 1980 Policy. Office directors, regional administrators, and Agency staff now possessed an official directive for creative actions not previously sanctioned. Perhaps staff would not be chastised for ignoring the Policy in a particular circumstance; but conversely, the Policy implied staff would not be penalized for actualizing it in appropriate situations. So, like the trust responsibility, the Policy had value to tribes more as a persuasive consideration counseling atypical Agency responses than as a remedial tool forcing particular results. Time would tell whether EPA and the tribes would make effective use of it.

Judicial Deference for EPA's Indian Program

Before the Agency had any opportunity to begin implementation of the new Indian Policy, its underlying premise that states lack regulatory jurisdiction on Indian reservations and its primary tenet for direct federal implementation instead of state delegation were judicially confirmed. The same court that in *Nance* upheld the Northern Cheyenne air quality redesignation in the first challenge to EPA's Indian program also handed EPA its second win. In *State of Washington, Department of Ecology v. United States Environmental Protection Agency*,[48] the Ninth Circuit Court of Appeals found no error in the Agency's rejection of a state's application for delegation of the federal hazardous waste program on Indian reservations.

Like all of the early environmental statutes, the Resource Conservation and Recovery Act, which among other things regulated the treatment, storage and disposal of hazardous wastes, was silent on Indian country implementation. EPA had indirectly addressed the issue just a few months before issuing the first Indian Policy in 1980 when it promulgated regulations for approving state permit programs under the Act and other regulatory statutes. Those rules said EPA would "assume that a State lacks authority [over Indian lands] unless the State affirmatively asserts authority and supports its assertion with an analysis from the State Attorney General."[49] EPA would directly implement the federal programs for Indian country where the state government could not show jurisdiction.

EPA's willingness to consider state claims was consistent with its position in 1973 that approved state water programs did not extend to Indian activities on Indian lands except pursuant to independent sources of authority. Read together, the two rules made clear that EPA approvals of state programs did not encompass Indian country unless the question had been explicitly raised and resolved in favor of state implementation. What was not clear were the possible bases supporting a state claim; neither regulation explained the legal reasoning behind the Agency's assumption that states lack jurisdiction in Indian country in most cases.

In 1982, the State of Washington tested EPA's unstated rationale and its resolve for actualizing the 1980 Indian Policy. The State affirmatively claimed authority over all hazardous waste facilities within the State, including those on Indian lands, in its application for delegation of the federal program. Included with the application was the required Attorney General's statement, which argued the State's legal basis for claiming authority over Indian lands was the Resource Conservation and Recovery Act itself. The Act did not specifically authorize state authority in Indian country, but its cooperative federalist preference for state implementation and comprehensive regulatory focus on all persons involved in hazardous waste handling suggested a congressional intent that states regulate the entire geographic territory within state borders. The Act also contained a provision common to the other environmental statutes that specifically preserved states' inherent authority to impose requirements more stringent than the federal regulations.

No similar provision preserving inherent tribal powers over environmental management appeared in the statute. The Act's only reference to Indian tribes came in their unusual, and unexplained, inclusion within the definition of municipality.[50] That odd association of sovereign tribal governments with subdivisions of state governments had also appeared without explanation in the regulatory statutes other than the Clean Air Act whose 1977 amendments adopted the state-like air quality role EPA proffered for tribes in 1974.

EPA's disagreement with the State's interpretation of the Act revealed the assumptions driving its early Indian program actions and the permit program regulations. It viewed Congress' general references to states' primary responsibilities for environmental management as applicable to areas over which they possessed inherent authority rather than an implicit authorization for implementation of federal programs in Indian country. The permit regulations envisioned state legal analyses based on other sources of jurisdiction like specific treaties or special jurisdictional statutes rather than arguments over the meaning of the ambiguous environmental statutes. Washington offered no independent basis for its claim so EPA disapproved the State program as to Indian lands, retaining authority for that territory itself.[51]

Washington's judicial challenge to the Agency's decision was rejected by the Ninth Circuit in an opinion written by Judge William Canby, probably the court's most experienced jurist on Indian law issues. Canby clerked for Justice Charles Whittaker of the United States Supreme Court in 1959 when it issued the termination era case of *Williams v. Lee*, which iterated the long held policy of leaving reservation Indians free from state regulation but also opened the Indian country door to state law that did not infringe on "the right of reservation Indians to make their own laws and be ruled by them."[52] Working on that case sparked Canby's interest and he later joined the law faculty at Arizona State University to teach one of the nation's first courses in federal Indian law and help found the University's well-known Indian Legal Program. Just after his appointment to the federal bench by Jimmy Carter in 1980, and shortly before he wrote *Washington Department of Ecology*, Canby published a widely read mini-treatise on federal Indian law.[53]

Judge Canby began the court's opinion by noting the statutory language relied on by Washington made no mention of state authority over Indians or Indian country. The Act's legislative history was "totally silent" on whether state programs approved "in lieu of" the federal program applied in Indian country. The Act's sole reference to Indian tribes as municipalities, which were defined in turn as regulated persons, subjected tribes and Indian country to the Act's regulatory requirements but shed no particular light on which government Congress expected would enforce them. In short, Congress' intent on this preliminary Indian program question was not clear.

The parties' contrary interpretations of the Act's ambiguity—Washington discerning implicit authorization for state implementation and EPA finding none—raised an important and timely administrative law issue. During the twentieth century courts addressing competing views of the scope of regulatory statutes vacillated between exercising independent judgment on the questions of law presented and giving preferential weight to the positions taken by administrative agencies charged with implementing those statutes. The year before the Ninth Circuit decided *Washington Department of Ecology*, the Supreme Court issued what would become a bellwether administrative law case. *Chevron, U.S.A. Inc. v. Natural Resource Defense Council*[54] held that a court's first inquiry should always be congressional intent, but where the requisite clarity was lacking, the court's role was not to substitute its independent judgment for that of a previously announced agency position, especially in complex regulatory schemes involving reconciliation of conflicting policies. The Court reasoned that by leaving a statutory gap, Congress implicitly delegated discretion for filling it to the agency, so that the question for the court was simply whether the agency's interpretation of the ambiguous statute was reasonable and not whether other policy positions (argued by those challenging the agency) might be more appropriate in the court's view.

The Ninth Circuit found EPA's rejection of Washington's hazardous waste program over Indian lands appropriate for *Chevron* deference. Congress' intent on the matter was not clear, forcing the Agency to rely on its expertise in regulatory program implementation and its discretion in reconciling Indian and environmental policies. The reasonableness of EPA's position that the Act did not extend state authority to Indian country was demonstrated by federal Indian law and the Agency's policies and past practices.

Judge Canby offered a succinct summary of the "well-settled" Indian law principle that states are generally precluded from regulating Indians in Indian country unless clearly authorized by Congress. That rule derived in part from the existence of a broad federal authority over Indian affairs and the concomitant federal trust responsibility for protecting Indian rights often against encroachment by states. Conceivably, direct implementation of the Act's program could discharge the federal trust by ensuring tribal lands would not become "dumping grounds" for hazardous waste generated off-reservation, an early Indian country environmental justice concern raised by several Washington tribes and others who filed a friend of the court amicus curiae brief in the case.

The general prohibition against state regulation of Indians was also informed by the long tradition of tribal sovereignty and self-government. Although tribal regulatory authority over hazardous waste was not at issue in *Washington Department of Ecology*, the court could not help observing that tribal self-determination was rapidly infiltrating the heretofore state-dominated cooperative federalist environmental law paradigm. Its earlier decision in *Nance* validated the 1974 tribal air quality program role that EPA created despite the absence of specific congressional authorization and in the face of statutory language preserving state governments' authority over their entire geographic area. Congress codified that state-like air quality role and EPA's similar tribal pesticide applicator certification role in the late 1970s, and inserted in a third statute a proviso disclaiming any intent to alter the jurisdictional status of Indian lands by subjecting federal facilities to state regulation. EPA's 1980 Indian Policy and 1983 Discussion Paper espoused a commitment to primary tribal management roles consistent with President Reagan's 1983 exhortation for a national policy of true tribal self-determination through delegation of federal programs to tribes. The court was apparently unaware of and did not note the more recent 1984 Indian Policy, which made plain the Agency's desire to work with tribes directly rather than through state governments, perhaps because the Policy was adopted two months after the case was argued to the court.

Neither Congress nor EPA had yet taken a position on tribal implementation of the hazardous waste program, but the court had seen the writing on the wall and Judge Canby specifically said the court did not wish to foreclose that possibility. Subordinating tribes to state regulation seemed clearly at odds with tribes' governmental interests and the emerging federal policy encouraging tribal assumption of or involvement in the administration of federal programs in Indian country. EPA's decision to retain federal authority, on the other hand, could promote the self-government policy through tribal consultation on program decisions like siting new waste disposal facilities, perhaps building tribal capacity leading to eventual program operation, as well as helping discharge the federal trust responsibility for protecting the Indian country environment.

The court thus turned away the State's invitation to second-guess EPA's judgment on how best to achieve national environmental protection in light of the Indian country regulatory gap. *Chevron's* black letter administrative law specifically described a limited judicial role for resolving statutory ambiguities in regulatory programs Congress charged administrative agencies with implementing, and that deferential standard of review would play a crucial role in many of the Agency's Indian program successes in court over the coming years. Even before *Chevron, Nance* had accorded great weight to EPA's conclusion that tribal regulatory roles were not inconsistent with states' primary regulatory responsibilities. Like *Nance*, the challenged decision in *Washington Department of Ecology* reflected a permissible view of an ambiguous statute and was consistent with previously declared Agency polices. EPA's rejection of the State's hazardous waste application for Indian lands in the absence of clear congressional authorization was not unreasonable.

Explicit congressional authorization, however, was not the only way for states to enter Indian country. After the allotment era ushered in a new wave of non-Indian immigrants, the Supreme Court backed away from its earlier absolute prohibition on state authority in Indian country believing the presence of non-Indian state residents increased state interests there. So while the policy of protecting Indians from state regulation remained deeply rooted, the modern rule was that even without Congress' express permission states could nonetheless exercise authority over non-Indians in Indian country so long as doing so did not infringe on tribal self-governance and was not preempted by federal Indian law.

EPA's decision on Washington's program application followed the precedents set in the 1980 regulations and the 1980 and 1984 Indian Policies of blending those two separate Indian law rules together to form a general statement of states' limited Indian country jurisdiction and insistence on a state showing of express congressional authorization. The Agency similarly glossed over the distinction between the Court's clear support for tribal sovereignty over tribal citizens and its distinctly less favorable treatment of tribal jurisdiction over non-Indians. Commenting on the draft 1984 Policy, the United States Department of Justice cautioned EPA saying that "[g]eneralizations about jurisdiction over lands and activities on Indian reservations are particularly dangerous."[55] The United States Department of the Interior's comments were more explicit:

> The draft [Indian Policy] statement announces that EPA will not delegate program responsibility to a State on an Indian reservation in the absence of an express grant of jurisdiction. When no significant tribal interests are affected, however, the State—not the Tribe—has jurisdiction over conduct by non-Indians on a reservation. The State will frequently have jurisdiction simply because no significant tribal interests are involved even though there is no express statutory grant of jurisdiction to the State.[56]

The Ninth Circuit also hinted at EPA's potential overreaching in *Washington Department of Ecology*:

> It is important at the outset to define the issue raised by the State of Washington's petition. Washington sought EPA authorization to apply its hazardous waste program to both Indian and non-Indian residents of Indian reservations. In the Attorney General's analysis of state jurisdiction and again before this court, Washington contended [the Resource Conservation and Recovery Act] confers on the state the right to regulate all hazardous waste activities within the state, with no exceptions for Indian tribes or Indian lands. We hold today that the EPA Regional Administrator properly refused to approve the proposed state program because [the Act] does not authorize the states to regulate Indians on Indian lands. We do not decide the question whether Washington is empowered to create a program reaching into Indian country when that reach is limited to non-Indians.[57]

Washington caught the hint and submitted an amended petition to EPA asserting authority over only non-Indian hazardous waste activities on Indian lands. Perhaps reading too much into the court's comment, the State offered no supporting legal argument. EPA apparently erred to the opposite side in intuiting the court's intent. It rejected the State's claim in three sentences by simply equating "Indian lands" with "Indian country" that encompassed dependent Indian communities, Indian land allotments and all lands within Indian reservations, including lands owned outright or in "fee simple" by non-Indians.[58] Curiously, the State did not challenge that decision in court.

Shortly thereafter, Washington applied to EPA for approval under the Safe Drinking Water Act of its underground injection program on non-Indian fee simple lands within Indian reservations in the State. This time, the State explicitly asserted such authority existed because it would not infringe on tribal self-government and was not preempted by federal law. That correct statement of the law, however, did not carry the State's burden to show non-infringement and lack of preemption. Washington offered no analysis of the various interests at stake. EPA said the federal and tribal interests associated with tribal self-determination in the Act and the Agency's Indian Policy were significant, and would be hindered by state regulation. EPA rejected the State's application on that basis,[59] and again Washington lodged no challenge.

Washington's failure of proof made the Agency's decision easier than it otherwise would have been. The Court's Indian preemption test involved a subjective calculus of the pervasiveness of federal regulation and the relative state, federal and tribal interests at stake. The environmental context offered persuasive arguments for state preemption, but the issue's lack of clarity was ripe for lengthy court battles.

EPA saw an opportunity to blunt such claims in a management concept raised in the 1983 Discussion Paper and expanded on by a tribal comment made during the public meeting on Washington's underground injection program application:

> All lands within the Reservation regardless of ownership are to be regulated by EPA under Federal law. *The need for unitary management of water sources on Indian reservations is without question*, as the dangers posed by [underground injection] activities to underground aquifers as well as to surface waters *demand the imposition of a single comprehensive management scheme* by EPA. This conclusion is grounded in the knowledge that actions taken on one parcel of land, no matter whether owned by an Indian or a non-Indian, can have an important environmental consequence on adjacent parcels on the reservation.[60]

The notion of a single reservation-wide program made perfect sense for common mobile resources like air and water. In theory, it would improve the administrative efficiency of program implementation. The approach also accorded with the Supreme Court's not infrequent comment that checkerboard regulation of Indian country is impractical and not favored in the modern era.[61] "Jurisdiction dependent on the 'tract book' promises to be uncertain and hectic."[62] Perhaps most importantly, it could minimize or preclude litigation causing long-term jurisdictional uncertainties undermining effective program implementation.

In 1991, EPA issued a "state-tribe concept paper" reaffirming the 1984 Indian Policy and setting out additional guidelines and procedures for federal program delegation and implementation. The paper was largely an iteration of the earlier Policy, with one important exception: the Agency announced its adoption of an anti-checkerboard policy for Indian reservations:

> Consistent with the EPA Indian Policy and the interests of administrative clarity, the Agency will view Indian reservations as single administrative units for regulatory purposes. Hence, as a general rule, the Agency will authorize a tribal or state government to manage reservation programs only where that government can demonstrate adequate jurisdiction over pollution sources throughout the reservation. Where, however, a tribe cannot demonstrate jurisdiction over one or more pollution sources, the Agency will retain enforcement primacy for those sources.[63]

States recognized the anti-checkerboard policy for what it was: an absolute bar masquerading as a neutral rule. EPA well knew the Supreme Court almost never tolerated direct state regulation of Indian tribes and reservation Indians. That rule was the genesis of EPA's conclusion that a regulatory void existed in Indian country and called for a special alternative approach. But that meant states could never show jurisdiction over all pollution sources on reservations. The anti-checkerboard policy thus ostensibly foreclosed state delegations even for reservations with very high non-Indian populations and percentages of fee lands. EPA incorporated the policy into nearly all of its Indian program regulations in the 1990s, and time would reveal its important contribution to obtaining courts' continued deference to the Agency's Indian program.

CHAPTER 3

FAR UNDERGROUND: PROTECTING INDIAN COUNTRY DRINKING WATER

Uncontaminated drinking water is second only to clean air in importance to human health. In the United States drinking water is typically derived from two sources: waters on the earth's surface, like rivers and lakes, and underground aquifers. The national population draws its drinking water about evenly between the two sources although on volume over ninety-five percent of the nation's fresh water is underground. In rural areas like Indian country, nearly ninety percent of drinking water comes from underground.

Groundwater quality is vulnerable to a host of current and historic surface land uses. Millions of pounds of pesticides, herbicides and fertilizers are applied to farmlands, golf courses and lawns annually and some 100,000 solid waste landfills and millions of underground storage tanks have leaked contaminants. Rainwater and snowmelt facilitate the migration of these pollutants from surface and subsurface soils into groundwater.

A more direct threat is the intentional injection of wastes and other liquids into subsurface soils. For decades the petroleum industry has injected fluids underground to increase pressure forcing petroleum to oil wells. Often the liquid is concentrated saltwater brine generated as an unwanted byproduct of the oil and gas development itself. Other industries also use subsurface geologic layers for waste disposal. The chemical, petrochemical, wood preserving, minerals, metals, agricultural and energy industries have pumped millions of tons of nonhazardous, hazardous, toxic and radioactive liquids into tens of thousands of underground wells.[1]

In 1970, EPA's predecessor in water pollution control, the Department of the Interior, recognized underground waste injections potentially threatened subsurface water supplies. Interior adopted a policy against deep well injection conducted without water supply protections, which EPA adopted after assuming Interior's water program. But neither Agency possessed clear authority for imposing underground injection controls.

Congress responded in 1974 by enacting the first federal statute addressing groundwater pollution. The Safe Drinking Water Act focused on public drinking water systems, whether drawn from surface or subsurface sources, requiring they maintain particular health-based levels of purity. The Act also required permits for certain land uses, including underground injection, which might endanger drinking water sources.

The Safe Drinking Water Act employed the cooperative federalism model spawned by the 1970 Clean Air Act and repeated in the 1972 Federal Water Pollution Control Act (later called the Clean Water Act). Congress explicitly envisioned a joint federal-state system to regulate the discharge of pollutants into underground waters from injection wells. Congress directed EPA to promulgate regulations setting minimum requirements for states to seek "primacy" or primary responsibility for implementing their own injection control programs under EPA supervision. If a state did not apply for primacy, or failed to develop and enforce a program consistent with the minimum federal requirements, then EPA was to develop and implement a federal injection program.

Federal Underground Injection Control Programs in Indian Country

Federal backup authority was necessary to ensure states did not repeat their historic inattention to environmental protection, and because "the causes and effects of unhealthy drinking water are national in scope."[2] Congress was also well aware that contaminated groundwater could cross state boundaries and anticipated a need for injection programs in all fifty states. Indeed, "[i]t is readily apparent from the legislative history that the [1974 Act was to apply] throughout the country, border to border, ocean to ocean."[3] And yet, like the early Clean Air and Clean Water Acts, Congress left a gaping hole in its geographic coverage: no provision of the 1974 Safe Drinking Water Act referred to whether or how it should be implemented in Indian country.

The omission of Indian country was curious for two other reasons. One was Congress' contemporary acknowledgement of the need for clean drinking water in Indian country. The committee report accompanying the Act noted existing Indian Health Service grant programs for the construction of sanitation and drinking water systems for Indians and Alaska natives. But the committee suggested those programs might not adequately ensure safe drinking water,[4] implying its expectation the Act's anticipated benefits would extend to Indians. That concern for extending the benefits of federal environmental law to low income communities of color was a progenitor of the modern environmental justice movement that would begin nearly twenty years later.

The second reason the Safe Drinking Water Act's silence on Indian country was curious was its sole and unexplained reference to Indian tribes as "municipalities." Congress defined the term as "a city, town or other public body created by or pursuant to state law, *or an authorized Indian tribal organization.*"[5] That strange appellation for sovereign tribal governments was even more odd for its association with traditional state subdivisions. It first appeared in the U.S. Code—also without explanation—in the 1970 Resource Conservation and Recovery Act and in the 1972 Clean Water Act. Under both statutes, the municipal designation rendered tribes eligible for particular financial grants relating to environmental planning and demonstration projects, required EPA consultation on specified federal initiatives, and, because municipalities were defined in turn as legal "persons," subjected tribes to the acts' pollution prohibitions and requirements as regulated entities.

The reference to tribes as municipalities, and the consequences of that designation, clearly implied Congress intended those pollution laws to apply in Indian country. Less clear was how they should be implemented there. Only EPA and states, not municipalities, were authorized to run the core regulatory components of both statutes—the pollution discharge permit programs. Additionally, the statutes contained general references to states as having primary responsibility for pollution control.

In later years, states and others would argue those general references implied Congress expected state implementation everywhere including Indian country. The State of Washington took that position in the early 1980s in *Washington Department of Ecology.* As it has consistently done across its many programs, EPA rejected the argument and the State's application for delegation of the federal hazardous waste program on Indian lands despite Congress' silence on Indian country. As noted in Chapter 2, the Ninth Circuit upheld the Agency's decision, deferring to its reasonable interpretations of the ambiguity Congress left in the statute.[6]

The reasonableness of EPA's general position was supported by a 1973 Supreme Court opinion reciting the well-established rule that state laws do not apply to reservation Indians unless Congress expressly authorizes such authority.[7] EPA took its first Indian program action just two months after that Supreme Court decision. In May 1973, EPA promulgated a regulation detailing how states could receive delegation of one of the Clean Water Act's pollution permit programs. The Agency said it would not delegate the program to states for Indian activities on Indian lands because Congress had not explicitly authorized state implementation.[8]

A year later, presumably aware of the Court's insistence for explicit state authorization and EPA's interpretation of the Clean Water Act as failing that test, Congress enacted the Safe Drinking Water Act. Like other federal environmental statutes, the Safe Drinking Water Act contained a general reference to states' primary responsibility for pollution control. And as the Clean Water Act did, its definition of municipality included Indian tribes but was otherwise silent on Indian country implementation. It was thus not surprising that EPA followed its sense of the Clean Water Act with an interpretation that the Safe Drinking Water Act did not authorize state implementation on Indian lands. In fact, EPA said it would "assume that a State lacks authority unless the State affirmatively asserts authority and supports its assertion with an analysis from the State Attorney General."[9]

A state's assertion and analysis, of course, had to be more that a claim the Safe Drinking Water Act implicitly authorized state implementation on Indian lands. But that did not mean a state could never prove Indian country jurisdiction. Courts have long claimed for Congress a broad Indian power, including the authority to delegate Indian country jurisdiction to states. Such delegations are rare and typically specific to a particular state or tribe, often made as a concession in settling Indian land claims. For example, the Puyallup Land Claims Settlement Act of 1989 ratified a settlement agreement that specifically provided Washington State authority over non-Indian lands inside the Puyallup Tribe's reservation.[10] Similarly, the Maine Indian Land Claims Settlement Act of 1980 ratified a settlement agreement that consented to state jurisdiction over certain Indian reservation lands in Maine.[11]

Only once, in a particularly infamous instance, has Congress made a broader delegation of Indian country jurisdiction to states. In 1953, President Dwight D. Eisenhower took office, taking with him Republican majorities in both Houses of Congress, partly on a platform of guarding against the purported danger of big government. An early and easy target was dismantling the federal government's extensive management of Indian affairs, ostensibly so that Indians could be "freed from Federal supervision and control and from all disabilities and limitations specifically applicable to Indians."[12] Terminating the political government-to-government relationship of tribes and the federal government, it was asserted, would entitle Indians to the same "privileges and responsibilities" applicable to other citizens. It would also subject Indians to the same laws.

A key component of the so-called Termination Era was a 1953 congressional act commonly known as Public Law 280.[13] It addressed a perception of rampant lawlessness in certain parts of Indian country by transferring criminal jurisdiction from the federal government to five specific states, and offering the same authority to any other state electing such responsibility. Public Law 280 also provided that the "civil laws of such State" would apply in Indian country. In 1976, the Supreme Court decided that provision encompassed the rules of decisions state courts use in deciding civil cases, but did not authorize the application of state regulatory laws to Indian country.[14] Although the federal environmental laws all carry criminal sanctions for certain violations, they are quintessentially civil regulatory statutes and thus not authorized by Public Law 280 for state implementation in Indian country.

Congress' initial silence in the Safe Drinking Water Act, then, meant that states generally lacked jurisdiction requisite to implement the Act's regulatory programs in Indian country at least as to Indian activities. That conclusion was buttressed in 1977 by Congress' reference that amendments to the Act subjecting federal facilities to state regulation did not affect the status of or sovereignty over Indian lands.[15] The consequence for the cooperative federalism paradigm was noted in EPA's first Indian Policy, adopted in 1980 just months after the Agency promulgated regulations for approving state underground injection control programs:

> [W]ithout some modification, our programs, as designed, often fail to function adequately on Indian lands. This raises the serious possibility that, in the absence of some special alternative response by EPA, the environment of Indian reservations will be less effectively protected than the environment elsewhere. *Such a result is unacceptable.* The spirit of our Federal trust responsibility and the clear intent of Congress demand full and equal protection of the environment of the entire nation without exceptions or gaps.[16]

This was the Agency's first official articulation, though not in name, of Indian country's unique environmental justice challenge: unlike other communities of color, the threshold environmental justice question in Indian country was not whether federal programs were applied and enforced as vigorously or fully as other areas, it was whether they were implemented at all.

The Indian Policy's preferred solution envisioned filling the Indian country regulatory gap through program implementation by tribal governments. EPA would promote opportunities for tribes to assume central implementation roles consistent with the national policy of tribal self-determination. That was a long-range goal, however, because with two narrow exceptions the environmental laws at the time did not authorize program delegation to tribes. So, until the laws were amended, EPA would fill the unacceptable regulatory gap in Indian country through direct federal implementation. However, its "special alternative response" would not follow the old model of federal decision-making without tribal consultation; EPA claimed its work would be informed by the close involvement of tribal governments in a manner consistent with tribal self-determination.

Indian country has seen more than its fair share of high-sounding but unactualized policy pronouncements. In fact, due in part to administration changes shortly after its adoption, EPA largely failed to implement the 1980 Indian Policy across the Agency and its programs. Yet, strains of the Policy did appear in various program-specific actions. One of the first appeared in EPA's federal underground injection program.

The Safe Drinking Water Act directed that EPA publish regulations for state underground injection control programs containing minimum requirements Congress felt necessary for preventing endangerment of underground sources of drinking water. EPA's 1980 regulations set out extensive technical requirements beyond Congress' minimums for five classes of injection wells, but the Agency did not require state programs be identical. Nonetheless, the oil and gas industry saw the federal requirements as potentially burdensome, and pressed Congress for more lenient treatment. Congress let EPA's requirements stand, but obliged the industry by providing an alternative method for states to show their injection programs for Class II oil and gas wells would prevent endangerment of underground water supplies.[17]

States' flexibility in designing injection programs generally and Class II programs specifically were paradigmatic symbols of modern cooperative federalism. Apart from specific federal mandates or prohibitions, states are generally free to achieve national goals through whatever means they elect. One reason states seek primacy is to avoid having EPA directly implement a generic federal program developed without consideration of site-specific circumstances and the priorities of local communities. States' freedom to differ from federal programs, however, raised unique and previously unconsidered issues for Indian country.

EPA's requirements for state injection programs essentially doubled as the Agency's generic program. Where a state did not develop an injection program, or where its program fell short of protecting underground waters, EPA would directly implement the generic federal program. EPA's assumption that states lacked jurisdiction in Indian country meant that EPA would be respon-

sible for regulating underground injections there even if the state had an otherwise acceptable program. The possibility of two different programs running
simultaneously in the same state evoked the specter of increased complexity
and compliance costs for operators of multiple injection wells.

Interestingly, a related issue was the reverse of the state/federal programs
challenge. In states lacking approved programs, EPA initially proposed applying the generic federal program on both Indian and non-Indian lands. That
"one-size-fits-all" approach would promote consistency in the federal program
and save EPA time and resources that would otherwise be devoted to site-specific development. But the generic program was not developed with Indian
country in mind and could not be adapted to particular tribal interests or concerns in a manner similar to states' alternative programs.

In the spirit of the Indian Policy, EPA developed a special alternative response to these issues that emphasized tribal participation. Where appropriate, the Agency said it would adapt the generic federal program on specific Indian reservations or lands using the same flexibility states possessed.[18] EPA
promised to give "special consideration" to the interests and preferences of the
affected tribe consistent with the government-to-government relationship between tribes and the United States. Other factors influencing a program's design would be the goals of simplifying regulatory requirements on well operators and maintaining consistency among the federal programs.

The Agency's good intentions for federal injection programs tailored to the
unique circumstances and needs of Indian country then ran headlong into the
wall of practical reality. The National Wildlife Federation sued EPA for sitting
idle in the face of some thirty states' failures to develop injection programs.
EPA settled the suit by promulgating two large packages of federal programs
in 1984. Seventeen of the states covered by the programs contained Indian
lands. Public hearings did not identify a consensus approach for the Indian
country programs and, facing court-imposed deadlines, EPA opted for the
generic program in all but a few instances.

EPA again came under fire for slow action two years later. Congress was
clearly dissatisfied that twelve years after enacting the Safe Drinking Water Act,
EPA had only scratched the surface of protecting Indian drinking water
sources. Statutory amendments in 1986 directed EPA to prescribe injection
programs for every tribe lacking one within nine months.[19] With little time
for tailoring specific programs, EPA promulgated the generic program for Indian country within twenty-seven states.[20]

These actions moved the Agency's general Indian program forward, albeit
modestly, despite their generic nature. They sent a clear message to states and

well operators that federal rather than state injection programs would control in Indian country. An important Indian law case in 1981 indicated the Supreme Court placed great weight on the extent of past state regulation of non-Indians activities in determining whether tribal jurisdiction extended to those activities.[21] Direct federal implementation effectively limited states from developing regulatory histories, thus strengthening (or at least not undermining) potential future tribal claims of jurisdiction.

The federal injection program also illustrated how the Indian Policy's arguably rhetorical commitment to enhancing tribal roles could have concrete practical consequences. EPA promulgated its generic program in states lacking programs and in states with approved programs not applicable to Indian country. In states without programs, EPA rebuffed state and industry pleas for adapting the generic programs to related local laws in part because a nationally uniform federal program would be easier to administer. For Indian country programs, however, national uniformity, as well as EPA's interest in minimizing inconsistencies with state requirements, gave way to tribal preferences. Harkening back to its early Indian program actions in the 1970s under the air and pesticides acts and the 1980 Indian Policy, EPA cited its newly adopted 1984 Indian Policy in support of this view:

> [I]t was and is Agency policy to accommodate the wishes of the Tribal governments as far as possible, to deal with them on a government-to-government basis, and to assist them in developing the capability to manage their own environmental programs.[22]

EPA also took its Indian Policy commitment for expanded tribal outreach more seriously in the injection program than it had in developing the official Indian Policies and prior Indian country regulations. Copies of proposed programs were distributed to tribes and public hearings were held in cities closer to Indian country than Washington D.C. (although not on reservations). Few tribes, however, showed interest in tribe-specific programs. EPA took those that did at their word. EPA excluded the Seneca Nation from its generic program for Indian country in New York because the Tribe initially indicated a desire for working with EPA on a tailored program. Later, when the Tribe's priorities changed, EPA amended the generic New York program to add Seneca. EPA developed injection programs different or more stringent than the generic program for Indian country in Minnesota, Wisconsin and Wyoming, and for certain tribes in Utah and New Mexico, including the Navajo Nation whose reservation extends beyond those two states into Arizona and Colorado. EPA also tailored an injection program for certain tribes in the oil-rich state of Oklahoma.

Black Gold and Groundwater Contamination in Oklahoma

In many respects the history of oil production in Oklahoma's Indian country is emblematic of the avarice that formed the core of federal Indian law, policy and action. Western contact with North American indigenous peoples occurred precisely because of European desires for more land and their appurtenant natural resources. The infamous and logically indefensible Doctrine of Discovery ensured that imperial nations' claims to "new" lands would not be unduly hampered by the inconvenient fact of their prior possession by others. Immigrants' insatiable desires for land beyond the eastern seaboard, particularly those in the Cherokee territory where gold was discovered in the early 1800s, led directly to the forced removal of some 16,000 Indians in the winter of 1838–39. The internationally recognized embarrassment of the Trail of Tears pushed many tribes far from their lush southeastern homelands to a new and comparatively desolate Indian Territory west of the Mississippi River.[23]

Federal promises to prevent incursions by white settlers into the new homelands evaporated with the discovery of black gold just decades later. Reports by Indian agents of oil appearing in surface water springs in the 1940s were confirmed in 1959 by the accidental discovery of oil in a deep saltwater well. Limited drilling began in the 1880s, and by the turn of the century, oil had shown in wells on lands occupied by the Cherokee, Choctaw, Chickasaw and Osage Nations.[24] Oil companies and wealthy non-Indians rushed to secure development leases from tribes and tribal citizens who owned individual allotments of former tribal lands. Just south of Osage the Indian town Tulsa boomed as the oil capital of the world, and in 1907, the Indian Territory entered the Union as the State of Oklahoma.

Oklahoma's success in oil production garnered less propitious national attention when the modern environmental era took hold in the late 1970s. The Safe Drinking Water Act tasked EPA with listing states where underground injection programs might be necessary to prevent endangering drinking water sources. EPA considered state populations, reliance on groundwater as a drinking source, well numbers and injection volumes. Liquid brines associated with oil and gas production, along with certain other injections, present relatively greater potential for endangerment, so the Agency weighted Class II wells in its calculation. Oklahoma ranked eleventh out of the fifty states and six U.S. territories, and was listed as one of twenty-two states needing either a state or federal injection program.[25]

Many of the states on the list dragged their feet for years, leading to the National Wildlife Federation's 1983 lawsuit forcing generic federal programs in 1984. Oklahoma did not. The State proposed and EPA approved an alternate injection program for Class II wells in 1981,[26] thus sparing Oklahoma's important oil and gas industry from extensive federal requirements. The program included the territories of five of the State's thirty-six Indian tribes. A 1947 federal act expressly subjected the lands of the Choctaw, Cherokee, Chickasaw, Creek and Seminole Tribes, sometimes collectively referred to as the Five Civilized Tribes, to the State's oil and gas regulations. Oklahoma did not seek authority for other portions of Indian country, lending credence to EPA's view that states lacked authority absent express congressional permission. Interestingly, however, EPA announced (without explanation) its intention to develop for all but one of the remaining tribes a joint injection program where the state would perform technical and administrative activities while EPA issued permits and conducted enforcement. The remaining tribe — the Osage Tribe — was already consulting with EPA for a separate federal injection program.

Oil production at Osage has a long and sorted history. A major well drilled in 1896 on northeastern Osage lands narrowly missed the distinction of being Oklahoma's first commercial well. A non-Indian company drilled that well and several others under leases made with the Osage Tribal Council and approved by the Secretary of the Department of the Interior. Interior dissolved the Tribal Council in 1900 when conflicts arose over the issue of allotment. Full-blooded Osage citizens rejected the assimilative policy of breaking communally owned tribal lands into small "allotments" conveyed to private ownership by individual tribal citizens. Mixed-bloods, some of questionable ancestry alleged to have bought or bribed their way onto the tribal rolls, urged allotment in anticipation of wealth from private oil leases.

Congress spoke to both interests in a 1906 Act that authorized individual allotments of surface lands but reserved oil, gas, coal and other minerals to the Tribe.[27] A provision in the allotment act required payments and royalties from tribal mineral leases be paid directly to tribal citizens rather than residing in a trust account managed by the Bureau of Indian Affairs. Payments would shortly net individual Osage citizens tens of thousands of dollars annually, with total per capita payments running well into the tens of millions. The dramatic shift from a turn of the century average per capita income of $200 to extreme wealth generated fanciful media descriptions of the Osage as the richest people on earth. It also brought all manner of unscrupulous non-Indians to northern Oklahoma, who conned, bilked and defrauded Indians out of their money. Where business deception failed, many non-Indians married into money.

The Osage allotment act reinstated the Osage Tribal Council, and recognized its pre-existing authority to lease rights for developing the so-called Osage Mineral Reserve, subject of course, to federal approval. Regular reports of new oil discoveries at Osage and throughout the Indian Territory brought an international flood of fortune-seeking non-Indians, reminiscent of the Heavy Eyebrows who first paddled into Osage territory in the late seventeenth century. The Osage Council tapped the market excitement with periodic oil lease auctions beginning in 1912. Prices skyrocketed. The original 1896 Osage lease was for the entire reservation and promised only a royalty of one-tenth of the oil produced and $50 per well annually. In 1922, a 160-acre lease sold for nearly $1 million with royalties of one-fifth of the oil and annual well payments of $35–100. Media reports of the auction, held outside under a shady tree, ran colorful headlines on the "Million Dollar Elm." Just a few years later a 160-acre lease went for nearly $2 million. One commenter on oil development in the southeastern United States characterized these auctions as an Osage Monte Carlo, but with a far greater exchange of money than Monaco.[28] Another author called this time simply The Great Frenzy.[29] By 1927, the Osage Tribe had leased over 530,000 acres for oil exploration and development.

Two key figures in the Osage oil boom were brothers Frank and L.E. Phillips. Frank Phillips, a shop owner from Iowa, came to the area as a bond salesman and holder of oil and gas leases. He formed a bank and trust company in Bartlesville, Indian Territory in 1905. L.E. Phillips joined him shortly thereafter to monitor their joint oil and gas properties, which they incorporated into the Phillips Petroleum Company in 1917. The Company boomed with the market. At the start it had twenty-seven employees, $3 million in assets and lease rights to 11,200 acres in Kansas and Oklahoma, most of which were on Osage lands. By 1947, the Company had grown to 16,000 employees and $500 million in assets, with oil and gas lease rights to 4.4 million acres throughout the southeastern United States. Phillips' involvement in the huge 33-square mile Burbank wellfield at Osage in the 1920s contributed significantly to this tremendous leap into the cadre of Oklahoma's major oil producers. (The 1920 discovery of Burbank is attributed to E.W. Marland, whose oil business became the Continental Oil Company (Conoco) in 1928, which merged with Phillips Petroleum to become ConocoPhillips in 2002.)

Sixty years later, Phillips' extensive investments in Oklahoma oil and gas production meant the issue of underground injection program jurisdiction in Indian country was not simply a theoretical jurisprudential question. Phillips'

Osage wells had historically been regulated by the Bureau of Indian Affairs, the agency responsible for overseeing leasing of Indian lands held in trust by the federal government. The Bureau's role was akin to a property manager, with a focus on ensuring lessees performed their contract obligations to Indian owners and did not unduly damage Indian property.[30] Its program had well operation and closure requirements potentially beneficial to the environment, but their protections were nowhere near as extensive as EPA's generic program. Implementing the Safe Drinking Water Act would add a new, complex and potentially expensive layer of environmental regulation for the owners of some 3,600 Class II injection wells at Osage.

So when EPA and the Osage Tribe began developing a tailored federal program for the Osage Mineral Reserve in 1980, EPA went beyond its normal required public participation processes. The Agency specifically notified Phillips of its intentions. It shared a draft copy of the federal program with the Company in 1982, and then met with Company officials to discuss it. The next year EPA held a public hearing on its proposed program for other Indian lands in Oklahoma. Finally, four years after informing Phillips, EPA formally proposed the federal Osage program in May 1984 and opened a forty-five day public comment period.[31] Company representatives appeared and testified at a public hearing in June, and requested an additional thirty days to file written materials. EPA declined to extend the comment period, and Phillips managed to submit extensive comments anyway. On November 15, 1984, the Agency promulgated the final Osage underground injection control program for Class II oil and gas wells.[32]

The Osage program made full use of EPA's declared flexibility for designing Indian programs. Some components were drawn directly from the Bureau of Indian Affairs' program. EPA promised to work with the Bureau to harmonize implementation of both programs, and noted its intention to accept a single permit containing both Bureau and EPA conditions. Other aspects were borrowed from the State program. EPA acknowledged many well operators like Phillips had facilities both in Osage territory and other locations in the state. Incorporating portions of the Bureau's and State's programs into the Osage program would help minimize disruption and promote relative uniformity across jurisdictional lines. Finally, portions of the generic federal injection program were also used.

Coincidentally, just one week before issuing the Osage program, EPA finalized its second official Indian Policy, which promised increased collaboration with tribes for program implementation. Many of the injection program components the Agency attributed to desires of the Osage Tribe. For example,

EPA followed the Tribe's suggestion that operators of existing saltwater disposal wells not endangering drinking water sources not be required to seek EPA permits, though they would still be subject to various EPA conditions. EPA also used the State's one-year measurement for finding an inactive well abandoned and thus requiring plugging instead of the generic federal program's six-month period at the Tribe's request. An Osage official testified in support of the federal program at the public hearing, and the Osage Tribal Council passed a resolution of support.

The most significant and controversial provision required pressure tests on the mechanical integrity of each operating well. Mechanical integrity in this context meant the well, when subjected to artificially elevated liquid pressures, evidenced no significant leakage that could allow contaminants to escape and thereby threaten underground waters.

This provision generated more industry comments than any other proposed element of the Osage program. Oil producers complained the requirement was excessive. Their overarching concern stemmed from the age and relatively unsophisticated construction of many wells at Osage. Some of them were turn-of-the-century artifacts built with hollow logs, corrugated sheet metal or other casing materials vulnerable to corrosion from saltwater brines generated in the oil production process. Newer wells incorporated more resilient materials consistent with the Bureau of Indian Affairs' regulations, but lacked the modern industry standard of concrete casings around steel piping. In short, after six or more decades of operation, many of the wells at Osage were of questionable integrity. Producers protested these older wells would likely fail the mechanical integrity test, or that the test pressure itself might cause well leaks, and urged more passive methods of showing integrity, like monitoring for leaking fluids at the surface or changing fluid levels at the base of underground waters.

EPA made some minor concessions in response to industry comments, but generally rejected the passive testing means proffered. The Agency viewed affirmative evidence of integrity under pressure, rather than simply the absence of obvious leakage, as a fundamental regulatory requirement. EPA would not waive testing requirements, nor would it allow operation of wells showing significant leakage. The final Osage program retained the mechanical integrity pressure test requirement.

Phillips perceived a triple threat to its bottom line. Initial testing of each well would take time and money previously devoted to production priorities. Wells that were strong producers but failed the test would have to be taken off-line for expensive retrofitting or repair. Upgrade expenses for marginal wells that leaked could be avoided by shutting them down, but that meant decreased production and additional costs for plugging and monitoring the abandoned wells. The Company sought protection from these expected increased compliance costs and decreased production profits by challenging the federal program in *Phillips Petroleum Company v. United States Environmental Protection Agency.*[33]

Although the Company had been involved for nearly four years in the development of the Osage program, once in court it raised for the first time a standard administrative law argument: irrespective of whether EPA's Osage program had independent merit, the Agency simply lacked authority to promulgate it. EPA strenuously urged the court reject the argument out of hand since it had not been raised during the Agency's rulemaking proceedings. The court noted Phillips had long been aware of and had participated in the program's development, characterizing the Company's argument as an apparent "afterthought" that did a "disservice to the agency, other affected parties, and to an orderly rulemaking process." Nonetheless, the court felt such a basic jurisdictional issue must be addressed despite its "unfortunate" timing.

Phillips' argument relied on a literal interpretation of the pre-1986 Safe Drinking Water Act. In 1984 when EPA promulgated the Osage program the Act recited the common cooperative federalism refrain of state-federal partnerships, and specifically authorized direct federal implementation when state programs failed to satisfy the Act's minimum requirements. Agreeing with EPA that Oklahoma lacked jurisdiction at Osage, Phillips attempted to bootstrap that concession into a conclusion EPA's backup authority thus did not apply there either.

The court acknowledged the Company's literal argument was strong "[f]rom a technician's standpoint." But it was contradicted by the Act's legislative history. Congress set a clear goal of nationwide coverage and had shown specific concern for drinking water protection in Indian country. The extent of oil and gas production across Indian country, and specifically at Osage where Congress had been involved since 1906, meant Phillips' view would eviscerate the Act's goals by creating what the court called a "vacuum of authority."

Of course, filling Indian country regulatory gaps was precisely what motivated EPA's early Indian program activities and its Indian Policies. Just one year earlier, that practical need had been a significant factor leading the *Washington Department of Ecology* court to uphold direct federal implementation of hazardous waste programs on Indian reservations in Washington when EPA concluded the State lacked jurisdiction.[34] Like *Phillips Petroleum, Washington*

Department of Ecology found EPA's choice of direct implementation a reasonable application of a statute silent on Indian country implementation.

Congressional modifications to the Safe Drinking Water Act indirectly buttressed that view. In 1977, Congress proposed an amendment subjecting federal agencies to state regulation under the Act. The Osage Tribe objected the amendment might be understood as giving states jurisdiction over Indian lands since federal agencies were intimately involved in Indian country mineral development. Congress responded by excluding Indian tribes from the definition of federal agency, and specifically stating sovereignty over Indian lands was to be unaffected by the amendment.[35] The *Phillips Petroleum* court saw the proviso as an explicit limitation on state authority in Indian country, though it did not directly answer whether EPA thus had implementation authority for filling the regulatory gap.

Congress answered that question affirmatively in the Act's 1986 amendments. Its directive that EPA prescribe injection programs for every tribe lacking one made clear the Agency's direct implementation power in Indian country. But that order could not be the source of the Agency's authority for promulgating the Osage program two years earlier. Phillips argued the amendments implied EPA lacked authority before 1986. The court disagreed. Congress sometimes amends existing laws to clarify its prior intentions, strengthen particular provisions, or codify agency interpretations. The legislative history was mute on the point, which the court found more consistent with EPA's position than the Company's view that Congress vested such power in EPA for the first time in 1986. Ultimately, Phillips' various arguments could not overcome the respect courts pay to agencies' perceptions of their statutory responsibilities.

Administrative law's rule of judicial deference was also the death knell for Phillips' substantive challenge to the mechanical integrity pressure test requirement. The Company argued the test violated Congress' directive, adopted under industry pressure, that injection programs not impede oil and gas production unless necessary to protect underground sources of drinking water. Phillips asserted its compliance with Bureau of Indian Affairs' regulations meant underground waters were protected without any need for confirmation by testing, and argued the pressure test would hamper development because marginal wells would be shut down. Although EPA repeatedly asked for evidence supporting the threatened economic impact, Phillips produced none during either the Agency's processes or the court case.

The court concluded Congress' overriding concern was environmental protection rather than economic profit. EPA studies and analyses indicated that concrete casings with mechanical integrity were essential for groundwater protection because without them corrosive fluids like brines could attack well tubing that could serve as a conduit for fluid migration from salty formations to drinking water sources. Phillips' argument essentially asked the court to substitute its view of environmental risk for the Agency's expert judgment, which contravened well-established principles of administrative law. It was also simply unpersuasive in light of the Company's bold admission of a "very large number of very old injection wells [at Osage] with questionable integrity." The court upheld the Osage program, finding EPA considered the relevant factors and made no clear error of judgment.

Transitioning to Tribal Program Implementation

EPA's success in *Phillips Petroleum* went far beyond simply approving a particular injection program for one tribe's territory. The Indian program had now prevailed in three consecutive cases decided by three different courts across three different media programs: underground water protection, hazardous waste regulation, and air pollution prevention. Those cases represented clear judicial approval of the Agency's tripartite approach to Indian country environmental programs: an aversion to state delegation, a commitment to direct federal implementation with special attention paid to tribal preferences, and an aspiration for full or partial tribal regulatory roles.

EPA had also seemingly won legislative approval for its program directions in the 1970s and mid-1980s. Congress almost immediately ratified EPA's approaches via amendments to the air and drinking water laws in the face of pending judicial challenges at Northern Cheyenne and Osage. Congress codified the apparently uncontroversial tribal authority EPA created under the pesticides law,[36] and added several important tribal roles to the Superfund program for the cleanup of hazardous substances released into the environment.[37] The only major environmental statute not amended with provisions for tribal regulatory powers was the hazardous waste law at issue in *Washington Department of Ecology*.

The various amendments confirmed EPA's assumption Congress did not intend EPA delegate federal environmental programs for Indian country to states. In some cases, like the Safe Drinking Water Act, there were specific references to federal implementation authority. But the amendments' primary mechanism was the creation of tribal regulatory roles identical to or parallel with state roles. A 1977 Senate committee explained the Clean Air Act amendments as giving tribes the same powers as states, but it was the 1986 Safe Drinking Water Act amendments where Congress first used EPA's formulation of tribal regulatory roles as state-like. "[EPA's] Administrator ... is authorized to treat Indian Tribes as States under this title."[38] Congress specifically authorized treatment-as-a-state for the underground injection control program,[39] and left to EPA's judgment which other drinking water programs were appropriate for tribal roles.

Congress imposed certain threshold eligibility criteria for tribal applications that would be repeated in one form or another in later amendments to other environmental statutes. EPA could partner only with a "federally recognized" Indian tribe—one with whom the federal government maintained political relations—that had a governing body exercising "substantial" governmental powers and duties. The tribe must show technical capacity adequate for operating the particular program consistent with minimum federal requirements and standards. And, the tribe must have jurisdiction over the area or the activities to which the program would apply.

The legislative histories of the Safe Drinking Water Act and the other environmental laws do not clearly reflect Congress' reason for imposing the threshold eligibility criteria in the tribal treatment-as-a-state provisions. Some tribes suggest the criteria simply emphasize tribal programs must be at least as rigorous as state programs. Some states and others opposed to tribal regulation view the criteria, especially the criterion requiring tribal jurisdiction, as setting the bar higher for tribes than states, implying that EPA's review of tribal applications should be especially demanding.

In reality, the criteria effectively asked little more of tribes than states. EPA regulations for state delegations uniformly require evidence of the state's technical, governmental and legal capabilities for implementing a desired program. Neither states nor tribes can be effective local partners without such capacity. Jurisdiction over polluters and the geographic areas affected was a cornerstone of EPA's first Indian program action vis-à-vis state delegation; it only made sense the same criterion applied to tribes seeking delegated programs.

Federal Indian law has always been about jurisdiction. The foundation cases like *Worcester* were fundamentally about the respective powers of the federal, state and tribal governments. A threshold question in those cases was determining the extent of Indian country. The geographic boundaries of Indian country essentially demarcate the jurisdictional line where state authority contracts, and tribal sovereignty and federal Indian law arise. Finding that line, however, is more difficult than pulling out a Triple-A roadmap. Indian country is a confusing patchwork of formally designated reservations, informal reservations, non-reservation lands owned by tribes and tribal citizens, and so-called dependent Indian communities. The Court's approach for identifying those areas and their geographic extent relies on a relatively subjective view of congressional intent often divined from century-old actions taken with no thought for future jurisdictional consequences. That ambiguous and therefore unpredictable guideline for the venerable stakes of governmental sovereignty and/or business profit margins fosters frequent disputes over whether particular actions occur within Indian country or without.

EPA anticipated Indian country status disputes in both the tribal treatment-as-a-state and direct federal implementation programs implementing the Safe Drinking Water Act. The former had potential for tribal-state disagreements over authority for public water systems and/or underground injections on particular parcels; the latter for federal-state claims. Either case could result in drawn out legal battles leaving important sources of underground drinking water in the lurch for years.

The treatment-as-a-state rule posited two approaches for limiting that prospect. One was a process for addressing the issue administratively at a program's outset. EPA would notify "all appropriate governmental entities" when it received a tribal application for particular lands. Those governments—primarily states, but in some cases adjacent tribes—would be invited to comment specifically on the tribe's asserted jurisdiction (but on no other issue). If the tribe's claim was disputed, EPA would consult with the Department of the Interior, which houses the Bureau of Indian Affairs, before acting on the tribe's application. Parties dissatisfied with the final decision could of course seek judicial review, but the Agency seemed hopeful that a deliberative administrative vetting would lessen that risk.

The other approach rested on an ostensible narrowing of the treatment-as-a-state program's geographic extent. The proposed rule did not define the Safe Drinking Water Act's ambiguous reference to Indian "lands." One commenter suggested equating the phrase with federal Indian law's "Indian country" term as EPA had done in an earlier direct implementation rule. EPA declined, saying the complicated dependent Indian community component of Indian country was rife with jurisdictional dispute potential. In contrast, the Agency perceived "substantial support" for the general proposition that tribes have jurisdiction over their reservations. It also read the twenty-two comments received from tribes as interested primarily in reservation programs.

Yet, the final rule did not limit tribal programs to reservations. EPA explicitly said tribes were not precluded from seeking treatment-as-a-state for any lands over which they showed jurisdiction.[40] It did not admit that position presented precisely the risk supposedly avoided by leaving the Indian lands phrase undefined. Nor did it acknowledge the same risk was inherent in the direct implementation rule that asserted federal program coverage over all of Indian country. *Phillips Petroleum* and *Washington Department of Ecology* had just demonstrated that federal programs could suffer the same lawsuit-related delays as tribal programs. Amazingly, the Agency justified the different program approaches by asserting it had a broader need for Indian country protection than tribes.

Despite a lack of forthrightness, EPA was clearly aware of the continuing litigation risks. It developed a creative strategy aimed at managing them just one month after finalizing the treatment-as-a-state rule. The context was the promulgation of direct implementation programs for injection wells on Indian lands in Oklahoma (other than Osage and the Five Civilized Tribes) and several reservations in the four corners region of the southwest.[41] The proposed programs generated relatively few public comments. EPA made no mention of jurisdiction, but two commenters asked how Indian land boundaries would be determined. One commenter urged they be established at the outset rather than later on an ad hoc basis.

The Agency conceded the logical appeal of advance decisions, but promulgated the final programs without specifically identifying the particular Indian lands covered. The reasons were practical. The programs covered 913 injection wells scattered among the lands and reservations of seventeen tribes located in five states. Determining the Indian country status of each well's location before finalizing the entire program would significantly delay implementation for many wells. Moreover, and perhaps most importantly, a meta-decision for all wells could provoke an untold number of legal challenges. States and tribes (and those they represent) often have divergent views about the status of particular lands. Suits attacking various individual decisions issued as part of a package could conceivably postpone the effective date of the entire program.

Disputes would of course arise as decisions were made later on individual wells. The final program notice casually mentioned an untried creative approach for avoiding resulting program delays in those instances: EPA would simply continue to assume the disputed land was Indian country, and implement the federal program there until a contrary judgment was reached. A single objection for a particular parcel thus would not create a temporary regulatory gap. An additional benefit of the approach was that it effectively shifted what would otherwise be EPA's initial burden of justifying the program's application to disputed lands. Challengers could seek temporary injunctions against federal programs but they would be required to show a likelihood of succeeding ultimately on the suit's merits.

Environmental Justice
Challenges at Church Rock

Perhaps fittingly, the first test of EPA's disputed lands approach occurred near a site made infamous by the country's largest spill of radioactive materials. Church Rock, New Mexico sits near the southern border of the Navajo Indian Reservation, about seventeen miles northeast of Gallup, New Mexico. From 1977 to 1982, the United Nuclear Corporation operated a uranium ore processing mill at Church Rock and several uranium mines in the area. United Nuclear, a Virginia corporation, was at that time the largest privately owned uranium processor in the world; the Church Rock mines were its largest holdings.

The Church Rock mill site included approximately 100 acres occupied by discarded mill tailings—the sand-like material left after uranium is extracted from the ore. Over ninety-five percent of ore becomes tailings containing around eighty-five percent of the original ore's radioactivity. The tailings were disposed of in a massive wastewater lagoon contained by an earthen berm twenty-five feet high and thirty feet wide. For its time, the dirt dam was state of the art and had been recommended by the federal agency responsible for radioactive materials regulation.

The Company did not however follow the agency's design criteria, or its expectations for the usable life of the dam, or its maximum recommended liquid waste levels. The dam was not regularly inspected, even after significant cracks became apparent. On July 16, 1979, a twenty-foot section breached and released a toxic flood of nearly 100 million gallons of hazardous liquids and over 1,000 tons of radioactive solid wastes that spilled into a dry arroyo, ran down a small tributary, and then flowed down the Rio Puerco. Toxic metals were detectable as far as seventy miles downstream, and residues of radioactive uranium, thorium, radium, and polonium, as well as metals like cadmium, aluminum, magnesium, manganese, molybdenum, nickel, selenium, sodium, vanadium, zinc, iron, and lead could be found along the 125 miles affected. The media ran stories on the spill and government agencies posted warning signs, but many of the traditional Navajo sheepherders who used the stream and river spoke and read only Navajo. It didn't really matter though; there were few alternative sources of water.

EPA immediately issued an order against United Nuclear for unauthorized discharges in violation of the Clean Water Act, and in 1981 listed the mill and tailings pond as a hazardous substance cleanup site under the newly enacted Superfund law. In five years of operation United Nuclear disposed 3.5 million tons of mill tailings on-site. Tailings fluid not spilled in the 1979 catastrophe leaked underground contaminating the Upper Gallup Aquifer. The site was added to the Superfund National Priorities List in 1983, and extensive remedial work continues today.

United Nuclear's environmental problems were compounded by significant declines in the international uranium market in the early 1980s. Decreased profits and increased regulatory costs led the Company to close the mill and its nearby Church Rock mine in McKinley County. The mine site was sold to Hydro Resources, Incorporated, a New Mexico corporation that proposed in the late 1980s to begin *in-situ* leach uranium mining. In contrast to more expensive strip or pit mining that digs massive quantities of ore rock from the ground and transports it off-site for processing, *in-situ* leach mining combines extraction and initial processing in one on-site step. Large volumes of acid or alkaline solutions are injected underground to leach uranium from the ore rock. The uranium-containing fluid is then pumped back to the surface where the valuable minerals are extracted.

Proponents of leach mining claim it is less harmful to the environment than traditional mining and milling methods. Mine site surfaces are disturbed far less, and mill sites feature none of the dangerous tailing piles and ponds. They also assert underground injection of hazardous fluids can be accomplished without contaminating groundwater.

Nonetheless, when Hydro Resources applied for injection permits it also sought exemptions from the Safe Drinking Water Act's prohibition on contaminating groundwater, asserting the aquifers beneath the Church Rock mine site would never be used for drinking water. The Company submitted its applications to the State of New Mexico's Environmental Department, which had implemented the Act's underground injection program since 1983. EPA's approval of the State's program, though, specifically excluded Indian lands, and EPA had promulgated a direct implementation program for those lands in 1988. Program responsibility for the proposed mine site thus depended on its Indian country status.

That issue is itself emblematic of the long history of environmental justice challenges at Navajo. In an 1868 Treaty, the Navajo Nation ceded most of its expansive territory to the United States and reserved for itself a much smaller area in Arizona and New Mexico. Water supplies and livestock forage were scarce in the Navajo reservation's desert ecosystem, so many traditional Navajo sheepherders remained on formerly aboriginal areas east and south of the reservation. Those lands, however, were now considered part of the United States' "public domain" open to immigrant settlers. White and Mexican-American stockmen moving there at the turn of the century asserted superior rights to the limited water holes.

By 1907, racial tensions were nearing dangerous proportions. Navajos complained to federal agents of being driven forcibly from their homes and from watering holes they had used for generations. New Mexico's Territorial Governor and Legislature demanded the federal government keep Navajos on the reservation and forbid them from watering sheep on public domain lands. President Theodore Roosevelt intervened on the recommendation of the Commissioner of Indian Affairs. He issued an Executive Order withdrawing the eastern lands from the public domain and adding them to the reservation.[42] The idea was that Navajo citizens would receive first choice of 160-acre allotments—that is, lands with prime watering locations—free from competition with white settlers.

The non-Indian New Mexico delegation did not give up after losing the first battle. It pressed the Commissioner to allot lands only to Navajos already living in the eastern area. As soon as the allotments were completed, it clamored for the remaining lands. In 1911, President William Taft "restored" the unallotted lands to the public domain.

Taft's order did not address the jurisdictional issue that would become crucial eighty years later when Hydro Resources proposed its leach mine: whether subsequently acquired non-Indian lands remained Indian country. One year after the Company applied to the State for its mine permit, an unrelated federal case held Taft's ambiguous order terminated or "disestablished" the area's status as Navajo reservation.[43] A few years later in a case involving another tribe in Utah the Supreme Court unequivocally stated that federal restoration to the public domain "stripped [Indian lands of their] reservation status."[44]

But following Taft's 1911 order, the Bureau of Indian Affairs continued treating the eastern area similar to other communities on the Navajo reservation. It created the Pueblo Bonito Agency, later called the Eastern Agency, for the provision of federal services to Navajos there. It purchased lands for building Indian schools. In 1927, the federal government organized the Church Rock Chapter as a division of the Navajo government.

Today, ninety-seven percent of the Church Rock Chapter population is Navajo. The Navajo Nation runs several federal human services programs, a Head Start school and a public water system there. Navajo police provide public safety services, and the Navajo tribal court system provides a forum for dispute resolution. The federal government provides medical care through Indian Health Service facilities located there, and owns approximately eighty percent of the land in trust for the Navajo Nation or its citizens. Among the remaining twenty percent are the two parcels where Hydro Resources proposed its leach mine.

One of the parcels in the Eastern Agency, located in Township Section 17, was a split estate; the United States owned the surface, which it held in trust for the Navajo Nation, and Hydro Resources owned the subsurface minerals through its purchase from United Nuclear. The other parcel, located in Township Section 8, Hydro Resources owned outright, and it sought an injection permit there first. The State approved the Company's proposed injection plan and requested EPA exempt the underlying aquifer from the protections of the Safe Drinking Water Act. EPA approved the State's request without inquiring as to the parcel's Indian country status.

Three years later, Hydro Resources requested its permit be extended to the adjacent Section 17 parcel, and the State asked EPA for a second aquifer exemption. This time the Navajo Nation's surface rights piqued EPA's attention to the jurisdictional question. EPA declined the exemption on the ground the parcel was Indian country.

That decision spurred a five-year process of correspondence and meetings between New Mexico's Environmental Department, the Navajo Nation and EPA. At points in the process the parties discussed the possibility of a joint federal-state permitting process, but the State was not particularly cooperative and the Navajo Nation objected to the proposal. Navajo representatives argued forcefully that both the Section 17 and Section 8 parcels were within Indian country. EPA eventually invoked its disputed lands rule in 1997 because of concern that delays were negatively affecting the Company. But, in what must been an unwelcome surprise for the Company and the State, EPA treated both parcels as disputed. That decision effectively reversed the Agency's 1989 approval of the State's aquifer exemption and injection permit for the Section 8 parcel.

Hydro Resources did not immediately send applications for permits and aquifer exemptions to EPA as required by the disputed lands rule. It sent a civil summons and legal complaint instead, as did the State. A host of procedural and substantive claims were aimed at establishing the mine site was not Indian country. The goal, of course, was to put regulatory authority over the mine in the State's hands, which had already shown its tolerance for the Company's desired underground injections. The Navajo Nation intervened to protect its jurisdictional interests.

In *HRI, Inc. v. Environmental Protection Agency*, the court sided with EPA and the Navajo Nation on the specific question of whether the status of the two parcels was disputed.[45] More broadly, and perhaps more importantly, the court's rationale validated EPA's disputed lands approach and marked several guiding principles for the Agency's general Indian program.

The Company and the State were particularly troubled by EPA's switched position on the Section 8 parcel. They argued the 1989 approval of the State's aquifer exemption meant the State program applied there, at least until a tribal program took its place. The 1986 treatment-as-a-state amendment provided the "currently applicable" underground injection program continued until a tribal program became effective. In 1994, EPA approved the Navajo Nation's injection program for the reservation, but determined the Nation did not adequately demonstrate jurisdiction over the Eastern Agency.

The court said the Company misunderstood EPA's authority. Only Congress can change the Indian country status of particular lands. If the Section 8 parcel was Indian country, EPA's contrary assumption in 1989 could not have changed its status. Nor could the Agency's failure to object to the State's assertion of authority defeat the federal government's independent legal duty to protect tribal lands. The federal trust responsibility to Indians, the court said, applies with greater force to jurisdictional disputes implicating the "core sovereignty interests" of tribes. Hence, despite EPA's prior approval of the State's aquifer exemption, New Mexico's program could not be currently applicable to the Section 8 parcel once EPA determined a status dispute existed.

The Company and the State sought to postpone that determination by arguing it violated the public notice and comment procedures required when EPA revokes or revises existing state programs. The Agency argued those requirements applied only to wholesale revocations and substantial program revisions. The court accepted the Agency's view and its conclusion that excluding 160 acres from the entire state program was an insubstantial revision. EPA's interpretations of its program regulations and their application here were clearly matters within the Agency's expertise entitled to the court's deference.

Traditional judicial deference for administrative decisions could not, however, extend to the Agency's federal Indian law conclusions. By necessity, EPA had been analyzing federal Indian law issues since 1973. But, strictly speaking, Indian law questions were not environmental matters within EPA's expertise. EPA thus invoked the administrative safe harbor of the disputed lands rule in requiring federal permits on the Section 17 parcel even though it believed the parcel was Indian country. The court handed the brass ring to the Agency anyway; the Section 17 parcel is in fact Indian country as an informal Indian reservation.

The Supreme Court has read Congress' definition of Indian country as including informal as well as formally designated Indian reservations.[46] What constitutes an informal Indian reservation is unclear, but the Court has said land outside a formal reservation but held in trust for an Indian tribe could qualify.[47] The surface of the Section 17 parcel is tribal trust land. The United States purchased title and associated water rights in 1929. Ironically, the U.S. paid $1.2 million to the Santa Fe Railroad for property originally given to the Railroad for free to encourage westward expansion. Adding insult to injury, the Railroad retained the valuable subsurface mineral rights, profiting from its later sale to United Nuclear who in turn sold to Hydro Resources.

Out of caution the Tenth Circuit did not rely solely on the Section 17 parcel's trust status to find it an informal reservation. It also applied the Supreme Court's two-part test for determining dependent Indian communities. First, by its purchase the federal government had set the land aside for the use of Indians. The purchase was part of continued efforts to ensure Navajo sheepherders in the Eastern Agency had access to water increasingly appropriated by non-Indian settlers. Second, the government maintained significant supervision over the parcel. The federal government retained title and the Bureau of Indian Affairs controlled acquisition of interests in and uses of the land. The split nature of the surface and subsurface estates did not alter the court's conclusion the parcel was Indian country; the court found EPA's direct implementation regulations reasonably provided the federal program would apply if either estate constituted Indian lands.

In the end, the court upheld the Agency's requirement the Company obtain federal permits. The Section 17 parcel was Indian country as an informal reservation and/or a dependent Indian community, and the Section 8 parcel was in dispute. The court intimated the Section 8 parcel was probably also Indian country as a dependent Indian community, but remanded for EPA's final decision. The court was unsympathetic to Hydro Resources' complaint of additional delays in its mining plans; the Company could have sought federal permits at any point over the eight-year dispute.

EPA did not immediately move forward following the court's remand because the Company apparently abandoned plans for leach mining on the property. It seems likely the market had more to do with the decision than any fear Hydro Resources had for federal injection permits. The market price of a pound of yellowcake uranium, which hovered around $10 a pound in 1989 when the Company applied for its first permit, dropped to an all-time low of $7 in 2001. Two years later it skyrocketed to $65 and then in 2005 to $75 a pound. Hydro Resources promptly sent a second permit application for the Section 8 parcel to the New Mexico Environmental Department.

The State had no choice but to ask EPA for a final decision on the Indian country status of the parcel. This time EPA issued a public notice and sought public comment. Twenty-five parties submitted written comments on whether the Section 8 parcel was Indian country as a dependent Indian community. Five commenters, including the Navajo Nation, the Church Rock Chapter, and a tribal environmental justice organization called Eastern Navajo Diné Against Uranium Mining, urged finding the parcel Indian country. Fifteen commenters, including Hydro Resources, the National Mining Association, the Uranium Producers of America, several mineral extraction companies and state officials, and a collection of individual Navajo allottees interested in economic development in the Eastern Agency, argued against Indian country status. Five parties submitted off-topic comments railing against or for uranium mining.

The commenters' primary disagreement was whether the Agency's analysis should be limited solely to the Section 8 parcel or encompass the broader Church Rock Chapter. A prior Tenth Circuit case, *Pittsburg & Midway Coal Company v. Watchman*,[48] said a threshold issue for determining dependent Indian communities was identifying the appropriate "community of reference." *Watchman* criticized the lower court for focusing narrowly on the property at issue and ignoring the surrounding area. Several commenters cited *Watchman* in support of their claim EPA should consider the Church Rock Chapter as the relevant community of reference.

Opposing commenters cited the more recent decision of the Supreme Court in *Alaska v. Native Village of Venetie*,[49] which set out a two-part test for determining dependent Indian communities—federal set-aside and federal superintendence—without referring to a community of reference analysis. The commenters argued that *Venetie* implicitly vitiated *Watchman's* standard. The *HRI* court, however, had explained the *Venetie* Court's silence as due to the issue not being presented, and said the community of reference standard continued as binding law in the Tenth Circuit. Two later cases in the circuit had directly or indirectly applied *Watchman's* standard.[50]

EPA consulted with the Department of the Interior's Solicitor's Office after considering the comments received. Interior took the position that binding Tenth Circuit law applicable to EPA's decision required community of reference analysis. Interior concluded the Church Rock Chapter was the appropriate community to be considered. It had specific geographic boundaries, it was a unified cohesive community dominated by Navajo residents, and effectively constituted a mini-society with its own governmental infrastructure and services. In February 2007, EPA announced its final decision that the Section 8 parcel is Indian country because it is located within the dependent Indian community known as the Church Rock Chapter of the Navajo Nation.

Hydro Resources refused to concede. By month's end it had sued EPA again. The Company's public announcement simply insisted it believes EPA got the parcel's status wrong. Its underlying motivation for waging the decade-long battle is unclear. A local Gallup Independent news report implies the Company fears EPA will listen to mine opponents and impose conditions more stringent than the State might, or perhaps deny the permit altogether. Coincidentally, just as the Company was preparing its second state permit, the Navajo Nation enacted a law banning all uranium mining within Navajo lands. Since EPA decided in 1994 the Navajo Nation had not shown jurisdiction over the Eastern Agency, it is unclear what effect the ban might have on EPA. At the very least, the federal trust responsibility and EPA's Indian Policy would suggest EPA consider the ban in making permit decisions. That is, assuming the Company ever applies for a federal permit.

CHAPTER 4

THE SOURCE OF LIFE: HONORING TRIBAL WATER QUALITY VALUES

Like groundwater, the nation's human population has historically utilized its surface waters—lakes, rivers, streams, wetlands, and similar waters—for two seemingly incongruous purposes: supporting beneficial uses like drinking, irrigation, industrial, commercial, recreation and aesthetic values, and as a ubiquitous and inexpensive system for the disposal of solid and liquid wastes and toxic substances. The need for balancing those uses in the post-industrial age led Congress to enact the Federal Water Pollution Control Act of 1948, which has been amended several times and is now commonly referred to as the Clean Water Act. For over thirty years the Act's overall goal has been to maintain or restore the chemical, physical and biological integrity of surface waters, but EPA has estimated some 20,000 river segments, lakes and estuaries, 300,000 miles of rivers and shorelines, and five million acres of lakes—over forty percent of waters that have actually been surveyed—do not meet applicable water quality expectations.

The primary mechanism of the Clean Water Act is similar to the Safe Drinking Water Act: certain kinds of water pollution discharges are flatly prohibited unless done pursuant to and in compliance with regulatory permits issued by EPA or states with delegated programs. The main permit program is the inaptly titled National Pollution Discharge Elimination System that authorizes pollution discharges from so-called "point source" conveyances like pipes, outfalls, ditches, storm drains and similar features typically associated with commercial and industrial facilities. Congress completely exempted indirect "nonpoint" sources of water pollution and certain agricultural point sources, which account for an estimated fifty percent of water quality impairment, from the Act's permit requirements in a tremendous concession to the farm lobby.

A permit's specific effluent limitations restricting the quantity, rate, and concentration of chemical, physical, biological and other constituents discharged from an individual point source reflect the modern era's cooperative federalism. Some limitations are derived from national standards set by EPA for various classifications of industrial facilities like pulp and paper mills, petroleum refiners, or electroplaters. Allowable discharges are established for each pollutant by calculating the reduction a source could attain by employing certain pollution control technologies designated by EPA as appropriate for that kind of facility and/or pollutant. The technology-based standards are uniform for individual facilities within industrial classifications and do not account for differences in the quality of the lake or river receiving the pollution discharge.

Congress left consideration of site-specific factors like natural water quality, other pollution sources, and human uses to states. Section 303 of the Act required states develop water quality standards reflecting two local value judgments: the desired uses of particular waters or segments of waters, and the scientific and policy conclusions on the maximum concentrations of pollutants consistent with maintaining or achieving the designated uses. Congress mandated at a minimum that state standards seek water quality levels adequate for supporting healthy fish and wildlife populations and human recreational uses, but specifically preserved states' inherent public health and welfare powers to set standards more stringent than needed for preserving those minimum fishable and swimmable uses. Where the application of EPA's technology-based effluent limitations will not ensure a facility's compliance with water quality standards at the point of discharge or downstream, additional conditions must be added to the permit.

Indian Country Surface Water Protection

By 1987 when Congress substantially amended the Clean Water Act, EPA's vision of cooperative federalism in Indian country, as articulated in its 1980 and 1984 Indian Policies, was taking shape. The year before Congress had explicitly adopted EPA's tribal treatment-as-a-state approach in amendments to the Safe Drinking Water Act and in the remedial Superfund statute that imposed cleanup liability for unpermitted releases of hazardous substances into the environment. Shortly thereafter *Phillips Petroleum* interpreted the former provision as evidencing Congress' intent that EPA implement federal programs in Indian country only until such time as tribes took them over. EPA lobbied Congress to replicate the approach for surface water regulation, as did some tribes anxious for assuming increased regulatory roles in their territories.

Congress continued the trend in section 518 of the Clean Water Act amendments,[1] which was fully consistent with EPA's Indian Policies and the Safe Drinking Water Act. Eligible tribes could play key regulatory roles in the implementation of federal pollution programs. The tribal roles, like their state counterparts, spanned the spectrum from pollution prevention planning to construction of wastewater treatment facilities to full permit program operation. An intermediate role, which would soon form the core of EPA's Indian program and attract the largest degree of tribal interest, was the development of tribal water quality standards. Like tribal air quality redesignations under the Clean Air Act, once approved by EPA tribal water quality standards could influence the stringency of conditions in pollution discharge permits issued both in and near Indian country.

Section 518 also contained a set of threshold eligibility requirements for tribal program roles much like the Safe Drinking Water Act had:

> The Administrator is authorized to treat an Indian tribe as a State for the purposes of [specified water programs] to the degree necessary to carry out the objectives of this section, but only if—
> (1) the Indian tribe has a governing body carrying out substantial governmental duties and powers;
> (2) the functions to be exercised by the Indian tribe pertain to the management and protection of water resources which are held by an Indian tribe, held by the United States in trust for Indians, held by a member of an Indian tribe if such property interest is subject to a trust restriction on alienation, or otherwise within the borders of an Indian reservation; and
> (3) the Indian tribe is reasonably expected to be capable, in the Administrator's judgment, of carrying out the functions to be exercised in a manner consistent with the terms and purposes of this Act and of all applicable regulations.[2]

The first and third criteria tracked the Safe Drinking Water Act. Only tribes truly functioning as governments and possessing the requisite technical capabilities could be effective local partners for EPA. The second criterion, however, was distinctly different. The Safe Drinking Water Act required a showing that "the functions to be exercised by the Indian Tribe *are within the area of the Tribal Government's jurisdiction*."[3] Federal Indian law had long acknowledged tribal jurisdiction over Indian lands and tribal citizens, but the existence and extent of tribal sovereignty over non-Indians was an unclear matter. The Safe Drinking Water Act's requirement had tripped up the Navajo

Nation's underground injection program; EPA decided the Nation had not adequately demonstrated its jurisdiction over the Eastern Agency's intermixed Indian and non-Indian land.

The Clean Water Act's second criterion did not use the term jurisdiction. Instead, it applied the tribal roles to two types of water resources: those "held" by a tribe, a tribal citizen or the United States on their behalf, and waters "otherwise" inside Indian reservations. Standing alone, the first category implied a narrow conception of tribal governmental powers limited to Indian property ownership. The category of waters "otherwise within the borders of an Indian reservation" was not so limited. Its broader territorial view was made clear by section 518's verbatim recitation of the first element of Congress' definition of Indian country: "Federal Indian Reservation means all land within the limits of any Indian reservation under the jurisdiction of the United States Government, notwithstanding the issuance of any patent, and including rights-of-way running through the reservation." Numerous Supreme Court decisions made clear Congress' reference to patents and rights-of-way included non-Indian property interests.

That conclusion, however, did not clearly answer the question naturally arising from the contrast with the Safe Drinking Water Act's explicit requirement of showing jurisdiction. Had Congress delegated authority over non-Indians such that tribes need not show an independent jurisdictional basis for receiving program primacy? Or did Congress simply mean to clarify EPA could approve tribal water programs applicable to non-Indians over whom the tribe demonstrated its inherent jurisdiction?

EPA glossed over these issues without explanation when it proposed the first substantive section 518 regulation in 1989. It simply equated the Clean Water Act's reference to reservation waters with the Safe Drinking Water Act's jurisdiction requirement.

> [The criterion] concerning Tribal authority, means that EPA may treat an Indian Tribe as a State for purposes of water quality standards only where the Tribe already possesses and can adequately demonstrate authority to manage and protect water resources within the borders of the reservation. The Clean Water Act authorizes use of existing Tribal regulatory authority for managing EPA programs, but it does not grant additional authority to tribes.[4]

The Agency's interpretation of Congress' intent was duly noted by six congressmen who submitted letters along with other members of the public during the comment period on the draft rule. One house representative and two senators supported EPA's view that section 518 did not expand tribes' authority over non-Indians, making reference to legislative history that specifically disclaimed any intent to expand tribal property rights in water quantity. Three other senators argued to the contrary. They asserted Congress did intend to expand tribal powers via delegation of authority over non-Indians, which was shown in part by legislative materials reporting tribes' regulatory powers over non-Indian owned fee lands and resources on reservations. The senators also observed that in a recent tribal case testing the scope of inherent tribal authority for zoning non-Indian land uses, four Supreme Court justices cited section 518 as an example of an express congressional delegation of authority over non-Indian fee lands.

Two of the senators supporting delegation held key positions for EPA's Indian program. Daniel K. Inouye, a Democrat from Hawaii, was Chairman of the Senate Select Committee on Indian Affairs. John McCain, a Republican from Arizona, was Vice-Chair. Two months before EPA proposed this regulation, Inouye and McCain called an historic first oversight hearing on the implementation of EPA's Indian Policy.[5]

Inouye's introductory comments at the hearing explained its purpose was to address the "widely-held perception" that not enough was being done about Indian country's many environmental problems. McCain commented that "abundant" evidence showed serious threats to reservation environments. Tribal witnesses echoed these sentiments, and posited a lack of funding as a primary reason for the Agency's slow progress. Inouye emphasized that point with dramatic numbers. EPA's budget for Fiscal Year 1988 was $5.5 billion and it spent only $6.9 million, just over one tenth of one percent, on Indian issues. The Agency's long-term track record was worse; out of a $48 billion budget over fifteen years, only $25 million, or *less* than one tenth of one percent, was devoted to Indians.

Much of that money had been spent on water issues. Inouye specifically asked William Whittington, Deputy Administrator of EPA's Office of Water, whether all regulations for implementing section 518 had been issued. Whittington said three of six had been completed: grant rules for constructing water treatment facilities and conducting water quality planning, and procedures for initial treatment-as-a-state. He asserted the Agency had prioritized "getting the money out to tribes," but did not mention the primary regulatory mechanisms of the Act—water quality standards, water pollution discharge permits and permits for dredging and filling waters—had yet to be addressed.

Within two months of the hearing EPA proposed the water quality standards rule. Inouye's and McCain's responses arguing delegation put the Agency in a delicate situation. They constituted the leadership of the Select Committee, which was clearly unimpressed with the pace of the Indian program. Inouye had concluded the oversight hearing saying he was optimistic it would not be the last one. But a final rule interpreting section 518 as a delegation was sure to draw an immediate lawsuit from tribal sovereignty opponents. The Agency's ability to cite the rule as concrete forward progress would be postponed.

The final rule very carefully explained why EPA decided not to interpret section 518 as a delegation of authority over non-Indians. The congressmen's letters were fully considered, but they were contradictory and courts had previously warned against relying on subsequent statements from legislators. The contemporaneous legislative history was ambiguous and at times contradictory as well. The Supreme Court opinion that had referred to section 518 as an example of delegation was not a majority opinion and had not analyzed the confusing legislative history. Finally, EPA felt if Congress had truly intended to expand tribal jurisdiction over non-Indians it would have addressed the issue more explicitly. Hence, candidly admitting trepidation in the face of congressional and judicial uncertainty, EPA promulgated the final rule requiring tribes to show jurisdiction over non-Indian polluters through their inherent sovereignty.

Inherent Tribal Sovereignty

In 1831, the year before John Marshall famously declared in *Worcester* that Georgia's laws had no force in Cherokee Territory, the Court addressed another jurisdictional dispute between the State and Tribe. Marshall described the Cherokee Nation "as a [nation-]state, as a distinct political society, separated from others, capable of managing its own affairs and governing itself."[6] The governmental sovereignty inherent in the Tribe's political organization, which pre-existed the United States and was evidenced by long political relations with the federal government, formed a measure of Marshall's justification for invalidating Georgia's later prosecution of the non-Indian missionary Samuel Worcester for entering Indian country without the State's permission.

Scholars generally regard *Worcester* as a key foundation case in federal Indian law, but its practical impact on tribal and state sovereignty was and is largely academic. Worcester was saved from breaking rocks in the state penitentiary by the State Governor's pardon, not by enforcement of Marshall's decision. The introduction of European diseases and federal control had greatly reduced the power of the sophisticated Cherokee governmental structures; the Tribe was not governing non-Indians in the modern sense of regulation. In fact, other than insolent missionaries and federal Indian agents, there were few non-Indians in Indian country for tribes or states to control. Extensive federal enactments and treaties protected Indian lands from state taxation, precluded state regulation of commerce in Indian country, and preempted state criminal laws there. Governmental services to Indians were the exclusive province of the federal government, and there were no state residents clamoring for state services.

The federal government's turn-of-the-century allotment policy changed the face of Indian country forever. Its primary consequence was the loss of close to 100 million acres of tribally owned land. An equally pernicious result was the flood of non-Indian settlers encouraged by federal actions in direct violation of earlier treaty promises of preserving tribal homelands in perpetuity. Suddenly the perceived legitimacy of states' purported interests in Indian country heightened. The new immigrants demanded state services available to other state residents. States in turn sought to tax non-Indian properties and incomes and regulate their activities in the same manner as in other areas.

The federal government also induced non-Indian natural resource development companies to locate in Indian country in the mid-1900s. As trustee, the federal government was legally obligated to manage tribal resources for the benefit of the tribes, but on occasion its zeal for revenue and the political connections of non-Indian companies led to below market lease and royalty payments. Prospects for increased profit margins, possible insulation from state taxation, and comparatively weak federal regulation helped spur strip and pit mines, clear-cut timber harvests, and power plants. Many of these activities and facilities were located on tribal lands, but just as often they appeared on lands sold or given to non-Indians during the allotment era.

The prospect of tribal regulation of non-Indians arose in a concrete way as the tribal self-determination era gathered momentum in the late 1980s. Newly constituted tribal governments, some traditional but most based on Euro-American models, began adopting laws for preserving the public health and welfare. Like states, tribes developed criminal codes and civil regulatory laws, taxed business activities and controlled land use, building, housing, and hunting and fishing.

American descendents of the early immigrants and their successors objected vociferously to any suggestion tribal sovereignty might somehow constrain their desired actions. They argued tribal regulation was tantamount to taxation without representation, which their public education posited as one impetus for the United States' origin. Regrettably, their history books overlooked the comparative irony of the federal government's unilateral assertion of absolute power over the continent's original inhabitants without their representation.

The Supreme Court, staffed by Euro-American Justices whose more distinguished education was similarly lacking, was sympathetic to non-Indian complaints. Recognizing the sovereignty of indigenous nations at the country's origin had been a necessity. Practically speaking, the tribes were more adept militarily than the nascent nation who could not afford to fight Indian and international wars at once. Legally, the Supreme Court had staked the United States' claim to property rights in tribal lands on principles of international "law" that recognized tribes as sovereign nation-states in important regards.[7] But once the new country gained political and military strength, and European disease decimated tribal populations, honoring the "platonic notions of Indian sovereignty"[8] became less compelling if not downright inconvenient.

The Court did not overtly overturn its foundation Indian law cases however. As EPA's Indian program began in the 1970s the Court continued to describe tribes as possessing territorial sovereignty extending beyond their citizens.[9] In the early 1980s, the Court twice upheld the imposition of tribal taxes on non-Indians who entered into business transactions with tribal entities on Indian lands. Taxation as a form of civil regulatory authority was "a fundamental attribute of [inherent tribal] sovereignty"[10] properly exercised over non-Indians who "avail[ed] themselves of the 'substantial privilege of carrying on business' on the reservation."[11]

It was a different matter for non-Indians on non-Indian lands. Those actors, or their predecessors, had entered Indian country at a time when no one seriously considered the prospect of tribal regulation of non-Indians. The federal and state governments, in fact, fully expected Indian country and Indian tribes would cease to exist in fairly short order. When they did not, a new rule, or more accurately, a significantly revised old rule, was necessary for the protection of non-Indians who had not voluntarily submitted themselves to tribal jurisdiction.

The starkest example of the Court's revisionist approach was the 1978 decision *Oliphant v. Suquamish Indian Tribe*.[12] Two non-Indians prosecuted by the Tribe for criminal acts committed on the Port Madison Reservation in western Washington sought immunity in federal court. A well-established rule counseled that tribes retain all aspects of their inherent sovereignty save those specifically taken away by congressional enactments or surrendered in treaties. No federal law or treaty spoke to the Tribe's criminal authority over non-Indians on its reservation. The Supreme Court nonetheless invalidated the tribal convictions. It revised the general rule to read: "Indian tribes are proscribed from exercising both those powers of autonomous states that are expressly terminated by Congress *and* those powers '*inconsistent with their status*'" as domestic dependent nations.

Non-Indians and states praised what to them was an eminently reasonable conclusion. Tribes were "communit[ies] separated by race and tradition." They were not bound by the federal Constitution's protections for criminal defendants, or for that matter, any of the individual rights ensconced in its first ten amendments. To hold otherwise, the Court said, would subject non-Indians to:

> the restraints of an external and unknown code ... which judges them, not by their peers, nor by the customs of their people, nor the law of their land, but by ... a different race, according to the law of a social state of which they have an imperfect conception.[13]

Tribes and Indian law scholars were apoplectic. The alleged unfairness of imposing an alien legal code on others had not bothered the Court when it was European law applied to deprive indigenous peoples of their lands and self-determination rights. The "inconsistent with their status" test rested on a gross perversion of early cases directed at establishing the United States' claims to the North American continent as among other European nations, not defining the scope of tribal sovereignty. Practically, the test's indeterminacy promised a wave of litigation asserting all manner of inherent tribal powers should be determined as implicitly divested by virtue of subjective judicial views of tribes' "proper" status. Those apprehensive of a "civil *Oliphant*" did not wait long before their fears were realized. Three years later the Court applied *Oliphant's* asserted implicit divestiture rule to tribal civil regulatory jurisdiction over non-Indians on reservation lands owned in fee simple by non-Indians.

Montana v. United States[14] involved a long-running dispute between the State and the Crow Tribe over the Big Horn River as it runs through the Crow Reservation in southern Montana. An 1868 treaty with the United States reserved an eight million acre reservation for the Tribe's "absolute and undisturbed use and occupation," and promised that no non-Indians "shall ever be permitted to pass over, settle upon, or reside in" the reservation.[15] Within half a century, the federal government had exercised its unilateral Indian powers to reduce the reservation to just over two million acres and transfer nearly thirty percent of its land from the Tribe to non-Indians.

Like their tribal neighbors, the non-Indian residents value the reservation's natural beauty and bounty of outdoor pursuits. They fish for trout and hunt ducks on the Big Horn River and its tributaries, and hunt deer and other game in upland areas. The legal dispute arose when the Crow Tribe and the State of Montana both claimed regulatory authority over non-Indian hunting and fishing on the reservation. The United States sued Montana as the Tribe's trustee. The parties' arguments, and the decisions of the trial court and the Ninth Circuit Court of Appeals, focused on the Tribe's rather than the State's authority, and used the term nonmembers rather than non-Indians.

The Supreme Court was not troubled by the Tribe's assertion of authority over nonmembers who entered lands owned by the Tribe or held by the U.S. in trust for the Tribe. On tribally owned lands, the Tribe could exclude nonmembers completely, or allow their entry conditioned on compliance with the Tribe's wildlife management rules, as any landowner could. That unremarkable conclusion, however, neglected the status of Indian tribes as sovereign governments and affirmed tribal control of only seventeen percent of the reservation. It could not support tribal authority over the remaining lands.

The United States asserted the Tribe's territorial sovereignty covered those other non-tribal reservation lands. The Court's carefully crafted disagreement was worthy of any politician's admiration. Yes, prior cases had noted tribes' inherent sovereignty over their territories as well as their members. But the most recent reference came in a case concerning a tribe's criminal prosecution of a tribal member. Tribal power over nonmembers had not been at issue. Most of the cases making broad statements of tribal sovereignty, in fact, involved only tribal members in clearly "internal" matters like domestic relations. Those areas were not within the aspects of tribal self-government *Oliphant* suggested were implicitly divested by the tribes' dependent status. "But exercise of tribal power beyond what is necessary to protect tribal self-government or to control internal relations is inconsistent with the dependent status of the tribes, and so cannot survive without express congressional delegation."

The *Montana* Court admitted *Oliphant's* rationale was developed in the fairly unique context of tribal criminal authority over nonmembers, but explicitly incorporated it into the tribal civil regulatory context nonetheless. The result appeared as a nearly absolute rule labeled as a "general proposition:" inherent tribal sovereignty does not reach the activities of nonmembers. The Court would later call *Montana's* rule "pathmarking," implicitly admitting it had departed from the prior course. A congressionally authorized report to the American Indian Policy Review Commission in 1976 deduced the opposite "general proposition" from federal common law: that tribes possess inherent civil authority over non-Indians even where Congress has legislated in the field and/or allowed state jurisdiction.[16]

Somewhat reluctantly, the *Montana* Court acknowledged that prior path by not completely barring tribal regulation of nonmembers:

> To be sure, Indian tribes retain inherent sovereign power to exercise some forms of civil jurisdiction over non-Indians on their reservations, even on non-Indian fee lands. A tribe may regulate, through taxation, licensing, or other means, the activities of nonmembers who enter consensual relationships with the tribe or its members, through commercial dealing, contracts, leases, or other arrangements.... A tribe may also retain inherent power to exercise civil authority over the conduct of non-Indians on fee lands within its reservation when that conduct threatens or has some direct effect on the political integrity, the economic security, or the health or welfare of the tribe.[17]

These two apparent exceptions to the general rule of no tribal authority implicitly defined the Court's reference to inherent powers over non-Indians that are "necessary to protect tribal self-government."

The first exception did not apply to non-Indian hunters and fishers on the Crow reservation because they had no commercial relationship with the Tribe. The fact of their land ownership inside the reservation did not qualify. The second exception's concern for nonmember impacts on tribal interests seemed more relevant. "Health and welfare" is a common catchphrase describing the legitimate goals of state governments' inherent police powers. Long ago the Court upheld a state's bird-hunting laws on the assumption they were rationally related to promoting the general welfare by preserving a common resource.[18]

The Crow Tribe did not receive the same treatment. The Tribe's legislative determination of the public interest in effective wildlife management garnered none of the deference state legislatures normally receive. The Court in fact showed absolutely no interest in the legislative history of the Crow laws at issue. Instead, it demanded proof that non-Indian hunting and fishing "imperiled" the Tribe's subsistence or welfare. Faulting the United States for failing to anticipate this dramatic new standard in its initial legal complaint, the Court found the Tribe's health and welfare interests insufficiently affected.

Equally unusual was the Court's reliance on the reservation's regulatory history. Montana had stocked the Big Horn River on the reservation with trout as early as 1928, and had also stocked upland birds and game in areas adjacent to the reservation. State game wardens had cited, and county attorneys had prosecuted, non-Indians who violated the State's wildlife laws on the reservation. The Tribe occasionally complained about the State's on-reservation enforcement, but it was not until the early 1970s when the Tribe and the federal government began developing joint wildlife management efforts that conflicts with the State ended up in court. By then it was too late. The Supreme Court characterized the failure to object earlier as the Tribe having "accommodated" itself to the State's jurisdiction, buttressing the Court's conclusion that non-Indian hunting and fishing did not affect tribal self-government. In contrast to the high evidentiary burden placed on the Tribe, the Court neither required nor offered a justification for the State's intrusion into Indian country in the first instance. And its decree forbidding tribal regulation of non-Indians on fee lands effectively sanctioned the State's continued exercise of regulatory authority in Crow territory without analysis.

Montana's result and tortured analysis provided little guidance on the scope of the health and welfare exception to the general rule of no tribal authority over non-Indians. EPA's 1983 Discussion Paper, which featured the Agency's first public legal analysis of Indian country jurisdiction, made no attempt to reconcile the inconsistencies. In fact, the Discussion Paper did not cite the general rule, nor did it mention the status of the health and welfare test as an exception rather than a presumption. It noted several lower court cases subsequent to *Montana* upholding tribal regulation of non-Indian water rights and land uses, and concluded tribes' inherent sovereignty extended to "control environmental activities of all people on *all* lands within reservation boundaries."[19]

The Supreme Court cast some doubt on that unqualified conclusion just two months before EPA proposed its first regulation under section 518 of the Clean Water Act. The issue in *Brendale v. Confederated Tribes and Bands of the Yakima Indian Nation*[20] was whether the Yakama[21] Indian Nation's zoning code applied to two parcels of non-Indian land on the Tribe's reservation. One parcel was located in an undeveloped forested area of the reservation owned mostly by the Tribe and closed to general public access. The trial court upheld the Tribe's authority because it found the non-Indian owner's plan to build ten summer cabins presented threats to air quality, soil stability, vegetation, wildlife, religious and cultural sites, and other tribal welfare interests. The court denied tribal authority over a similar development proposed on the other parcel, which was located in a developed area of the reservation occupied primarily by non-Indians, because it found no such environmental or welfare threats there. The Ninth Circuit Court of Appeals reversed the latter conclusion on the rationale that governmental zoning ordinances by their nature promote general health and welfare.

The nine Supreme Court justices split badly. Four viewed the Yakama Nation as a domestic dependent sovereign lacking inherent authority to zone any non-Indian property within its reservation, while three other Justices came to the opposite conclusion. Like the Ninth Circuit, the latter Justices saw tribal zoning power as a fundamental sovereign power central to the Tribe's health and welfare, particularly because of indigenous peoples' cultural connection to their lands. The two remaining Justices split the properties and the Court: for reasons different than the other Justices, they endorsed tribal control over non-Indian lands in the undeveloped portion of the reservation closed to the general public, but denied it in the reservation's so-called "open" area.

The strange mathematics of plurality decisions meant the result favored by two Justices became the Court's result; the Tribe prevailed on a 5–4 vote for the "closed" property, but lost the "open" property on a 6–3 vote. But the lack of a majority's agreement on the test for determining inherent tribal authority meant *Brendale's* status as binding precedent for future cases was technically and practically non-existent. So, rather than providing EPA with timely guidance for navigating *Montana's* confused pronouncements, *Brendale's* disjointed result threw an additional layer of unpredictability on the Agency.

EPA's Interim Operating Rule

The section 518 rule EPA proposed in 1989 governed the development of tribal water quality standards. Tribes treated as states could designate uses they desired to make of their waters and set criteria defining the levels of pollutants necessary for preserving the designated uses. The standards thus represented important tribal value judgments on water quality, but they were not self-executing; they offered tribes no direct regulatory control over non-Indians. Their legal effect came through incorporation in pollution permit conditions issued by EPA.

EPA nonetheless proposed requiring tribes whose waters could be impaired by non-Indian activities show inherent jurisdiction over non-Indians under relevant federal Indian law principles. Twenty-five people testified at three hearings across the nation and EPA received thirty-four written comments. The most significant attention was directed at whether and how EPA should require tribes demonstrate satisfaction of the second treatment-as-a-state criterion, and of course, *Brendale* was heavily cited.

Commenters opposed to tribal sovereignty read the case as foreclosing tribal regulation of non-Indians completely. They believed *Brendale* had overruled *Montana's* health and welfare exception. At the very least, they argued, the two cases together suggested EPA should impose on tribes the burden of submitting detailed factual analyses proving any purported health and welfare impacts.

Tribes and their supporters saw no need for any factual showing or explanation. Water quality management is quintessentially health and welfare regulation. Rather than demand proof of that obvious fact, they supported a per se rule presuming tribal jurisdiction in every case. They asserted *Brendale* had not diminished *Montana's* recognition of tribal sovereignty.

EPA had followed the path of caution on the issue of congressional delegation and it did the same here. It would proceed on a case-by-case basis, neither assuming tribes could always or could never show authority over non-Indians. *Brendale* did not bar EPA from recognizing tribal water programs for the simple reason there was no majority opinion. And the result of the case—upholding tribal authority over non-Indian activities threatening tribal interests but denying it where no such threat existed—appeared in line with *Montana's* health and welfare test.

By the same token, the Crow Tribe's loss in *Montana* meant the health and welfare exception was not the same test applied in state police power cases. Something more than a mere assertion of impacts on tribal welfare seemed necessary. Four of the *Brendale* Justices suggested the effects must be "demonstrably serious" and three others said they should implicate "a significant tribal interest." An unrelated Supreme Court case had recently commented tribal authority existed where its exercise was "vital" to tribal self-determination. The trend toward requiring more than some minor or de minimis showing of tribal impact appeared to be gaining momentum. EPA concluded it would be prudent in that light to adopt "an interim operating rule" requiring tribes show the potential impacts of non-Indian water pollution were "serious and substantial."[22]

The Agency's caution represented more than institutional inertia or reticence. Federal Indian law's principles for tribal sovereignty were matters outside its expertise. They were not unfamiliar; by this time the Indian program was nearly twenty years old. But they were not matters Congress specifically delegated to the Agency for implementation. As such, EPA's interpretations of *Montana* and *Brendale* and the like were not eligible for judicial deference, as *Phillips Petroleum* and *HRI* made clear in the underground injection context.

EPA's interpretations of the Clean Water Act and its expertise in environmental management were different. Congress had placed program responsibility squarely on the Agency's shoulders. Its conclusions on Indian country implementation had garnered judicial respect in every Indian country environmental case to date. EPA sought to bring future tribal claims of jurisdiction within that protective cloak by announcing a set of "generalized findings" on the relation of water pollution to health and welfare.

EPA viewed the Clean Water Act's passage as constituting a legislative determination that water pollution presents serious and substantial impacts on public health and welfare. Section 518 specifically represented Congress' preference for tribal regulation as the means for meeting the Clean Water Act's goals on Indian reservations. Tribal management was practically important because water pollutants are highly mobile. Once introduced into a water body, separating water quality impairment caused by non-Indian pollution discharges can be difficult if not impossible. The water transport mechanism also increases the likelihood tribal citizens will be exposed to pollutants released from non-Indian lands. Water quality management was thus directly related to protecting health and welfare, which EPA noted was a core governmental function whose exercise was critical to self-government.

These findings did not negate the interim operating rule's requirement that tribes show serious and substantial health and welfare impacts. Each tribe seeking treatment-as-a-state bore the burden of demonstrating its independent jurisdiction over non-Indians. But the generalized findings linking non-Indian water pollution to tribal health and welfare would effectively supplement the tribe's legal analysis. So, EPA said, a satisfactory tribal submission:

> will need to make a relatively simple showing of facts that there are waters within the reservation used by the Tribe or tribal members, (and thus that the Tribe or tribal members could be subject to exposure to pollutants present in, or introduced into, those waters) and that the waters and critical habitat are subject to protection under the Clean Water Act. The Tribe must also explicitly assert that impairment of such waters by the activities of non-Indians, would have a serious and substantial effect on the health and welfare of the Tribe.[23]

Once a tribe made this "simple showing," EPA would combine it with the generalized findings to presume an adequate demonstration of tribal authority over non-Indian lands had been made.

The presumption was rebuttable. The regulations created a new notice and comment process for jurisdictional objections. EPA would notify adjacent states and tribes when it received a tribal application and allow thirty days for comments specific to the tribe's claim of jurisdiction over non-Indians. Simple objections were inadequate. The challenger bore the burden of proving the tribe's lack of jurisdiction; in other words, that non-Indian water pollution did *not* present serious and substantial threats to tribal health and welfare.

Tribal Water Quality Judgments for Indian Country

From time immemorial, the twenty distinct bands of related indigenous peoples now referred to as the Salish and Kootenai Tribes claimed an aboriginal territory of well over twenty million acres in the north central portion of the United States and into Canada. In 1855, the federal government brought to bear the pressures so many tribes had suffered and would suffer in the country's history. The resulting Treaty of Hell Gate memorialized the Tribes' cession of nearly all its expansive territory; only 1.3 million acres in northwest Montana were retained as the Tribes' permanent homeland.[24]

The United States promised to respect their exclusive possession of the Flathead Indian Reservation and permit no non-Indians to enter without the permission of the Tribes. Fifty years later, through the exhortations of Missoula businessman and Representative Joseph M. Dixon, Congress opened the reservation to allotment and non-Indian ownership, paying about twenty-four cents on the dollar for the lands sold.[25] Non-Indians and the State now own about forty-two percent of the reservation; approximately seventy-five percent of the current reservation population is non-Indian.

The reservation is located at the bottom of the 8,800 square mile Flathead River Basin, just west of the glacially carved Mission Range that forms the continental divide in Montana. Some 500 miles of rivers and streams and over 120 lakes including seventy high mountain lakes dot the reservation. The most prominent feature in the area is Flathead Lake, the largest natural freshwater lake west of the Great Lakes. The southern half of the lake falls with the reservation's boundaries.

The reservation's higher elevations are relatively pristine and provide habitat for deer, elk, bears, turkeys and other upland birds. Stocked trout and native cutthroat and bull trout inhabit the rivers and lakes, as well as planted game fish in reservoirs and lakes. Tribal members make cultural and subsistence uses of the many plants, animals and fish on the reservation.

At higher elevations water quality is good to excellent. Lower in the valley a variety of human activity has degraded water quality somewhat. Logging, mining, agricultural operations, housing developments, cattle feedlots, dairies, auto wrecking yards, landfills, trailer parks, RV campgrounds, residential septic systems and publicly owned sewage treatment works all contribute to pollution loading in the rivers and Flathead Lake.

The Tribes have been developing their legal and administrative infrastructure for managing and enhancing the reservation's environmental quality since 1980, when they followed the Northern Cheyenne example and redesignated the reservation's air quality to Class I. In 1983, they created a Shoreline Protection Program regulating all dredging and filling and construction on lake and streambeds and banks and wetlands. In 1990, the Division of Environmental Protection was created within the Department of Natural Resources and assumed responsibility for the Shoreline and air quality programs and began a water quality program by obtaining grants from EPA for planning activities. In 1992, the Environmental Division applied for treatment-as-a-state for the water quality standards program.

A full year of inquires and discussion between officials at EPA's Region VIII and the Tribes followed the initial application. EPA clarified the Tribes' factual assertions and helped supplement them with information from state and EPA files reporting past pollution incidents involving non-Indians at Flathead. The Agency notified the Tribes it considered the application complete in July 1993.

EPA's first Indian regional administrator, a Crow citizen named William Yellowtail, formally notified Montana of the Tribes' application at that time. EPA's tribal water quality standards regulations required Yellowtail give notice of tribal applications to "appropriate governmental entities." Governments' comments were invited on the sole issue of the Tribes' assertion of regulatory authority to set standards for all reservation waters, including those adjacent to lands owned by non-Indians. EPA also posted a notice in the local newspaper, *The Missovlian,* directing the general public to convey their views to EPA through the State.

A distinguishing feature of modern administrative law in the United States is the broad opportunity for public involvement in many agency decisions. Any "interested person" is entitled to comment on most proposed actions affecting the environment. No specific interest in the proposal—economic, environmental or otherwise—is required. Nor must a commenter have particular qualifications or knowledge about the relevant environmental program or regulated activities.

The rise in the public's consciousness since the late 1960s has generated an increasing number of citizen comments on proposals for specific actions with direct environmental impacts. The not-in-my-backyard phenomenon means local citizens often weigh in on proposed timber harvests, mineral mines, landfills, hydroelectric dams, energy facilities and the like. Programmatic questions, however, rarely capture the average person's interest. That is particularly true of state applications for program delegation from EPA. Whether perceived as lacking direct effects on individuals' lives, or perhaps too complex for the average person to decipher, individual citizen comments on these actions are generally limited at best.

That has also typically been the case for EPA's programmatic actions in developing the Indian program. Most of the comments made on EPA's proposals for direct implementation of the water and underground injection programs came from states, municipalities, industry associations and individual businesses. On the other hand, a tribal treatment-as-a-state application seems to strike fear in the hearts of regular (non-Indian) folk everywhere. The State of Montana forwarded over 30 citizen comments to EPA on the Salish and Kootenai application for approval of their water quality standards.

To a person, the comments reveal little knowledge of or interest in the intricacies of program approval, or for that matter, the contours of federal Indian law as applied to the treatment-as-a-state approach. Instead, they parroted a flawed and irrelevant constitutional law argument, presumably transmitted through the cowboy boot telegraph in the coffee shops around Flathead. More than twenty letters, including two from the mayors of two reservation towns, specifically asserted the Tribes "have no constitutional right" to regulate non-Indian property owners. Presumably, what they meant to assert was that *they*, as non-Indians who could not vote in tribal elections nor hold tribal office, had federal constitutional rights not to be regulated by a government in which they could not participate. This of course was the taxation without representation argument that, unfortunately for the commenters, had been generally rejected by the Supreme Court on several occasions and specifically rejected by the Congress in the context of the Clean Water Act. And, there was no taxation here at any rate; EPA's approval of the Tribes' water quality standards had no direct regulatory impact on anyone, Indian or non-Indian.

But the commenters were unencumbered by the facts. They asserted federal approval of the Tribes' standards would be "devastating" and a "major threat" to non-Indian livelihoods, though they could not explain how the impact of the tribal standards was different from the nearly identical state standards. One letter asserted approval would constitute "another discriminatory act against the majority residents of this reservation." Several indicated their belief the Tribes would not administer their environmental programs fairly, and others were simply racist in their vehemence:

I say if [the Tribes] want to be treated as a sovereign nation, the borders will be gated just like any other national boundary. All benefits that the white man provides will be cut off from the tribes and let them support themselves. Then we'll see how long they thrive without us to support them. Most tribal members have no trade or college education how can they run a nation? They live from benefit check to benefit check.... I might add that there are very few full blood [I]ndians around. In fact, Mickey Pablo, who's the head chief is only 1/16 [I]ndian.[26]

The State's response was understandably more focused. It directly attacked the Tribes' assertion of authority over non-Indian water polluting activities. The primary thrust of its challenge, however, was not that such activities at Flathead presented minor or insubstantial risks to tribal health or welfare. Instead, it iterated objections made in 1989 when EPA proposed the regulations now controlling Region VIII's decision on the Salish and Kootenai application. The State asserted EPA had read the *Montana* health and welfare test too broadly and had not squarely addressed *Brendale's* impact on it. Montana also complained it had no opportunity to contest the Tribes' assertions of serious and substantial impacts, and demanded an administrative trial-type proceeding to do so. The State ignored the opportunity presented by its invited comment letter.

But Region VIII could do nothing with these misplaced attacks on the water quality standards rule promulgated two years earlier. EPA headquarters had rejected them in finalizing the rule and neither the State nor anyone else had challenged the rule. Region VIII was thus bound to follow the standard set by the interim operating rule and the process for obtaining comments from appropriate governmental entities on tribal assertions of jurisdiction.

The State's fears were realized in 1995 when EPA announced it had approved the Tribes' standards. The key finding, of course, was that the Tribes had showed jurisdiction over non-Indian water polluters. Central to that decision was the interim operating rule's shifted burden. The rule asked only assertions of the Tribes, whereas the State's burden was to prove the impossible: that water pollution did not present potentially serious and substantial health and welfare risks. EPA's explanation for its approval clearly illustrated the significance of the rule's shifted burden:

In accordance with [the interim operating rule] the Tribes have made a showing of facts that there are waters within the Reservation used by the Tribes or tribal members (and thus that the Tribes or tribal members could be subject to exposure to pollutants present in, or introduced into, those waters) and that the waters and critical habitat of the Reservation are subject to protection under the [Clean Water Act]. The Tribes have also asserted that impairment of such waters by the activities of nonmembers would have an effect on the health and welfare of the Tribes that is serious and substantial. Based upon the facts available to the Agency from the Tribes and other sources ... and in light of the generalized statutory and factual findings discussed above, the Agency believes that the Tribes have demonstrated that the protection of water quality sought to be carried out by setting water quality standards for water on [non-Indian] fee lands on the Flathead Reservation would protect against potential impacts on tribal health and welfare that are serious and substantial.[27]

Having thus determined the Tribes' met their burden of establishing a prime facie case of jurisdiction, EPA turned to Montana's objections:

The State of Montana's comments did not provide data pertaining to the Tribes' assertions that impairment of waters on reservation fee lands may have effects on the health and welfare of the Tribes that are serious and substantial. Since the Tribes' submittal met the initial requirement imposed on them by the regulation, the State's submittal should have presented any available data demonstrating that impairment of waters by activities on fee lands would not have potential effects on the health and welfare of the tribes that are serious and substantial. EPA carefully evaluated the State's submission and determined that the State did not provide information that would cause the Agency to conclude that the Tribes' assertions were unsupported.[28]

EPA's resulting approval of the Tribes' standards had no immediate legal effect on water pollution dischargers on the Flathead Reservation. Water quality standards take effect mainly through incorporation in the conditions of discharge permits. Existing permits can be reopened to take account of new or revised standards, but more typically they are revised as they come up for renewal in due course. Thus, the influence of the Tribes' standards would increase incrementally over time as permit renewals and application for new permits accrued.

Responsibility for translating the Tribes' standards into permit conditions for pollution discharges on the Flathead Reservation would fall on EPA. Section 518 offered the Salish and Kootenai Tribes the opportunity to assume that responsibility, but they were not required to do so as part of their application for the separate water quality standards program. When the Tribes submitted their standards EPA had not yet issued regulations for tribal permit program assumptions at any rate. In the absence of a tribal permit program, EPA's first Indian program action in 1973 made clear EPA was the permit-issuing agency in Indian country and would not delegate that responsibility to states absent a showing of independent jurisdiction.

And yet it is not difficult to find state-issued water pollution discharge permits on Indian reservations across the country. At Flathead, there were three in fact—the wastewater treatment facilities in the cities of Ronan and Hot Springs and the State's research facility at Yellow Bay all operated under the auspices of state permission. EPA was clearly aware of these permits. The program's general guidelines required state submission of draft permits to EPA for review and comment. Heretofore EPA had not objected to those permits even though Montana's approved permit program did not extend to Indian country.

EPA acknowledged some states were issuing water discharge permits in Indian country without authorization when EPA later issued regulations for tribal permit programs.[29] It took no responsibility for allowing states' regulatory machinery to creep into Indian country without showing jurisdiction, an omission clearly inconsistent with the Indian Policy and the federal trust responsibility.[30] State creep also violated binding regulations requiring states show Indian country jurisdiction before obtaining program delegation. Instead, EPA deflected attention away from its neglect by directing that tribal applications for program delegation describe an orderly process for transitioning from state to tribal permitting responsibility.

Until that time, and despite its repeated statements that states lacked regulatory authority in Indian country, EPA said it would assume that any existing permit issued by a state for discharges on Indian reservations contained enforceable limits:

> Until the [water pollution discharge permit] program is delegated to a tribe, or until EPA otherwise determines in consultation with a state and tribe that a state lacks jurisdiction to issue [such] permits on Indian lands, we will assume without deciding that those permits contain applicable effluent limits, in order to ensure that controls on discharges to reservation waters remain in place.[31]

EPA justified that assumption by claiming any contrary action would leave an unwarranted regulatory void over reservation waters. It did not acknowledge the perceived regulatory gap was exactly what motivated its 1973 decision not to delegate permit programs to states, and more generally, its entire Indian program. Nor did EPA address how a state lacking program approval in Indian country could issue a valid Clean Water Act permit there. EPA made the same curious assumption in the water quality standards rule, declaring it would "assume without deciding" that existing state standards were applicable to reservation waters until tribal standards were adopted.

Approval of the Salish and Kootenai Tribes' standards then meant EPA would no longer assume the State's standards applied to reservation waters. Presumably that did not preclude the State from continuing to issue discharge permits, though now they would have to be conditioned on compliance with the Tribes' rather than the State's water quality standards. There was no direct link between the parallel assumptions on state water quality standards and state permits, but EPA decided the state permits at Flathead had to go once the Tribes' standards took effect.

The State reacted strongly when the Agency informed the three state facilities they were now expected to apply for federal discharge permits. It had no basis to challenge EPA's authority to require a federal permit since the State's program was not authorized for the reservation, so it sued on EPA's approval of the Tribes' standards instead. Since the Tribes' standards appeared to have triggered the demand for federal permits, perhaps the State believed if it prevailed EPA would be content to leave the State permits in place. Again the State raised its arguments that EPA had misread and misapplied the *Montana* test.

Several individual farmers and ranchers, three irrigation districts and a state chartered entity governing water usage on non-Indian fee lands sought intervention as plaintiffs in the case. Reminiscent of the wide-ranging comments that individual citizens submitted on EPA's proposed approval of the Tribes' standards, the intervenors saw the approval as a harbinger of increased tribal control over non-Indian lands far beyond the impact of value judgments on water quality. They asserted losses of property value, rights to jury trials, local non-Indian governmental control over water use, and participation in governments that regulated them.

The federal district court in Missoula was perplexed by these vague assertions and denied the motion to intervene. The intervenors had no "significantly protectable" interest that could be impaired by the litigation; none possessed a water pollution discharge permit that might somehow be affected by the Tribes' new water quality standards. The Clean Water Act, in fact, specifically exempts irrigation return flows from the ambit of the discharge permit program. EPA's conclusion the Tribes' possessed adequate jurisdiction over non-Indians for purposes of approving the water quality standards did not somehow validate tribal control over all non-Indian activities within the reservation.

The district court also rejected the State's substantive arguments.[32] It initially observed the amicus argument submitted by the Assiniboine and Sioux Tribes of the Fort Peck Reservation in Montana that section 518 was a delegation of authority over non-Indian polluters of reservation waters. The court seemed favorably inclined toward the argument, noting *Brendale's* confirming reference, but did not decide on that basis since EPA had taken the cautious route in requiring tribal showings of inherent jurisdiction over non-Indians. It agreed with EPA that *Brendale* had perhaps narrowed but not overruled the *Montana* test, and deferred to the Agency's expertise in making the generalized findings and adopting its anti-checkerboard policy in the 1991 state-tribe concept paper.

The State and the intervenors appealed separately to the Ninth Circuit Court of Appeals. Both by geographic expanse and by number of states, the Ninth Circuit is the largest circuit in the country. In addition to Montana, it encompasses most of the western continental states—Washington, Oregon, California, Arizona, Nevada and Idaho—as well as Alaska and Hawaii. With large populations of indigenous peoples in each of those states, Ninth Circuit cases account for a significant portion of federal Indian law decisions. Ninth Circuit panels had decided *Nance* and *Washington Department of Ecology,* two of the first Indian country environmental law cases. The results of both cases were consistent with the court's reputation for favorable treatment of Indian claims. But the Ninth Circuit also had a history of its Indian cases being overturned by the Supreme Court: the tribes' key losses in *Oliphant, Montana* and *Brendale* had been victories in the Ninth Circuit. If the State of Montana could not convince the Ninth Circuit to overturn the district court, perhaps the Supreme Court would take the case and grant relief.

Montana's opening brief in the Ninth Circuit seemed crafted with Supreme Court review in mind. According to the State, the EPA action at issue was not its approval of the Salish and Kootenai Tribes' water quality standards, but rather its determination that "the Tribes possess inherent sovereign authority over the State of Montana and various of its political subdivisions" for purposes of the Clean Water Act. The State urged the court not to defer to EPA's reconciliation of environmental and Indian policies, and instead subject its reasoning to careful scrutiny, "given what hinges in the balance"—the right of citizens to participate in government and hold government officials accountable. Somewhat more on point, but still intended as a red flag, the brief asserted EPA's interim operating rule converted the Supreme Court's presumption against tribal authority over non-Indians "into an essentially irrebuttable one in *favor* of such authority."

The heart of the dispute was over the impact of the fractured opinions in *Brendale*. The lack of a majority rationale meant the case offered no clear precedent controlling future cases. EPA thus relied on the results of the case, which appeared consistent with *Montana's* health and welfare exception: the Yakama Tribe had jurisdiction in the closed area where non-Indian development threatened tribal welfare interests, but not in the open area where those interests were apparently not affected.

The State countered that *Brendale* was binding precedent despite the absence of a majority rationale because a holding could be divined by identifying the position taken by the Justices who concurred with the judgment on the narrowest ground.[33] Six of the Justices agreed in two opinions that the Tribe lacked jurisdiction over non-Indian development in the open area of the reservation. The State asserted their common frame of reference was a question that potentially preempted the *Montana* test: whether existing state or federal law regulated the non-Indian activities over which the tribe asserted jurisdiction. If so, the State argued, tribal law was foreclosed without any consideration of the potential impacts to tribal health and welfare. The tribe could protect its interests through a suit in state or federal court, but not by direct regulation of the offending activity.

In *Montana v. Environmental Protection Agency*,[34] the Ninth Circuit rejected all but one of the State's arguments: Montana was correct that judicial deference was not appropriate for assessing EPA's reading of the Supreme Court's tribal sovereignty jurisprudence. The court's independent or de novo review, however, revealed the correctness of the Agency's position. The court acknowledged *Brendale* had created confusion, but concluded a majority of the Justices treated the *Montana* health and welfare test as controlling. It could find no suggestion in the two opinions cited by the State that tribal sovereignty existed only where no other government could act. Nor was there any indication the two opinions somehow overruled *Montana*.

The Ninth Circuit found support in a unanimous Supreme Court decision issued after the parties submitted their briefs. *Strate v. A-1 Contractors*[35] denied tribal court jurisdiction over a car accident involving two non-Indians on a state highway running through a reservation. The result derived from direct application of the *Montana* health and welfare test, which flatly contradicted any claim that *Brendale* overruled the test eight years earlier. The Supreme Court ascribed no decisional weight to *Brendale*, observing in a footnote only that the *Montana* test had "figured prominently" in its fractured decisions. The *Strate* Court made no reference to a threshold inquiry of state or federal jurisdiction.

Strate did insist, however, the *Montana* test required something more than a simple showing of tribal health and welfare impacts. The Court conceded that careless driving by non-Indians on reservation roads "undoubtedly" jeopardized the safety of tribal citizens, but the Court read the cases upon which *Montana* relied as sanctioning jurisdiction over non-Indians only where necessary to protect tribal self-government or internal relations. It was not convinced an adequate nexus existed between regulation of highway accidents and "the right of reservation Indians to make their own laws and be ruled be them."

In contrast, the Ninth Circuit found tribal regulation of non-Indian water pollution had the requisite nexus with tribal self-government. In fact, it said the interim operating rule EPA adopted six years earlier adumbrated *Strate's* requirement of a nexus between tribal regulation of the non-Indian activity at issue and tribal self-government. EPA determined water pollution presents serious and substantial health and welfare risks, and properly found protection of tribal citizens from such risks is a core function of tribal self-government. That finding was consistent with a Tenth Circuit case in New Mexico upholding a tribe's sovereign right to set water quality standards more stringent than relevant federal criteria.[36] The nature of water as a "unitary" resource and the mobility of water pollutants meant pollution from non-Indian lands could affect tribal citizens on a scale much larger than a lone negligent non-Indian driver on a reservation highway. A prior Ninth Circuit case came to a similar conclusion in upholding tribal control over non-Indian water uses affecting tribal water rights.[37] In this regard, the court deferred as it should have to the Agency's expertise in environmental management and its reconciliation of environmental and Indian policies.

The Ninth Circuit also affirmed the district court's dismissal of the local intervenors because their allegations that the Salish and Kootenai standards would somehow violate non-Indian civil rights and undermine the constitutional republic held no water. The standards had absolutely no direct effect on the intervenors. The Clean Water Act did not regulate their ranching and irrigation activities; the irrigators held no water pollution discharge permits, and if they did apply for a permit, it would be issued by EPA. Any indirect impact on their property values was speculative and could not form the basis for an environmental claim like this one.

The intervenors did not seek Supreme Court review, but they filed an amicus brief on behalf of Montana which did petition for a writ of certiorari.

The State continued to pretend that EPA's approval meant the Tribes now had jurisdiction over the State and its local subdivisions, insisting the case presented important federalism concerns. No other circuit had decided the same issue, so there was no split of authority calling out for Supreme Court resolution. Montana clamored for space on the Court's limited docket instead by asserting the Ninth Circuit decision, which was "so obviously suspect," might improperly influence decisions on the some 210 tribes nationwide that had received or were seeking treatment-as-a-state status. Of those, however, only twenty-two were water quality standards applications; the overwhelming number simply sought grants for water quality assessment and planning that carried no regulatory impact.

An amicus brief submitted by eleven other states implicitly buttressed Montana's claim the case had national dimensions. The states attacked EPA's "pro forma" approval process as shifting the burdens of proof in a manner inconsistent with federal Indian law:

> Under EPA policy, states like the amici effectively have the burden of proving the absence of tribal jurisdiction in order to avoid the loss of authority states would otherwise possess under the Clean Water Act. Not only is this a burden the law does not require states to bear, but as formulated by EPA, the burden is one no state can ever carry.
>
> In its effort to promote the assumption of regulatory power by tribes, EPA has lost sight of the established precepts of Indian law, as well as the agency's own pronouncements. In place of careful, fact-intensive historical inquiry into the status of a reservation, EPA has concocted a simplistic, wooden formula under which no tribe could ever fail to receive state status under the Clean Water Act. EPA's approach to the issue of inherent tribal regulatory authority is wholly inconsistent with controlling precedent of this Court, which mandates a presumption against the existence of inherent tribal regulatory authority over nonmember activities.[38]

The brief offered as examples pending cases brought by Wisconsin challenging EPA's approval of four tribal water quality standards applications. The express point was that EPA had not conducted the fact-intensive analysis of each reservation the amici believed *Brendale* required. The reservations ranged from 200,000 acres to fewer than ten, and two of them were in urban or suburban areas on the outskirts of Green Bay and Madison, which the amici equated with the "open" area of the Yakama reservation. The implicit point, dropped in a footnote, was that impropriety pervaded the Agency's Indian program: an EPA lawyer and a staffer had backdated key administrative documents to cover their shortcomings in preparing the decision files for three of the tribal applications. The Agency ended up revoking the tribal program approvals and paying Wisconsin's legal costs in bringing the cases.

Salacious though it was, the story apparently did not have the intended effect. The Supreme Court denied the State of Montana's petition for review. The Ninth Circuit's validation of the Agency's interpretation of the *Montana* test as applied under the Clean Water Act remained the law of the western states. And *Montana v. EPA's* favorable treatment stands as the only national case directly addressing tribal sovereignty over non-Indian polluters in Indian country.

Tribal Environmental Program Influence outside Indian Country

Perhaps the Supreme Court recognized Montana's claim of being regulated by the Salish and Kootenai Tribes was overstated. The Ninth Circuit certainly understood the exaggeration. To the extent the Tribe's water quality standards affected the State facilities at all, they would take effect through conditions incorporated in permits drafted, issued and enforced by EPA not the Tribes. Yet, there was a kernel of truth to the State's fear of a tribal veto over its pollution discharges. While the permits' contents would be drafted in the exercise of a federal permit writer's best professional judgment, they could not be issued without the Tribes' approval.

Section 518 listed the Clean Water Act provisions Congress felt appropriate for tribal delegation. One of those provisions, section 401, was another reflection of the Act's cooperative federalism. In instances where a proposed pollution discharge would be permitted by a federal rather than state agency, the permit applicant was required to obtain from the state a certification that the discharge would conform to Clean Water Act requirements applicable to that location.[39] Among other things, section 401 offered the state an opportunity to confirm or correct the federal permit writer's interpretation of state standards more stringent than federal ones. The federal agency lacked discretion to reject any modified or new permit conditions the state determined were necessary to ensure compliance. And, if the state refused certification because it felt no additional condition could ensure compliance, the Act was very clear the federal permit could not issue.

Tribal treatment-as-a-state under section 401 offers tribes the same check on federal permit writers. Approval of tribal water quality standards triggers the Act's mandate that federal permits ensure compliance with the local government's water quality value judgments and tribal certification ensures the permit writer properly translates those judgments into specific conditions for particular facilities. If that cannot be accomplished in a manner protective of the tribe's water quality goals, then the permit may not be issued. Thus, as Montana had asserted, approval of tribal water quality standards in conjunction with treatment-as-a-state status under section 401 did create the potential for a tribal veto over proposed EPA-issued water pollution discharge permits on the Flathead reservation.

Outside Indian country, the impact of tribal water quality standards is less direct but still significant. Section 401's certification requirement applies only to the local government where the federally permitted discharge will occur. Downstream states and tribes potentially affected by discharges proposed upstream thus lack direct authority for imposing additional conditions on a permit or barring it altogether. However, they have valuable opportunities for influencing such upstream permits nonetheless.

Where a federal discharge permit is proposed, EPA must notify downstream states and tribes if the discharge may affect the quality of downstream waters. The downstream jurisdiction may object and request a hearing if it determines the discharge could violate its water quality standards. The permitting agency—EPA or another federal agency—has a mandatory duty to hold a public hearing upon receiving a timely request. If EPA is not the permitting agency, it evaluates the objection and recommends whether and under what conditions the permit should be issued. The permitting agency is not bound by EPA's recommendations, but the permit must meet all applicable water quality standards or may not be issued. EPA interprets the water quality standards of downstream jurisdictions as applicable Clean Water Act requirements.

The process is similar if the upstream permit is proposed by a state agency. The state must also give notice to downstream states and tribes, who may comment on the draft permit and request a hearing. The state must hold a hearing if requested. The state is not required to adopt recommendations submitted by downstream jurisdictions, but must explain to EPA's satisfaction why it did not. EPA may object if it determines the state's reasons are inadequate and the proposed permit will not ensure compliance with the water quality standards of a downstream jurisdiction. As it does for federal permits, EPA interprets the Clean Water Act as requiring such compliance.

EPA's interpretation was put to the test in a conflict between two states the year after EPA promulgated the tribal water quality standards rule. A newly constructed sewage treatment plant in the City of Fayetteville, Arkansas applied for a water pollution discharge permit from EPA because the State had not sought program delegation. The City proposed discharging some three million gallons of effluent per day into a small stream that flowed through a series of creeks for seventeen miles and then joined the Illinois River, which flowed twenty-two miles downstream to the Arkansas-Oklahoma border. EPA proposed a permit allowing the discharge, but conditioned it on ensuring the effluent would not violate Oklahoma's water quality standards for the Illinois River just downstream from the state border.

Both states challenged EPA's permit on various grounds, and the claims proceeded through a series of administrative adjudications and federal appellate courts before arriving at the Supreme Court's doorstep.[40] EPA argued the Clean Water Act required permit compliance with downstream water quality standards. A relevant portion of section 401 provided "[i]f the imposition of conditions cannot inure such compliance [with downstream standards] such agency shall not issue such license or permit." Since 1973, in the same water program rule where EPA took its first Indian program action, the Agency had consistently interpreted the Act as requiring discharge permits protect extra-jurisdictional downstream waters from harm.

While the Supreme Court said the statutory language "appears" to prohibit permits lacking adequate downstream conditions, it upheld the permit on a narrower ground. It specifically did not decide if the Act required that EPA veto a permit not complying with an affected state's standards, finding instead that the Act did not forbid EPA from imposing the downstream regulatory requirement. In other words, insisting on downstream water protection was within EPA's broad discretion even if the Act did not require it.

Extraterritorial environmental impacts between states were, after all, a primary stimulus for the rise of modern environmental law. Transboundary pollution migration implicated national interests. Cooperative federalism's reliance on minimum federal requirements implicitly addressed exported pollution at one level, but its respect for states' traditional prerogatives in environmental management also presented the opportunity for conflicts like those between Arkansas and Oklahoma. That dispute arose because the Clean Water Act allowed state water quality standards to be set anywhere over the minimum fishable and swimable goals of the Clean Water Act. The two states set different standards for adjacent reaches of the Illinois River. Fayetteville's proposed wastewater discharges complied with Arkansas' standards for the streams and Illinois River. It was only when the effluent arrived at an invisible line demarcating Oklahoma's territory some thirty-nine miles downstream that the question of its compliance with water quality standards arose. Had the evidence shown the discharge would cause a detectable violation of Oklahoma's water quality standards, EPA could have insisted Fayetteville conduct further treatment before discharging its effluent.

EPA exercised the same discretion the following year in drafting a permit for a wastewater treatment facility operated by the City of Albuquerque, New Mexico, sparking the first tribal-state conflict over the extraterritorial impacts of water quality standards. Albuquerque's facility was much larger than Fayetteville's, discharging fifty-five million gallons of wastewater each day into the Rio Grande just five miles upstream from the territory of the Pueblo of Isleta. The largest of the Rio Grande Pueblos, Isleta has inhabited the river valley since at least 900 A.D. In the hot arid country of central New Mexico, the river is the source of life and has always played a central role in tribal culture and spirituality. The Pueblo sought its protection by developing the nation's first tribal water quality standards, which EPA approved as consistent with the Clean Water Act just as Albuquerque's discharge permit came up for renewal.

Several Isleta standards were more stringent than those set by the State for the reach of the river just upstream, so conditioning the permit on compliance with New Mexico's standards would not ensure compliance with the Pueblo's value judgments. Consistent with the approach validated in the Arkansas case and with the Indian Policy, EPA prepared a draft permit incorporating several conditions directed at ensuring compliance with the Pueblo's standards, which the City complained would require over $300 million in capital improvements to the treatment facility. EPA was not dissuaded in part because the projected costs were largely due to the requirements of complying with New Mexico's water quality standards with only a fraction necessary for meeting the Pueblo's more stringent standards. At any rate compliance costs are not a legal excuse for ignoring federally enforceable water quality standards.

The Supreme Court's Arkansas decision confirmed the Agency's authority for imposing downstream compliance conditions, so a direct challenge to them would likely fail. The City chose a preemptory attack instead: it challenged EPA's approval of the Pueblo's standards that were more stringent than the minimum federal criteria. If the tribal standards were vacated wholly or at least to the extent they went beyond federal minima, there would be no need for additional conditions in the permit. But the Tenth Circuit rejected the City's multiple procedural and substantive claims and upheld the tribal standards in *City of Albuquerque v. Browner*.[41]

The court's decision was a paradigmatic example of judicial deference to administrative agencies in complex legal and technical matters. The City challenged EPA's interpretation of the Clean Water Act as allowing tribal water quality standards more stringent than the minimum federal criteria. In support of its approval of the Isleta standards, EPA cited section 510 that acknowledges states' inherent power to do so. But section 518's list of provisions appropriate for tribal treatment-as-a-state did not include section 510. The negative implication was clear to the City: Congress had not extended the authority states inherently possessed for establishing more stringent standards to tribes.

EPA was not troubled by the apparent inconsistency. The list in section 518 focused on the regulatory programs and grant opportunities Congress made available to tribes treated as states, not every provision somehow implicated by tribal governmental roles. Section 510 was not a program; it was essentially a savings clause that preserved pre-existing state powers to make value judgments beyond federal goals. Federal Indian law and the Agency's Indian Policy recognized tribes possessed similar sovereign powers. And the legislative history of section 518 revealed Congress intended the treatment-as-a-state terminology as more than a catch-phrase:

> The intent of the conferees as to assure that Indian tribes would be able to exercise the same regulatory jurisdiction over water quality matters with regard to waters within Indian jurisdiction that States have over their water. The conferees believe that tribes should have the primary authority to set water quality standards to assure fishable and swimmable water and to satisfy all beneficial uses. The Act also provides a mechanism for resolving any conflict between tribal standards and upstream uses or activities.[42]

Limiting tribal standards to the minimum federal criteria would frustrate Congress' goals. Tribes would not exercise the same regulatory authority states possessed over their waters, nor could they protect any beneficial uses beyond the minimum. EPA's judgments for protecting the minimum uses would become primary, largely making the tribes' values irrelevant.

Confronted with at least two plausible interpretations of the Act, the court concluded congressional intent was ambiguous, so judicial deference was in order for EPA's reasonable interpretations. Section 518, however, could not reasonably be read as implicitly including section 510 when it clearly did not and thus EPA's reliance on section 510 for approving Isleta's more stringent standards was misplaced. But the Agency's view of section 510 as a state savings clause accorded with the Supreme Court's observation in the Arkansas decision that section 510 was concerned only with preserving state authority and not constraining federal authority. It did not then affect inherent tribal sovereignty recognized by federal Indian law and policy, which EPA reasonably relied on in respecting tribes' independent value judgments on water quality, just as it respected state decisions.

In the trial court, the City had fallen back on a claim opponents of tribal sovereignty often urge as an alternative basis for limiting the impact of more stringent tribal standards. Congress specifically directed EPA develop a process for resolving "unreasonable consequences" arising from different standards set by a tribe and a state for common water bodies. On its face, the directive contemplated a neutral process for working out differences stemming from the independent judgments of two neighboring sovereigns. The City read the provision instead as a one-sided preemption mechanism barring approval of tribal standards and their application to upstream sources where unreasonable extraterritorial consequences would result. The district court did not dignify the argument by even mentioning it, and the City did not try again before the Tenth Circuit.

The City did attack the exclusivity of the dispute resolution process. Under the regulations, only a state or a tribe could initiate the process. The City could not request proceedings. Nor could EPA unilaterally begin them in response to the City's concerns. The State of New Mexico could have objected on the City's behalf, but it did not. In fact, the State submitted an amicus brief opposing the City's demand for a separate EPA-sponsored public comment period. The State argued it would be duplicative of the preceding tribal process and convert EPA's role from federal compliance assurance to substantive decision-making. That argument, like EPA's decision extending to tribes the same protection states enjoyed from dispute resolution processes initiated by regulated facilities, reflected substantive respect for the Pueblo's state-like status. The Tenth Circuit found EPA's interpretation reasonable.

Albuquerque was no more successful directly attacking the Pueblo's water quality standards themselves. The City was unhappy with many of the Pueblo's standards, but it was particularly incensed by the ammonia and arsenic standards, which were the primary bases for the expensive capital improvements EPA was demanding. In higher concentrations ammonia is toxic and arsenic is carcinogenic, and both are capable of causing a host of other serious adverse effects in living organisms. The Pueblo's value judgments on the acceptable levels of these pollutants in the Rio Grande were striking. The arsenic limit was some three orders of magnitude more restrictive than the federal Safe Drinking Water standard although the Pueblo did not use the Rio Grande as a source of drinking water. Isleta set a single absolute concentration for ammonia despite EPA's strong recommendation for a sliding calculation of legal levels depending on varying water temperature and pH. Neither standard contemplated variances during low water flows where concentrations would naturally increase.

Albuquerque considered the Pueblo's dramatic choices indefensible, and EPA's insistence on compliance irrational and futile. Without the sliding scale for ammonia, and especially during low flows, EPA had commented to the Pueblo its standard could be either overly stringent or not stringent enough. The arsenic standard seemed almost preposterous; current laboratory technology could not detect arsenic levels that low. The background concentration of arsenic naturally occurring in groundwater beneath Albuquerque was higher than the Pueblo's standard. Local agricultural activities not regulated by the Clean Water Act caused additional arsenic loading, suggesting the Pueblo might see no measurable water quality improvement even if the City's treatment facility installed the expensive pollution control technology EPA required.

As any lay observer would, the New Mexico federal district court found these issues "very troubling":

> The City cites technical information outside the administrative record to support its argument that the Pueblo standards are unattainable.... It is clear that the City raises realistic technical concerns.... Although under the standard of review ... I must uphold the agency decision in this case, I note that the City raises some very troubling issues here.... In this case, EPA is prepared to include limits in the City's [water pollution discharge] permit to ensure that discharged water at the facility outfall meets the water quality standards of the downstream state without first concluding that the quality of the river water five miles further downstream will be measurably improved. For example, the Pueblo's arsenic standard for the Rio Grande is three orders of magnitude (1000 times) more stringent than the federal Safe Drinking Water Standard, and is below the concentration that can be accurately measured by current laboratory equipment. EPA will impose this stringent limit on the City despite the fact that arsenic occurs naturally in Albuquerque's ground water at relatively high levels and is not discharged to the water by industrial polluters. If pure water is discharged at the City' outfall, it is possible that the arsenic levels in water flowing through the Pueblo will remain relatively high. I raise this issue of the agency's apparent inconsistency because it is one I find troubling.[43]

The court nonetheless deferred to the Agency, as did the Tenth Circuit. The City had not challenged EPA's proposed permit conditions. The question was

EPA's approval of the Isleta standards, which turned on the respective local and federal roles created by the Act's cooperative federalism. Congress clearly placed primary responsibility for determining desired uses of water and the criteria necessary for their protection on states, and once section 518 was added, on tribes. The Act specifically preserved states' authority to impose standards more stringent than the minimum federal requirements, and *Montana v. EPA* held that tribes also retained their similar inherent powers.

That Congress had envisioned their judgments on desired water quality might very well force technological advances through the adoption of more stringent standards was evidenced by EPA's circumscribed approval role simply to determine whether the proposed water quality standards satisfied the federal requirements. The Agency was not required to assess the attainability or scientific basis of standards that went beyond the regulatory floor and courts had repeatedly rejected claims that EPA should disapprove state water quality standards that were unattainable or caused significant economic impact. In other words, facilities that were unsuccessful in convincing local governments to adopt less stringent standards could not use EPA's approval process as a means for collateral attack by urging a federal reweighing of the local economic and social interests at stake.

The administrative record showed EPA had discharged its duty for ensuring the Pueblo's standards met the federal criteria and were sufficiently rational. While the Agency was not required to address the City's complaints about the costs of compliance, the record reflected extensive consultation over several concerns related to the stringency of the standards, leaving EPA satisfied the Pueblo's ultimate conclusions were the product of deliberative analysis. The Pueblo was particularly concerned about recent drought cycles and protecting its sensitive populations like elders and children. Lower river flows translated into higher pollution concentrations, and tribal members used the river more intensively during low flow seasons, especially for ceremonial purposes that were specifically designated uses.

The Pueblo would not detail the ceremonial uses its standards endeavored to protect, but did define them as religious and traditional uses involving immersion and intentional or incidental ingestion of water. The City seized on the standards' explicitly religious goals, arguing EPA's approval violated the federal constitutional prohibition on excessive entanglement of government with religion. Neither the district court nor the Tenth Circuit had any trouble with the Pueblo's sectarian purpose because EPA's approval served a clear secular goal: protection of human health from exposure to water pollutants. Federal First Amendment cases barred the government from advancing or promoting one religion over another but did not mandate insensitivity to religious groups and EPA's approval seemed consistent with federal policy for preserving American Indian religious exercises.[44]

CHAPTER 5

WINDS OF CHANGE: HONORING TRIBAL AIR QUALITY VALUES

Practically speaking, human health and welfare depend more acutely on uncontaminated air than other environmental media. Unlike contaminated soils or rivers or groundwater, we are all constantly exposed to the air. Geologic features do not contain air currents in the same manner as other media, and many air pollutants are widely dispersed and persist for hundreds or thousands of miles. Sulfur dioxide emissions from power plants in the Midwest have caused acid rain impacts as far away as Maine and Québec.

Scientific data on the health and environmental effects of particular air pollutants lag dramatically behind industry's tremendous capacity for generating an ever-expanding universe of conventional and hazardous air pollutants. Significant information does exist on the six ubiquitous pollutants that have garnered the most federal attention since the beginning of the modern environmental era. Sulfur dioxide, nitrogen oxides, ground level ozone and particulate matter are known to cause minor and severe respiratory problems in humans, damage vegetation, and impair water quality and visibility. Carbon monoxide damages cardiovascular and nervous systems, and airborne lead harms numerous internal organs and the brain. A host of more recently studied hazardous air pollutants have been linked to carcinogenic, mutagenic and toxic effects on humans and other biological organisms.

Human health concerns and the obvious transboundary nature of air pollution helped stimulate Congress' modern version of cooperative federalism that took form in the Clean Air Act of 1970, passed in the same month Nixon created EPA and in the first year of the period known as the environmental decade for its proliferation of major federal environmental enactments. Congress has substantially amended the Act several times since then, but protecting the public health and welfare by regulating mobile and stationary sources of air pollution through federal-state partnerships remains its primary goal.

EPA has two fundamental roles. One is setting uniform technology-based standards for sources of air pollution that are new or modified, or emit hazardous air pollutants. The other role is establishing maximum concentrations in the ambient air of pollutants emitted from numerous or diverse sources that can reasonably be anticipated to endanger public health or welfare. Somewhat like water quality standards, these national ambient air quality standards are value judgments representing a desired level of air quality that must be translated into legally enforceable emission limits applicable to individual pollution sources. Congress delegated that task to states.

Each state's primary role is controlling emissions from individual sources so they collectively do not cause air quality in various regions of the state to exceed the national standards. A state implementation plan sets out the mix of control strategies for all stationary sources, including emission limitations, timetables for compliance, permit programs, and requirements for sources to monitor and analyze their air emissions. Permits issued to individual facilities, usually by states or by EPA in lieu of approved state programs, contain the specific requirements from multiple air programs applicable to their construction and operation.

The Nation's First Air Quality Redesignation

The early federal air program was the genesis of the tribal treatment-as-a-state approach, but it occurred quite by happenstance. Congress unwittingly set the stage when it created the modern cooperative federalism model in the 1970 Clean Air Act targeting the country's worst air quality problems.

The Act's central state-federal partnership envisioned state control of individual air pollution sources so their collective emissions would not exceed levels of ambient air quality prescribed by national standards issued by EPA. Detailed provisions specified the consequences for areas within states that did not attain the national standards, but not clear was whether any particular restrictions applied to areas with good air quality in no immediate danger of exceeding the national limits. The Sierra Club feared industry would locate in these cleaner regions to avoid the costly emission control requirements applicable to nonattainment areas, and in 1972, convinced a federal court the Act implicitly required EPA prevent excessive degradation of existing air quality in such areas.[1]

EPA responded to the court's order by seeking public comment on four alternative approaches for implementing a "prevention of significant air quality deterioration" program.[2] The proposal did not address Indian country or Indian facilities even though it came just two months after EPA took its first Indian program step in the 1973 water pollution context. EPA went beyond its usual public comment processes and engaged state and local governments in separate consultations on their respective governmental roles to generate a more focused proposal. No comments were made on Indian country, and the Agency did not invite or seek the views of tribes or tribal organizations. Yet, an unprecedented state-like program role for tribes appeared in the second proposal.[3]

As the name implied, the overall program did not bar new pollution in clean areas; its goal was to prevent "significant" deterioration of existing air quality. Significance would be determined on an incremental scale calculated from baseline conditions associated with the classification of the airsheds affected by the emissions. In the relatively pristine air of Class I areas, nearly any negative change in air quality would be considered significant. Deterioration accompanying moderate well-controlled growth would be considered insignificant in Class II areas. And in Class III areas, deterioration right up to the national standard would be allowed. A preconstruction review and permit process would determine the conditions necessary for new and modified major sources to comply with the applicable deterioration increment.

Nearly the entire country was initially designated as Class II, but specific areas could be "redesignated" as Class I or Class III. Redesignation factors included anticipated and desired area growth, and the social, environmental and economic effects of redesignation on the area, the region and the nation. The primarily local (and highly political) nature of those considerations counseled against EPA redesignations, so the program put decision-making authority in the hands of states and federal land managers. EPA again assumed that states lacked authority for Indian reservations, but unlike the water program approach it did not posit direct federal implementation. Instead, it identified "Indian Governing Bodies" as the point of initiation for the redesignation.

The genesis of that innovative idea is unclear. States' lack of authority was its predicate and the only explanation offered. No tribe or tribal organization had publicly declared interest in such a role. EPA's initial consultations with states and local governments had not included tribes and the Agency's Indian program principle of direct outreach to tribal governments would not be formed for some years.

There was contemporary evidence of some tribes' concern over degradation of tribal air resources. The Jicarilla Apache Tribe and a chapter of the

Navajo Nation, along with a tribal environmental organization and several individual tribal members, filed an amicus curiae brief in the Supreme Court when EPA appealed the Sierra Club's win in 1972. They expressed concern their rights in air and water would be damaged by proposed coal-fired power plants in the Four Corners region that, without additional controls, would emit pollutants at levels far beyond those generated in Los Angeles, California, the nation's worst air pollution problem.

> While increases in air pollution of this magnitude would be cause for alarm anywhere in the United States, they are particularly tragic in the Four Corners region, an area of virtually unlimited visibility, unparalleled scenic splendor, and the most widespread Native American culture left in America. That culture and religion emphasizes the need for man to live in harmony with the beauty and order of nature. These amici believe that to allow their homeland to be engulfed by millions of tons of dangerous pollutants, at levels hovering just below those at which their soil, water, vegetation, wildlife, visibility and even their climate would be affected, would be a devastating blunder. They also assert that EPA, acting for the United States, has a "most exacting fiduciary duty" to preserve their environment. They believe that Congress, by means of the Clean Air Act Amendments of 1970, acted to make sure that this fiduciary duty would be carried out and that areas such as the Southwest would be preserved. The amici cannot conceive that Congress intended the Clean Air Act Amendments to serve as the vehicle for the transformation of their homeland into a dumping ground for the dirty industries whose pollution cities will no longer tolerate, but whose products they claim to need desperately.[4]

EPA's tribal treatment-as-a-state approach spoke to these issues at several levels, but Congress had not expressly authorized the prevention of significant deterioration program so it surely had not authorized tribal implementation of it. National Indian policy was swinging toward self-determination at this time, but its subjects were limited to education and human services programs carrying no real capacity to affect non-Indians. Similarly, the Supreme Court's contemporary statements of territorial tribal sovereignty appeared in cases not involving tribal control of non-Indians.

Legal battles over tribal environmental regulation of non-Indians would become a defining aspect of EPA's Indian program in the 1980s and 1990s. But even in 1974, as EPA contemplated the tribal air role, "the exercise of tribal jurisdiction over non-Indians [was] ... one of the most important issues in

Indian law."[5] A specially commissioned series of federal reports on Indian policy noted two years later that "no other issue in Indian law raises the emotional response from the non-Indian community as does the actuality of or the prospect of Indian tribes exercising jurisdiction over non-Indians," which "has generated much hostility and emotionalism in both the non-Indian community and Indian communities."[6]

EPA's proposal drew no hostility or emotionalism. In fact, EPA's dramatic new approach generated almost no reaction whatsoever. No individuals or businesses objected to the possibility their actions would be constrained by tribal redesignations. No state directly attacked EPA's unsupported assumption of tribal authority over reservation environments. The sole comment on the tribal role came from the State of New Mexico, which claimed EPA's decision "appeared" to take away states' alleged regulatory authority over air pollution on Indian lands. EPA's response was political and practical: it had no intent (or power) to alter existing legal relationships, so states remained free to regulate all areas for which they could show independent authority. EPA finalized the program with the tribal redesignation role as proposed.[7]

The final rule provoked the common American response: lawsuits. The Sierra Club felt the entire program was too lax; an assemblage of utility and energy companies saw it as too stringent. New Mexico's lone defense of state sovereignty in the rulemaking caught the attention of nine other states with Indian country, who joined New Mexico in arguing the tribal and federal land manager roles improperly trenched on states' primary responsibilities for environmental protection. They also correctly perceived the very real possibility their economic development plans might be hindered by tribal and federal redesignations. The court upheld the overall program but declined to rule on the states' sovereignty arguments.[8] The issues lacked the clarity of context because no federal land or Indian reservation had yet been proposed for redesignation.

A lawsuit joined by ten states made more sense than the near absolute lack of state comments on the original proposal. But if the states' lack of response was surprising, tribes' reactions were startling. Not one tribe or tribal organization commented on that groundbreaking first opportunity for wielding federally enforceable influence over impacts to the Indian country environment. Like the origin of the tribal air role itself, the reason for tribes' silence is unclear. Perhaps the most likely explanation was that because of the lack of EPA outreach for this brand new program tribes were simply unaware of the opportunity presented; ten years later only eight of seventy-four tribes surveyed reported familiarity with air quality classifications and their effects.[9]

The Northern Cheyenne Tribe, which resides on its reservation in south-central Montana learned of its redesignation authority in 1976.[10] That was about the time the mining industry focused its attention on Indian coal. The Clean Air Act's emission limitations on sulfur dioxide and new strip mining technologies had increased the economic attractiveness of generating electricity by burning western low sulfur coal. Northern Cheyenne owned substantial coal resources the government helped develop through leases with non-Indian companies. When the Tribe realized its federal trustee was selling its coal for less than the price of gravel, the Tribe successfully demanded a moratorium on further mining.

Outside the Tribe's reservation, however, the coal frenzy was in full swing. Strip mining on the adjacent Crow Indian Reservation unleashed huge quantities of "fugitive" particulate air emissions. The Montana Power Company and four northwestern utilities had proposed two 760-megawatt, coal-fired power plants in Colstrip, Montana, thirteen miles north of the Northern Cheyenne Reservation. Montana's Class II air status required only minimal emission controls, translating into hundreds of tons of hazardous emissions annually. Tribal citizens already suffered an unusually high rate of respiratory disease, and cultural and economic uses of vegetation, particularly Ponderosa pine forests, were perceived at risk.

The Tribe began the process of redesignating the reservation to Class I in 1976. It notified EPA of its intention, and then state and local governments and citizen groups. As required by EPA's regulations, it prepared a 200-page analysis of possible social, environmental and economic effects, and distributed it in advance of a public meeting at Tribal headquarters in Lame Deer, Montana in early January 1977. Testimony at the hearing and written comments submitted afterward—both supporting and opposing the proposal—were received from tribal citizens, non-Indian residents of the reservation, and others from the surrounding area. The Tribe analyzed the comments along with other required factors, and applied for EPA's approval. EPA then held its own extended public comment period, receiving sixty-two written comments. Some commenters asked for additional process, and others expressed fears the redesignation would adversely affect farming, coal mining and energy development. The Montana Power Company was particularly concerned; its Colstrip plant, as designed, lacked controls for sulfur dioxide emissions adequate to comply with the Tribe's Class I designation.

That same spring Congress was considering significant amendments to the Clean Air Act. Among the many issues on the table was the significant deterioration program EPA created under court order. No direct attention was focused on EPA's decision according tribes state-like roles, but the Northern Cheyenne Tribe urged Congress to preserve tribes' "traditional control" over reservation air quality and prevent states from redesignating reservations against tribal will.[11] The Tribe also sought to grandfather its pending redesignation.

Congress adopted the Tribe's proposed tribal role nearly verbatim: "lands within the exterior boundaries of reservations of federally recognized Indian tribes may be redesignated *only* by the appropriate Indian governing body."[12] The "treatment-as-a-state" phrase would not be coined for several more years, but the Senate Committee on Environment and Public Works noted under the provision "Indian tribes are given the same powers as States."[13] The Senate Committee also acknowledged the pending Northern Cheyenne redesignation in describing a provision preserving any redesignation approved before the amendments took effect. EPA approved the Tribe's redesignation just four days before President Jimmy Carter signed the 1977 amendments into law.

Once legally effective, the Northern Cheyenne redesignation triggered the Clean Air Act's transboundary pollution provisions. Those provisions were originally adopted to prevent upwind states from "exporting" their air pollution to downwind states. They contemplated permit conditions requiring sources comply with downwind jurisdictions' more stringent standards. Before the Montana Power Company applied for a permit and thus faced the risk of those more expensive permit conditions it and several other energy and coal concerns challenged EPA's approval of the Tribe's redesignation in court.

The 1981 decision in *Nance v. Environmental Protection Agency*[14] was notable for a number of firsts. It was occasioned by the nation's first redesignation, the only one done under the pre-1977 Act. It involved the first tribal exercise of a state-like role in federal program implementation, which presented for the first time the extraterritorial consequences of tribal roles in a federalist environmental management system. *Nance* was the first reported Indian country environmental law case addressing a tribal implementation role, and the first sanctioning EPA's policy of treating tribes like states.

The court gave "great weight" to EPA's interpretation that the silence in the pre-1977 Act did not subordinate tribes to state decision-making. The position was consistent with inherent tribal sovereignty, and its reasonableness was validated by Congress' 1977 codification of the tribal role. Noting neither the States of Montana nor Wyoming challenged EPA's approval, the court dismissed the companies' assertion that EPA's decision infringed state sovereignty, effectively placing tribal-state cross-boundary issues squarely within the realm of state compromises intrinsic to a federalist system. The extraterritorial impacts of concern to the court were not the alleged property rights of state residents, but rather the "dumping" of pollutants on the reservation from off-reservation lands. Non-Indian interests were protected from arbitrary tribal action by the checks contained in statutory and administrative standards and procedures for redesignations.

Nance was also the first case where an Indian tribe challenged another tribe's governmental decision to protect human health and environmental quality through federal program implementation. The Crow Tribe's economic interests in coal extraction aligned it more with the industry challengers than its Northern Cheyenne neighbors. The development of Crow mineral resources was clearly subject to the federal trust responsibility, which the Tribe said EPA ignored in approving the Northern Cheyenne redesignation. The court agreed that EPA's trust responsibilities extended to the Crow Tribe, but said they also ran to the Northern Cheyenne Tribe, thus confirming a key premise of the 1980 Indian Policy. But the court found those obligations satisfied by the program's requirements for public participation and tribal analysis articulated though a federally prescribed and supervised process. The Crow Tribe's economic interests could not automatically trump the Northern Cheyenne Tribe's public health and welfare interests.

The trust argument was also unavailing because the Crow Tribe did not officially object to the Northern Cheyenne redesignation. EPA's 1974 significant deterioration rule anticipated transboundary conflicts like those at Northern Cheyenne. Differing air quality classifications for immediately adjacent areas necessarily carried the potential for negative extraterritorial impacts, and thus, intergovernmental disputes. The rule required states and tribes proposing redesignation to account for the effect on neighboring jurisdictions, which EPA would accept unless the analysis was arbitrary or capricious. If an affected state or tribe lodged a formal objection, however, EPA said its review would expand and balance the competing interests in making a final decision.

The 1977 Clean Air Act amendments incorporated the idea of an express intergovernmental dispute resolution mechanism. An affected state or tribe could request EPA-initiated negotiations for resolving disputes over a proposed redesignation, or over a proposed permit for a major facility that could cause or contribute to violations of deterioration increments. EPA would make recommendations at the parties' request or resolve the dispute if they could not agree. In resolving disputes, the Administrator was to consider whether the lands to be redesignated "are of sufficient size to allow effective air quality management or have air quality related values of such an area."[15]

That provision, like the one Congress would later add to the Clean Water Act for resolving "unreasonable consequences" arising from differing state and tribal water quality standards, was neutral. Either a tribe or a state could invoke it in response to the other's action. It attempted to balance the authority of one jurisdiction to make value judgments on environmental quality in its territory with the legitimate interests of an adjacent government. Nothing expressly favored one government's interests over the other.

Opponents of tribal sovereignty sometimes read in exactly the opposite intention. They perceive the only appropriate resolution of state objections is forcing differing tribal values to yield. The air provision lent some credence to that view in that its redesignation objection process was specific to state-tribe conflicts whereas EPA's rule had applied the same process to disputes between two states. Congress' substantive standard of adequate land size and air quality values also implied doubt that all tribal lands would be appropriate for redesignation.

The Senate Committee, however, explicitly characterized the tribe-state dispute resolution process as replicating "the same authority that exists for resolving any classification dispute among States."[16] The legislative history also countered the implication of the land size provision:

> The conference bill provides that both States and Indian tribes will continue to have the power they now have to redesignate their lands to a new air quality classification.... But it is intended that the Administrator's review of [state objections to redesignations] by tribal governments be exercised with utmost caution to avoid unnecessarily substituting his judgment for that of the tribe. The concept of Indian sovereignty over reservations is a critical one, not only to native Americans, but to the Government of the United States. A fundamental incident of that sovereignty is control over the use of their air resources. Some statutes ... have encroached upon Indian sovereignty, eroding treaty rights negotiated at an earlier time. This is not such a bill....[17]

The dispute over the Northern Cheyenne redesignation did not go through administrative resolution processes. The Act's mechanism did not apply because the amendments took effect after the redesignation was approved. The process existing under EPA's prior rule was applicable, but neither Montana nor the Crow Tribe invoked it. It would be nearly twenty years before a tribal redesignation would go through the dispute resolution process and put Congress' intentions and tribal self-determination to the test.

The Act's provision for challenges to permits was invoked much earlier. The Montana Power Company sought federal permission for the Colstrip facility's expansion in 1979, and EPA announced its intention to issue a permit. The

Northern Cheyenne Tribe requested EPA initiate negotiations, which EPA did after the Tribe met its demand for a threshold showing of air quality impacts.

The parties met at EPA's regional offices in Denver, Colorado rather than in Colstrip or Lame Deer. The Agency conducted the "negotiations" more like a formal hearing, reflecting perhaps a view of the process as a procedural step toward permit issuance, rather than as assisting the parties in working toward a mutually agreeable solution. There was no opportunity for the parties to explain and discuss their respective interests except by means of formal opening statements, which were presented by the parties' lawyers, who dominated the legalistic de facto permit hearing. "Although the EPA managed the negotiations and fulfilled its statutory responsibilities, the rigidity of the format and the narrowness of the agenda prevented the parties from reaching a settlement."[18]

Although the Tribe has hoped its Class I status would prevent the plant expansion altogether, EPA issued the permit almost immediately after the meeting. It did impose conditions designed to protect the Tribe's air from significant deterioration, including requiring installation of expensive pollution control technologies resulting in tremendous reductions of annual emissions of sulfur dioxide and nitrogen oxides. In addition, the Tribe used a state legal process for siting new facilities to engage the Company in further negotiations leading to other concessions for assisting the Tribe in developing a state-of-the-art emissions monitoring system for reservation air quality.

Respecting Tribal Value Judgments

A thousand miles south of the windy plateaus of the Northern Cheyenne Reservation lay the arid desert lands of the Yavapai-Apache Indian Tribe, a federally mandated confederation of two distinct indigenous communities. Yavapai and Apache ancestors traveled relatively undisturbed over 2,000 square miles in the southwestern portion of the continent for a thousand years until that fateful day of discovery in 1863. This time it was yellow gold, and illegal immigrants flooded in seeking fortune and fame. Inevitable land conflicts led to U.S. military occupation of the area, but not to protect the original inhabitants or their lands.

President Ulysses S. Grant separated the rival factions by an 1871 executive order creating the Rio Verde Indian Reserve, reducing the Tribe's lands to about 800 square miles. That satiated non-Indian land hunger for almost four years. Then, in February 1875, the U.S. military forced the entire Tribe to leave its ancestral homeland and walk over 200 miles through mountain passes to the San Carlos Indian Agency in southern Arizona. About 150 of the 1,500 tribal citizens died on that forced winter march.

After twenty-five years of internment at San Carlos, about 200 Yavapai and Apache were released and made it back to the Verde Valley. They found the reserve gone and their lands occupied by white settlers. In 1909, the federal government purchased a fifty-five acre tract to replace the stolen 800 square mile reserve. The government subsequently purchased four other non-contiguous parcels and now holds the five tracts ranging in size from four to 458 acres in trust for the Tribe. The combined total of the Tribe's lands, which are not officially designated as a reservation, is about 635 acres.

The lands lie between the sprawling metropolis of Phoenix and the "red rock" country of Sedona and Oak Creek Canyon. Three National Forests— Coconino, Kaibab and Prescott—are nearby. The Sycamore Canyon Wilderness Area, a designated Federal Class I area, and three National Monuments— Castle, Montezuma Well and Tuzigoot—also lie within the Valley.

One of the Tribe's parcels is located near Clarksdale, Arizona. In the early 1990s, the Phoenix Cement Plant in Clarksdale, which coincidentally is owned by the Salt River Pima-Maricopa Indian Community, announced plans to burn used rubber tires as a supplemental source of the plant's energy needs. Sometime thereafter, the Tribe began analyzing the option of redesignating its lands to Class I. In September 1993, the Tribe completed an Air Quality Redesignation Plan, which the Yavapai-Apache Tribal Council unanimously approved. In October, the Tribe held a public hearing where forty-three people spoke in favor of the proposal, including thirty-seven non-Indians. No one opposed the redesignation. The Tribe submitted its final request to EPA in December.

EPA's regulations implementing the 1977 amendments required it offer a separate opportunity for public participation on redesignation applications. A one-month public comment period held in April 1994 satisfied the minimum requirement, but at the City of Clarksdale's request, EPA exercised its discretion to host a public hearing in the area. This time a few opponents appeared. Five commenters urged disapproval of the redesignation. Forty others, including twenty non-Indians, supported approval. EPA extended the time for additional written comments again at Clarksdale's request. Arizona's Governor Fife Syminton officially invoked the dispute resolution provision on the last day of the final extension.

The Governor's letter was illustrative of the misapprehension harbored and reflexive objections made by states and non-Indians faced with assertions of tribal sovereignty. The State offered no legal or technical dispute for resolution. Instead, having waited until the last moment of an eight-month process, the State sought further delays because it said stakeholders did not fully understand the effects of the redesignation. The prejudicial machine of coffee shop conversations and talk radio diatribes had begun. At Northern Cheyenne, farmers had feared restrictions on their agricultural operations. In Albuquerque, water users believed their monthly bills would skyrocket. Irrigators at Flathead were sure tribal water quality standards would destroy their livelihoods. And, in Clarksdale, non-Indians thought the Tribe's redesignation meant their woodstoves would be shut down and their cars "smog-checked."

EPA had explained in its public hearing that the program applied only to industrial stationary sources emitting huge amounts of a few specified pollutants; neither cars as mobile sources, nor woodstoves as minor sources, would be affected. To be fair, local residents could be excused for misunderstanding the complexities of federal environmental programs, especially since most of those complaining hadn't bothered to attend the hearing anyway. But too often objections made in these situations seem to have an air of self-righteous incredulity not seen in complaints about other governments' mandates. One commenter, for example, said it was "both unnecessary and possibly immoral" to allow "an extremely small minority of the population to impose [on regulated entities] a significantly higher level of bureaucratic regulation."

That the State's concern for improved public understanding was pretextual was made clear when it rebuffed EPA's offer to discuss additional public outreach. The real goal, of course, was to stop the redesignation and with it any possibility the Tribe's value judgment might affect economic development in the area. Clarksdale's cement plant was not really the motivating factor, however. A later letter from the Governor to EPA Administrator Carol Browner made plain the precedential effect of this redesignation was more troubling:

> [A]pproval of this redesignation may have effects far beyond the Verde Valley area. Twenty-one reservations are located, in whole or in part, in Arizona. A proliferation of redesignation requests and approvals for other reservations could have far-reaching consequences for the future of the State and its economic well-being.[19]

Two months after EPA pointed out that public confusion was not a basis for conducting a dispute resolution process, the State offered a new reason for initiation: to determine if the Tribe's lands were of sufficient size to allow effective air quality management or have air quality related values. The State having finally discovered the Act's triggering phrases, EPA had no choice but to begin the dispute resolution process. This time, unlike at Northern

Cheyenne, EPA played more of a mediator's role. The meeting was set near Phoenix rather than at EPA's regional office in San Francisco. State and Tribal representatives first met with the Agency separately, then together without EPA, and finally all three parties met.

The State's primary focus was on the size and nature of the Tribe's lands. The State asserted their relatively small size offered no important air quality related values. Their non-contiguous nature, spread over thirty miles, indicated to the Director of the Arizona Department of Environmental Quality that air quality management would not be effective. The resulting checkerboard relationship of Class I and II lands, the State asserted, portended difficulties in separating out the different air quality limitations in the context of permit proceedings. It also increased the chances of one jurisdiction "dictating" its health and welfare standards in a manner hindering growth in a neighboring jurisdiction.

The Tribe relied on a straightforward reading of the significant deterioration program. Congress directed review of an area's size and air quality values but did not impose an absolute limit on lands eligible for redesignation. Congress could not have meant to leave small states like Rhode Island and Delaware less protected than larger states. It was surely aware in authorizing tribal redesignations that Indian reservations varied greatly in size.

Not surprisingly, the parties did not come to agreement. EPA resolved the dispute by approving the Tribe's request. To do otherwise, the Agency said, would deprive the Tribe of its congressionally authorized power to make value judgments for reservation air quality. The report of the House Committee on Interstate and Foreign Commerce showed a state or tribe had broad discretion "to designate some parts class I and retain some class II areas, it may draw classification boundaries in any way it chooses—by entire air quality control regions, along county lines, or even along smaller subcounty lines."[20] EPA declined to do what Congress had not: adopt an arbitrary minimum size for local determinations. Similarly, EPA did not believe Congress envisioned redesignation only for areas with exceptional air quality related values; it was enough that the local manager felt existing air quality was important to preserve.

The State's position also rested on an unsupported assertion that the Tribe's small land base would result in an "untenable and unworkable" permit system because of the difficulties in distinguishing between Class I and II lands. EPA feigned confusion. Modeling and other management tools had grown quite sophisticated in recent years. Nonattainment areas as small as a few square kilometers or as large as the eastern seaboard had proven workable. In Arizona, overlapping attainment and nonattainment areas for individual pollutants made permitting challenging but not impossible. EPA's technical staff concluded existing modeling tools would make the job at Yavapai-Apache "relatively simple and practical." And at any rate, the proximity of the Sycamore Canyon Wilderness Area would likely require a Class I analysis for new permits regardless of the Tribe's land status.

Substantively, the Agency did not expect the redesignation would cause major impacts outside the reservation. If a conflict associated with a particular permit application arose, the dispute resolution process was available and would benefit from that more concrete context.

Predictably, Arizona did not wait for a permit application. It filed *Arizona v. United States Environmental Protection Agency*[21] in the Ninth Circuit to review both EPA's approval of the Tribe's redesignation and its ruling resolving the dispute in favor of the Tribe. The states of Wisconsin, California, Michigan, Montana, South Dakota and Utah filed an amicus curiae brief opposing EPA. Leaving the finer legal points to Arizona, their brief bluntly expressed a common non-Indian view of tribal self-determination in a federalist environmental system: EPA's decisions treating tribes as states "unlawfully impair[s] states' sovereignty over their air resources by transferring regulatory power from states to tribes." That position was political not legal, and unfortunately for the states, essentially moot. Congress had directly rejected it in providing explicit tribal program roles in the air, water and drinking water contexts.

But Arizona had by now done a bit more homework and made several pertinent legal arguments. Somehow it avoided losing on the general administrative law principle that reviewing courts generally will not consider arguments not first presented to the agency during the administrative process. Instead, Arizona lost all of its challenges on the merits.

During the Tribe's public comment process, the State's Department of Environmental Quality referred to the Tribe's lands as a reservation in arguing it was too small to be effectively managed. The State reversed its position in briefs to the court, arguing EPA erred in treating the separate parcels as a reservation as Congress used the term in the significant deterioration program. At oral argument on the case, the State flipped again, conceding that the Tribe's largest parcel, the 458-acre Middle Verde property, qualified as a reservation. The court accepted the State's concession and though the record was unclear on the status of the other parcels, said two were effectively protected by the Middle Verde parcel's status as Class I.

The State also challenged for the first time the Tribe's analysis of the environmental, social, health and energy effects anticipated from the redesignation proposal. The six-state amicus brief described the analysis as consisting of "general, unhelpful (and unsubstantiated) statements." Arizona demanded an explicit balancing of the different effects, and specific analysis on the extent to which redesignation might discourage economic and industrial development in the area including the Phoenix Cement Plant. EPA's acceptance of anything less was allegedly arbitrary and capricious, or in the words of the amicus brief, "pro forma."

The tremendous significance of the tribal treatment-as-a-state approach was made exquisitely clear on this issue. Congress is a national legislative body comprised of state representatives well attuned to the balance of federal-state power. The 1977 amendments specifically took from EPA the power it asserted under the 1974 rule to override reclassifications where it felt the local government had improperly weighed the environmental, energy or other factors. The Administrator could now disapprove a redesignation "*only* if he finds … that such redesignation does not meet the procedural requirements of this section."[22] The legislative history showed that text was intended to give greater latitude to local decision makers and prevent federal second-guessing.

Tribes treated as states benefited from the same respect for local value judgments. EPA was not to preempt tribal reclassifications on its contrary conclusions, say for instance, on a more traditional federal view the tribe would be better served by exploiting its natural resources for economic profit. And significantly here, adjacent jurisdictions would not have a veto over tribal value judgments. EPA's limited review, created at the behest of state representatives, would also insulate the Agency to some extent from the political pressures brought to bear by states invoking the dispute resolution process.

The 1977 amendments required only a "satisfactory" description and analysis of the redesignation factors, which EPA viewed as establishing a relatively low threshold. The court deferred to that reasonable interpretation and to EPA's conclusion that the Tribe's analysis conformed to it. Impacts on unknown future economic activities in the area, including possible tire incineration at the Phoenix Cement Plant, were speculative. *Nance* said the Act's strong presumption of maintaining clean air, and the nature of decisions for doing so, prevent exact predictions on redesignation consequences.

So the *Arizona v. EPA* court determined EPA had reasonably accepted the Tribe's analysis as adequate, and had not been arbitrary in approving the redesignation. Yet, the redesignation did not take effect. The Act made resolutions of redesignation disputes effective through incorporation in an "applicable plan." The court held that EPA wrongly promulgated the redesignation via a federal rather than a tribal plan.

The original Clean Air Act directed states develop plans for implementing EPA's national standards. State implementation plans constituted control strategies for ensuring the collective emissions of an area's air pollution sources did not exceed the required ambient air quality levels. Federal implementation plans could be developed as a fallback option where a state did not submit a plan or its plan was not consistent with the Act. No reference was made of course to Indian country plans.

The provisions for tribal redesignations in the 1974 rules and the 1977 amendments did not address the logical question of how they would be promulgated. The natural answer seemed to be federal implementation plans. EPA's first Indian program action in 1973 was direct implementation of the water pollution permit program in lieu of state delegation. EPA took the same course for the drinking water and hazardous waste programs in the early 1980s, and prevailed in *Phillips Petroleum* and *Washington Department of Ecology*. Like those other statutes, the silent Clean Air Act did not authorize state regulation in Indian country.

Strangely however, EPA had promulgated the 1977 Northern Cheyenne redesignation, without explanation, and without objection, as a revision to the State of Montana's implementation plan. Then, implementing the 1977 amendments, the Agency published regulations making all redesignations (including those by tribes) effective as revisions to state implementation plans.[23] Before the Yavapai-Apache dispute, EPA had received three redesignations under those regulations. All were from tribes—the Spokane Tribe of the Spokane Indian Reservation in Washington, the Assiniboine and Sioux Tribes of the Fort Peck Indian Reservation in Montana, and the Salish and Kootenai Tribes of the Flathead Indian Reservation in Montana—and all were approved as revisions to state plans.[24]

Congress substantially amended the Clean Air Act thirteen years later. The 1990 amendments followed the trend set in the Safe Drinking Water and Clean Water Acts and included a general treatment-as-a-state provision. Unlike the prior acts that listed eligible programs, EPA was responsible for determining which air programs were appropriate for tribal delegation. Of course, the 1977 amendments already identified the significant deterioration program. The 1990 amendments added one more: Congress included tribes in section 110 governing state implementation plans.

The theoretical question left open in 1977 thus seemed answered. Tribal redesignations would take effect through promulgation in tribal implementation plans. For the Yavapai-Apache, there was just one minor administrative obstacle: six years after the 1990 amendments, EPA still had not developed regulations specifying the required elements of tribal plans or the procedures for their approval. Hence, there was no tribal plan, or any immediate prospect of one, which could house the Camp Verde Reservation's Class I status.

Arizona, of course, had an available plan, and every previous tribal redesignation had been incorporated in a state plan. The 1978 regulation to that effect had not been revised or repealed. Administrative law requires agencies follow their substantive regulations no less than regulated entities, but EPA declined to do so here. That regulation, the Agency said, was adopted at an earlier time when it "had not clearly focused on the complex issues of tribal sovereignty." The regulation effectively treated tribes as state subdivisions, an approach explicitly rejected by the 1984 Indian Policy.

And, the Agency did not say, it made no sense. The original justification for the tribal role was the conclusion the silent Clean Air Act did not authorize state regulation in Indian country and thus federal environmental programs delegated to states did not apply there. Congress apparently ratified that view by codifying tribes' redesignation authority. But if a state's implementation plan was not applicable to Indian country in the first instance, it certainly could not give effect to a reservation redesignation adopted as a "revision" of the plan.

Some commenters had argued the regulation's internal inconsistency and the absence of a tribal plan meant there was no "applicable plan" to make the Yavapai-Apache redesignation operative. EPA agreed with their premises but changed the conclusion. In the same Federal Register notice reporting the Agency's final approval of the Tribe's redesignation, EPA announced it would be made effective through a federal implementation plan for the Camp Verde Reservation.

Arizona either overlooked or elected not to challenge the vulnerability this new development presented. The Arizona Chamber of Commerce, which had filed a petition similar to the State's, did not. The Chamber attacked EPA's failure to comply with its procedural rules for promulgating federal plans; the plan had simply appeared in the final announcement of the redesignation approval. There was no advance notice, explanation or opportunity for public comment. The Chamber also argued that federal plans were only proper to address deficiencies in applicable plans after notice and an opportunity for the local government to make necessary corrections. Here, there were no deficiencies for EPA to fix because Arizona's plan was inapplicable and there was no Yavapai-Apache plan.

That latter claim was a version of the "technician's" argument Phillips Petroleum pioneered in its challenge to EPA's underground injection program for the Osage Mineral Reserve. Phillips argued federal authority existed only to fix gaps created by inadequate state programs, but since Oklahoma's program did not apply at Osage, EPA's backup authority could not be activated. The Tenth Circuit rejected the Company's literal argument and deferred to the Agency's contrary interpretation of the Act because Phillips' view would create a vacuum of authority in Indian country inconsistent with Congress' goal for nationwide coverage. In the Arizona case, EPA argued *Phillips Petroleum* supported its view that federal plans were proper to fill Indian country regulatory gaps created by states' lack of jurisdiction.

The Ninth Circuit took a different view, although it should not have even considered the argument. The Chamber lacked standing because it had not participated in either the rulemaking or dispute resolution processes. The court dismissed the Chamber's petition at the outset for that reason, indicating it would address only the State's substantive arguments. The State lost every one of the claims it actually made, but the court mistakenly attributed the Chamber's federal plan argument to the State, which had not raised the issue, and the case turned on that argument.

The difference in *Phillips Petroleum*, as with many of EPA's key Indian program actions, was timing. The Agency's decision to implement a federal injection program at Osage was made before Congress added a treatment-as-a-state provision to the Safe Drinking Water Act so the Agency's options at that time were state delegation, federal implementation or no action. The silent Act did not authorize state programs in Indian country, and doing nothing left an unacceptable regulatory gap. The Tenth Circuit thus agreed with EPA that exercising its broad powers to carry out the Safe Drinking Water Act was necessary to close the circle of national protection.

But things had changed by the time *Arizona v. EPA* was decided. EPA promulgated its federal air quality implementation plan for the Camp Verde Reservation six years *after* Congress specifically authorized tribal implementation plans. There was no Yavapai-Apache plan because EPA had not yet developed regulations on how tribal plans would be reviewed and approved. Thus, the regulatory gap EPA sought to fill with the federal plan was not created by Congress' failure to provide a local partner as had been the case in *Phillips Petroleum*; in point of fact, EPA had frustrated Congress' intent by failing to give the Tribe an opportunity to submit its own plan.

A majority of the court thus invalidated the vehicle by which the otherwise valid tribal redesignation would have taken effect. Ironically, respect for the tribal regulatory role Congress preferred was the justification for rendering the Tribe's value judgment inoperative. One judge dissented from that anomalous result. It punished the Tribe for what he called EPA's "administrative sluggishness," and nullified the state-like autonomy the Act provided tribes, at least until the "relatively ministerial act" of producing regulations was completed.

Timing, as they say, is everything. For EPA, it has often meant the success or failure of its Indian program actions. *Arizona v. EPA* rejected *Phillips Petroleum's* endorsement of EPA's broad Indian country powers because of the temporal relation between Congress' treatment-as-a-state amendments and the Agency's actions. More prominently, the Agency had not developed rules for tribal plan approvals by the time of the Yavapai-Apache redesignation. A relevant regulation was adopted shortly before the case was argued to the Ninth Circuit, but could not validate EPA's earlier approval of the Tribe's redesignation. Its rationale, however, was directly supportive of EPA's position in court, though the Agency did not repeat the argument.

The "Tribal Authority Rule" had been proposed in 1994 about the same time Arizona requested dispute resolution proceedings. It was not directed at the Act's specific authorizations for tribal implementation plans and redesignations. It was proposed pursuant to section 301, the general treatment-as-a-state provision. In section 301 Congress called for EPA's determination of the Clean Air Act provisions appropriate for tribal delegation. Nearly six years after Congress' deadline, EPA finalized the rule identifying all but a few aspects of the Act appropriate.[25]

One provision excepted was section 110's authorization for federal implementation plans. EPA thought its two-year deadline for applying federal plans to states that missed statutory deadlines or submitted defective plans was not appropriately applied to tribes. Unlike state plans, Congress imposed no deadline for the development of tribal plans. Tribes were not required to develop plans at all. And, whereas states had been developing air quality management capacity with significant federal assistance since at least 1970, tribes just received express program authority in 1990 and had seen relatively little federal money or technical assistance.

By the same token, the nation's need for clean air could not depend on optional or lengthy tribal program development. Section 301 seemed cognizant of the conundrum:

> In any case in which the Administrator determines that the treatment of Indian tribes as identical to States is inappropriate or administratively infeasible, the Administrator may provide, by regulation, *other means by which the Administrator will directly administer such provisions* so as to achieve the appropriate purpose.[26]

The Tribal Authority Rule invoked EPA's direct authority by providing for the development of federal plans as necessary to protect air quality for tribes who did not submit plans "within some reasonable time" or whose plans were not approved.[27] Inserted quietly in the rule was one phrase anticipating the court's criticism of administrative procrastination in *Arizona v. EPA*: tribal plans were expected to meet the existing criteria for state plans. Tribal redesignations, therefore, could take effect either by way of a tribal plan approved under the same standards as states, or through a federal plan adopted in the absence of an approved tribal plan.

The 1998 Tribal Authority Rule could not save the 1996 Yavapai-Apache federal plan. It is curious, however, that EPA neither referred to nor argued its rationale for federal authority in the absence of a tribal plan. That analysis was more detailed and better supported that its bald assertions in court that federal authority was necessary to ensure national air protection. Perhaps it assumed *Phillips Petroleum* would carry the day. The difference in timing of the tribal roles was arguably offset by Congress' specific authorization of direct federal implementation where tribal roles did not accomplish national goals. At the very least, EPA could have protected itself on remand by seeking support from the court for re-proposing the Yavapai-Apache federal plan under the Tribal Air Rule.

Uncertainty over the means by which redesignations would become effective may explain why the groundswell of tribal requests Arizona feared did not materialize. No other Arizona tribe sought redesignation following *Arizona v. EPA*. The Yavapai-Apache Tribe did not prepare a tribal implementation plan or request EPA attempt a second federal plan under the new rule. Turnover in Yavapai-Apache staff and government officials led to different priorities, influenced in part by Phoenix Cement's subsequent decision not to incinerate tires as supplemental fuel.

Just last year EPA proposed for the first time since *Arizona v. EPA* using its direct implementation authority for a tribal Class I redesignation.[28] EPA had proposed approval of the Forest County Potawatomi Community's redesignation of its reservation in Wisconsin in the 1990s before the decision in *Arizona v. EPA*. Both Wisconsin and Michigan objected and requested dispute resolution proceedings. Wisconsin and the Tribe eventually settled their dispute through a Memorandum of Agreement specifying the conditions under which off-reservation major sources would perform Class I and air quality related values analyses. EPA's 2006 proposal promised to abide by those terms, interpreting the Clean Air Act as not requiring EPA approval where parties successfully settle their disputes. The proposal noted it would decide Michigan's dispute, which was not settled, following its consideration of public comments on giving effect to the Tribe's redesignation through a federal implementation plan. To date, that is the sole instance a federal plan has been proposed in the tribal redesignation context, although facility and program-specific federal plans have been proposed and promulgated for some reservations.[29]

Federal Delegation as the Source of Tribal Regulatory Authority over Non-Indians

The classic legal question of inherent tribal sovereignty over non-Indians did not play a central role in *Nance* or *Arizona v. EPA*. The challengers' arguments left no doubt the motivation for suing was their fundamental objection to the possibility non-Indians might somehow or someday be constrained by tribal value judgments different from state expectations. The potentially affected non-Indians, though, were outside Indian country and thus not subject to direct tribal control; non-Indians own less than one percent of land on the Northern Cheyenne Reservation, and the Camp Verde Reservation has no non-Indian land. Thus, the complaint was really directed at Congress' federalism decision giving legal effect to one jurisdiction's value judgments even where they might affect an adjacent jurisdiction.

Airshed redesignations are indirect by their nature at any rate. An area's classification has relatively little legal significance until a permit is sought for a new or expanded major facility. Neither the Northern Cheyenne nor the Yavapai-Apache issue Clean Air Act permits for on-reservation facilities; EPA retains that authority. And certainly the Tribes would never be delegated permit programs for facilities outside Indian country; the state or EPA would issue those permits. So the tribes' sovereignty over non-Indians was not directly at issue. *Nance* nonetheless foreshadowed how the issue would later take center stage in the air program and take the Agency's Indian program forward dramatically.

The industry petitioners made two related federal constitutional claims in attacking the extraterritorial impacts of the Northern Cheyenne redesignation. One asserted the due process clause prevented EPA's approval because it was for the Tribe's private benefit. The other argued Congress unconstitutionally delegated its legislative authority to tribes via the redesignation power. The court rejected both arguments as resting on unnecessarily crabbed interpretations of federal Indian law; tribes are not mere "private voluntary organizations," but are governments with sovereignty over their citizens and their territories.

> Certainly the exercise of sovereignty by the Northern Cheyenne will have extraterritorial effect. But another element must be considered,

namely the effect of the land use outside the reservation on the reservation itself. This case involves the "dumping" of pollutants from land outside the reservation onto the reservation. Just as a tribe has the authority to prevent the entrance of non-members onto the reservation, a tribe may exercise control, in conjunction with the EPA, over the entrance of pollutants onto the reservation. We do not, however, decide whether the Indians would possess independent authority to maintain their air quality. *"It is necessary only to state that the independent tribal authority is quite sufficient to protect Congress' decision to vest in tribal councils this portion of its own authority...."*[30]

That conclusion harbored tremendous potential for the Indian program. Its crowning quotation came from *United States v. Mazurie*,[31] a 1975 Supreme Court decision unique in several respects. The Mazuries were non-Indians who operated the Blue Bull Bar on their fee-owned land within the Wind River Indian Reservation in Wyoming. For a time, the Eastern Shoshone and Northern Arapahoe Indian Tribes had allowed liquor sales if made in compliance with state law, and the bar possessed a state license. The Tribes later amended the law to require a tribal license, but denied the Mazuries' application because of increasing reports of sales to minors and violence at the bar. The federal government successfully prosecuted the Mazuries for operating the bar in violation of a federal law that criminalized liquor sales in Indian country unless made in conformity with state and tribal law.

The Tenth Circuit overturned the convictions, holding the federal law improperly delegated regulatory authority over non-Indian businesses on the reservation to the Tribes, which the court viewed as "private, voluntary organization[s]." "It is difficult to see how such an association of citizens could exercise any degree of governmental authority or sovereignty over other citizens who do not belong, and who cannot participate in any way in the tribunal organization."[32]

The Supreme Court unanimously rejected that view and reinstated the convictions. Then Justice William Rehnquist, in just his third year on the bench, wrote the opinion endorsing the tribe's congressionally approved authority over non-Indians in Indian country. Dozens of prior cases showed that tribes were "a good deal more" than private organizations; they were in fact governmental entities with aspects of sovereignty over their citizens and territories. He gave barely a nod to the Mazuries' "taxation without representation" complaint, suggesting the Court had long guarded tribes' powers over their reservations and it was Congress' sole prerogative to strip such powers from tribes.

At any rate, irrespective of whether the Shoshone and Arapahoe Tribes' independent authority extended itself to the Blue Bull Bar, it was a sufficient foundation upon which to locate federal power. The Constitution's limitations on delegations of Congress' legislative authority are "less stringent in cases where the entity exercising the delegated authority itself possesses independent authority over the subject matter."

That was probably the only time Rehnquist wrote clearly in support of tribal sovereignty. Three years later he penned *Oliphant's* implicit divestiture rule positing in the Court's hands the very power he ascribed only to Congress in *Mazurie*. *Oliphant* immediately spawned *Montana's* general bar against tribal jurisdiction over non-Indians, marking a path for judicial activism over the next two decades that made the Rehnquist court synonymous with dismantling inherent tribal sovereignty.[33]

Yet, in a broad sense *Mazurie* was entirely consistent with *Oliphant* and *Montana*. The latter cases explicitly relied on the absence of congressional authorization for the asserted tribal criminal and wildlife jurisdiction over non-Indians. *Mazurie* addressed one of the few times Congress had exercised its extensive Indian powers by a general delegation of regulatory authority over non-Indians to tribes.

Importantly for EPA, *Mazurie* seemed directly analogous to the environmental context. In involved a subject (Indian country liquor sales) implicating significant federal interests and featuring extensive federal regulatory involvement. The challenged action (criminal prosecution) was a federal one animated by a tribal value judgment (requiring tribal liquor licenses) made effective through federal guidelines (BIA approval of the tribal law). The federal interests in national environmental protection were similarly high and EPA's regulatory machine even more extensive. Tribal environmental quality value judgments, made effective through specified federal approval processes, influenced federal permits and prosecutions. And in one environmental law — the Clean Water Act — Congress used the same definition of Indian reservations found in the liquor statute.

EPA's 1991 water quality standards rule considered but did not follow *Mazurie* in interpreting the Clean Water Act's tribal treatment-as-a-state provision. Some of the relevant statutory language was identical, and four Supreme Court justices in *Brendale* had cited it as a delegation. But the potential impact of tribal environmental regulation on non-Indian business went far beyond that at stake for a few Indian country taverns. The Agency elected instead to require tribes show inherent sovereignty over non-Indian polluters until Congress spoke more clearly on the matter.

EPA found that clarity in the air program. As it had done for the Safe Drinking and Clean Water Acts, Congress included threshold eligibility criteria in section 301's general authorization for tribal treatment-as-a-state. The tribal governance and capacity criteria were essentially the same, but the second criterion was somewhat different. The Safe Drinking Water Act applied to areas over which the tribe had jurisdiction, and the Clean Water Act focused on water resources within the exterior boundaries of the reservation. EPA viewed both as requiring a showing of inherent tribal sovereignty.

The Clean Air Act's second criterion authorized tribal management functions for "air resources within the exterior boundaries of the reservation *or other areas within the tribe's jurisdiction*."[34] While not a model of clarity, the disjunctive phraseology surely suggested a tribe could implement federal programs over two kinds of air resources: those within reservations, and those in non-reservation areas over which the tribe showed its inherent authority. In other words, Congress arguably delegated authority over the entire reservation airshed regardless of non-Indian land ownership.

EPA offered that interpretation when it proposed the Tribal Authority Rule in 1994. The proposed rule generated sixty-nine comments, twice the number submitted on the 1991 water rule. Indicative of tribes' increased awareness and interest in federal program implementation, over sixty percent of the comments came from tribes or tribal representatives. State governmental entities submitted thirteen; business and industry sent ten comments.

No issue in the proposed rule had more practical impact on the development of tribal environmental programs and environmental justice in Indian country than delegation. If Congress had delegated authority over on-reservation non-Indian air polluters, then EPA could approve tribal applications for federal program primacy on reservations without a showing of their independent jurisdiction. In other words, neither the tribe nor EPA needed to analyze the *Montana* test. That saved time and energy, obviated the need for an additional governmental comment period for jurisdictional objections, and constricted the issues that could trigger administrative dispute resolution processes.

More fundamentally, delegation foreclosed the most likely judicial challenge to individual EPA program approvals. The 1997 decision in *Strate v. A-1 Contractors*,[35] which said a reservation car accident that nearly killed the mother of five tribal citizens did not implicate the health and welfare of the Three Affiliated Tribes, emboldened states and non-Indians. The judicial tea leaves foretold of the Court's consistent rejection of tribal attempts to meet *Montana* in the early 2000s. The Agency's water quality rule that arguably eased tribes' burden by buttressing them with generalized findings of health and welfare impacts would soon prevail in *Montana v. EPA*, but that case and others showed the possibility that every tribal approval could draw a time-consuming suit. Delays in getting tribal programs operating exacerbated environmental injustice in Indian country. And administrative apprehension over provoking such responses, which translated into approval processes for tribal water program applications stretching into years, had the same effect.

Predictably, tribal comments favored the proposed delegation approach while states and industry objected to it. Tribes asserted their independent authority was sufficient to regulate air pollution apart from congressional delegation, but they acknowledged the value in avoiding case-by-case litigation over every claim of inherent sovereignty. Delegation's territorial approach was consistent with their view of federal Indian law and Congress' intent in the Act.

States and industry necessarily mounted a defensive offense. They argued delegation was not supported by the statute's plain text. The phrase "within the tribe's jurisdiction" could be read as modifying both "other areas" and reservations so that tribes must always show their independent authority. The language was similar to the water acts and a Senate report equated the process for approving tribal air programs with the water acts. The opponents noted in those acts EPA had not found delegations. They also argued *Mazurie* required tribes show pre-existing jurisdiction over non-Indians to receive Congress' delegation.

EPA's prior interpretation of the Clean Water Act as not delegating authority over non-Indians was bothersome. The language and programs of the two statutes were similar in key respects. The trial court in *Montana v. EPA* issued its decision upholding EPA's interim operating rule requiring tribes show jurisdiction by asserting non-Indian water pollution seriously affected tribal welfare interests while EPA was pondering public comment on the proposed Tribal Authority Rule. Ironically, the court commented in dicta that the Clean Water Act "seems to indicate plainly" a congressional delegation.[36]

The legislative history of the Clean Air Act was conflicted of course. The summary of one Senate Report said tribes would need to show jurisdiction for all programs sought. That same report later said the Act was "an express delegation of power to Indian tribes."[37] Strange as it seems for an entity whose power is circumscribed by statute, congressional confusion can be quite comforting for an agency in federal court. Directly conflicting viewpoints imply Congress was not of one mind on a matter, or show Congress was not clear on it. Reconciling competing and conflicting goals in implementing complex regulatory schemes is a category of administrative action that routinely benefits from judicial deference. And statutory ambiguity theoretically shifts the court's inquiry from independently determining congressional intent to asking whether the agency's view is unreasonable.

Clearly, Congress had not rejected delegation by imposing the jurisdictional criterion found in the Safe Drinking Water Act, and it had used language fundamentally different than the Clean Water Act, perhaps to overcome EPA's initial hesitance there. The Clean Air Act's treatment-as-a-state provision was the more recent congressional expression on tribal programs. Its disjunctive second criterion reasonably implied a delegation to tribes for reservations, and an authorization for off-reservation programs where tribes showed independent jurisdiction. The argument for delegation was more than plausible.

The final Tribal Authority Rule adopted the delegation approach in February 1998. The following month the Ninth Circuit rejected Montana's attack on EPA's approval of the Salish and Kootenai water quality standards. Within five months, the Tenth Circuit would reject Arizona's complaint over the Agency's approval of the Yavapai-Apache's airshed redesignation, although it would order promulgation through a tribal plan. The Tribal Authority Rule had more direct and binding national implications than the Agency's decisions at Flathead and Camp Verde, so it was no surprise that several petitions for judicial review were filed.

Claims that EPA's view impinged on states' sovereignty peppered each suit, but curiously, no state or state environmental agency lodged a petition. The State of Michigan did intervene in a national industry association's action, and when it later sought Supreme Court review three other states—South Dakota, Nevada and New Mexico—submitted an amicus brief.

But the main attack came from a potpourri of thirteen business and utility groups whose operations and profit margins could be greatly affected by effective air pollution management in Indian country: Salt River Project Agricultural Improvement and Power District; Nevada Power Company; Public Service Company of New Mexico; Tucson Electric Power Company; Oklahoma Gas & Electric Company; Arizona Public Service Company; National Mining Association; National Association of Manufacturers; American Forest & Paper Association; The Timber Producers Association of Michigan and Wisconsin; Michigan Chemical Council; and Rhinelander (Wisconsin) Area Chamber of Commerce. Four Indian tribes with emerging air programs— Gila River Indian Community, Navajo Nation, Salt River Pima-Maricopa Indian Community, and Shoshone-Bannock Tribes—intervened on EPA's side. The D.C. Circuit consolidated the various petitions into one case, captioned *Arizona Public Service Company v. Environmental Protection Agency.*[38]

The petitioners followed the time-honored non-Indian strategy of presenting a cannonade of arguments. Their main challenge was directed at delegation, which could preclude nearly every jurisdictional challenge to individual reservation air program approvals in the future. They complained it was simply unfair that tribes might regulate non-Indians while states were prohibited from regulating reservations.

The D.C. Circuit found EPA's interpretation comported with the statute's text, structure, purpose and legislative history. The second criterion's disjunctive text was a "clear distinction" implying Congress considered all reservation areas "to be *per se* within the tribe's jurisdiction." It accorded structurally with the Act's other provisions that tribal redesignations and tribal implementation plans applied to all areas within the exterior boundaries of reservations. A fragmented parcel-by-parcel checkerboard approach would not serve the Act's purpose of effective air quality management because air pollutants are highly mobile, disperse widely, and present significant health and welfare risks.

The legislative history offered some support for the delegation conclusion. The original provision limited tribes to management functions "within the area of the tribal government's jurisdiction."[39] The version enacted, of course, expanded tribal functions so they applied "within the exterior boundaries of the reservation or other areas within the tribe's jurisdiction." No explanation appeared for the change, but the court felt it "strongly suggested" Congress viewed all areas within reservations as subject to tribal jurisdiction. The earlier provision also showed Congress knew how to draft language requiring tribes show jurisdiction to qualify for treatment-as-a-state.

One judge dissented from that view. He thought the change was more likely to authorize tribal air roles in non-reservation parts of Indian country. As EPA had opined in the water context, it just seemed reasonable to assume Congress would be clear when it delegated tribal authority over non-Indians. The dissent read such intent in section 110. Tribal implementation plans were authorized over "*all areas* ... located within the exterior boundaries of the reservation, *notwithstanding* the issuance of any patent, and including rights-of-way running through the reservation."[40]

That same "notwithstanding" proviso was a key part of the liquor control program over non-Indians that *Mazurie* said Congress had delegated to tribes. At the time of *Arizona Public Service*, *Mazurie* was the only case directly confronting the issue of tribal delegation. Another Supreme Court decision, addressing state regulation in Indian country under the same liquor program, repeated *Mazurie's* conclusion that the notwithstanding proviso represented a tribal delegation.[41] And, of course, four justices in *Brendale* referred to the Clean Water Act's definition of reservation, which included the notwithstanding proviso, as a delegation.

The *Arizona Public Service* dissent thus characterized the notwithstanding proviso as the "gold standard" for tribal delegations. Its appearance in section 110, the dissent argued, meant tribal implementation plans for reservations applied to non-Indian lands without any need for showing inherent tribal authority. But the broader section 301 lacked the gold standard. Its "never-before-attempted" formulation of express delegation, in comparison with section 110, suggested something less than delegation to the dissent. Arguably buttressing that view was Congress' rejection of an earlier bill that provided "the Administrator … may delegate to [] tribes primary responsibility for assuring air quality.…"[42]

That sort of delegation, however, was different from the delegation at issue in *Mazurie* and *Arizona Public Service*. It authorized EPA to hand over to tribes (and states) responsibility for operating particular federal regulatory programs—water quality standards, airshed redesignation, pollution permit issuance, etc. Delegation of program primacy was dependent on a showing of the local government's regulatory authority. The source of that pre-existing regulatory power—either inherent or congressional delegation—was the delegation issue in *Arizona Public Service*, not EPA's power to approve tribal operation of particular air programs.

The majority rejected the asserted gold standard. *Mazurie* did not say there was only one formulation for congressional delegations to tribes, and a single case hardly qualified as establishing an exclusive rule de facto. That Congress used different language in the 1990 Clean Air Act amendments was thus not dispositive. Indeed, the difference might have been motivated by EPA's hesitation in 1989 to read the Clean Water Act's notwithstanding proviso as a delegation. EPA had exercised caution there because of the Act's ambiguous and inconclusive legislative history, which the court found was not true for the subsequent Clean Air Act amendments. The court concluded the Tribal Authority Rule's provision for approving tribes' reservation air programs without a prior showing of independent jurisdiction over non-Indians was valid.

Federal Delegation or Confirmation?

A subsequent Ninth Circuit decision following the D.C. Circuit's delegation analysis in a different Indian country environmental case caused some confusion on the meaning of federal delegation. A non-Indian landowner on the Hoopa Valley Reservation in northern California argued her timber harvesting was exempt from the Hoopa Tribe's environmental regulations. Tribal law required mitigation of damage caused by timber activities and forbid harvests within an identified buffer zone adjacent to ancient dance grounds still used by the Tribe. The Tribe asserted a congressional delegation of jurisdiction over non-Indians through a land claims settlement act that "ratified and confirmed" the Tribe's governing documents. The Tribal Constitution asserted jurisdiction over all reservation lands and specifically contemplated tribal laws affecting nonmembers by requiring federal approval of them.

The district court accepted the Tribe's delegation argument, but on appeal an initial panel of three Ninth Circuit judges reversed.[43] Congress' ratification and confirmation was wanting, the panel wrote, because it failed the delegation gold standard of the dissent in *Arizona Public Service*. The Tribe successfully urged the Ninth Circuit to consider the conflict with the D.C. Circuit by rehearing the case en banc. En banc review is the full court's check against an errant three-judge panel whose decision would otherwise stand as the law of the circuit.

A new opinion issued from a panel of eleven Ninth Circuit judges reinstated the district court's delegation conclusion in *Bugenig v. Hoopa Valley Tribe*.[44] *Bugenig* expressly agreed with the majority's analysis in *Arizona Public Service*, saying "no particular verbal formula" is required for delegation. The phrase "ratified and confirmed" had been interpreted in other Indian law cases as reflecting Congress' intention to give to some prior agreement or decision the force and effect of law. When combined with the Hoopa Tribe's Constitution, the court held Congress had expressly delegated authority over non-Indian land uses within the Hoopa Reservation. The Hoopa Tribe, therefore, had no need to argue and win the *Montana* test in order to regulate the environmental consequences of logging on non-Indian lands within its territory.

Bugenig's result was correct, but its rationale wrong. The statute's language was plain. The Tribe's territorial sovereignty was expressly acknowledged, not granted. The statute's real consequence, arising from Congress' ratification, was to make the Tribe's pre-existing powers effective as a matter of federal law. In a sense, the Hoopa settlement act added a tribe-specific exception to *Montana's* general rule: the Hoopa Tribe could regulate non-Indian land use activities on fee lands within its reservation consistent with powers identified in its constitution. The federal court thus properly rejected the non-Indian's federal Indian law challenge without requiring the Tribe satisfy the *Montana* test, but it should not have relied on the term delegation to do so.

That was the Supreme Court's fault. *Mazurie's* characterization of the liquor statute as a delegation was particularly misplaced. The Tribe's power over non-Indians was not directly at issue. The challenge was to the federal government's authority to define actions taken in violation of tribal law as a federal crime. Or said differently, the case involved Congress' power to make an Indian tribe's value judgment about reservation liquor sales effective as a matter of federal law. The Tribes' independent territorial jurisdiction—essentially their status as sovereign governments—was the necessary touchstone validating Congress' authority. But once Congress specifically confirmed the particular tribal regulatory power, there was no need to identify its bounds by resort to federal Indian law principles created for instances where Congress had not spoken.

Another federal criminal case recently brought this somewhat less patronizing view of delegation into specific relief. The federal government prosecuted a citizen of the Turtle Mountain Band of Chippewa Indians for punching a federal officer on the neighboring Fort Totten Indian Reservation in North Dakota, home of the Spirit Lake Nation. The defendant argued the federal prosecution was unconstitutional double jeopardy since the Spirit Lake Nation previously prosecuted him for the same act. He asserted the Tribe had exercised federal power under a law that confirmed tribes' criminal jurisdiction over all Indians in Indian country.

The unique context in which that law was passed underscored the alternative view of federal delegation. In 1990 the Supreme Court extended *Oliphant* to conclude that tribes lack inherent sovereignty over crimes committed by Indians from other tribes.[45] A political uproar over the decision's practical consequences for Indian country forced a nearly immediate congressional response. Four months later Congress passed a temporary amendment to the Indian Civil Rights Act, which was made permanent the next year.[46]

The amended law defined tribes' powers of self-government in part as "*the inherent power of Indian tribes, hereby recognized and affirmed*, to exercise criminal jurisdiction over all Indians."[47] Only two years earlier, Congress used the remarkably similar "ratified and confirmed" phrase in the Hoopa settlement act that *Bugenig* would later call a delegation of federal power.

Yet, the language of the Indian Civil Rights Act amendment seemed clearly directed at overriding the Court's conclusion that tribes' inherent sovereignty no longer included criminal jurisdiction over non-member Indians. The amendment effectively restored that power, but it could not accomplish that goal through delegation. Delegation implied tribal prosecutions would be exercises of federal power, barring later federal prosecutions as double jeopardy.

So Congress filled the legislative record with explicit references to restoring and affirming tribes' inherent governmental powers. The House conference committee explicitly disclaimed a delegation. Senator Inouye, who was at the same time pressing EPA to find a federal delegation in the Clean Water Act, stated the amendment "affirms the inherent jurisdiction of tribal governments over nonmember Indians."[48] Others offered similar affirmations.

The Supreme Court accepted those characterizations in *United States v. Lara*,[49] which identified the source of the Spirit Lake Nation's criminal power over nonmember Indians as inherent rather than delegated authority. Congress passed the law to "adjust the tribes' status" following the Court's earlier decision that tribal jurisdiction was lacking. The Court could find no constitutional principle limiting Congress from relaxing restrictions put on tribes by "judicially made" Indian law.

Lara's implications for the Clean Air Act and other federal environmental statutes are not clear. The pre-existence of inherent tribal sovereignty was important in *Mazurie, Arizona Public Service* and *Bugenig*. Perhaps Congress had simply readjusted inherent sovereignty rather than delegated federal authority. The Hoopa settlement act in *Bugenig* was not all that different from the Indian Civil Rights Act amendment in *Lara*. The Clean Air Act was different though, and its legislative history was not as clear as the Indian Civil Rights Act, which was passed at nearly the same time. Most significantly, it was far more likely to be viewed as impacting state sovereignty interests. *Lara* made clear it was not deciding whether the Constitution might limit Congress' Indian powers where their exercise involved an "interference with the power or authority of any State."

Defining the Geographic Scope of Indian Country

Indian law questions nearly always have a geographic component. EPA's success in interpreting the Clean Air Act as a delegation rested on Congress' distinction between Indian reservations and other geographic areas under tribal jurisdiction. Tribes escaped the burden of preparing and the risk of losing *Montana* health and welfare arguments for air program assumptions over territories denominated Indian reservations. *Arizona Public Service* validated one other significant geographic issue EPA put forth in the Tribal Authority Rule: a broad view of what constitutes an Indian reservation.

The Camp Verde "Reservation" illustrated the conundrum. The Yavapai-Apache Tribe's lands had never been officially designated an Indian reservation, although the Department of the Interior referred to them that way. Many other tribes, particularly the pueblos of the southwest and the Oklahoma tribes, also reside on lands not labeled reservations but effectively treated by the federal government as such. The policy question was whether those tribes were eligible for the same delegation benefit as tribes with so-called formal reservations.

The Clean Air Act referred to Indian reservations in three provisions, but did not define the term. EPA explained it would resolve the apparent ambiguity by resort to Supreme Court case law. Long ago the Court held the southwestern pueblos, which are held communally in fee simple under land grants made with the Spanish government, constitute Indian country.[50] More recently, it had said the "common understanding" of reservation included trust lands validly set apart for the use of a tribe even though not formally designated as a reservation.[51] The Tribal Authority Rule thus indicated EPA would consider tribal trust lands and pueblos as reservations so that tribes residing on them were excused from showing jurisdiction under *Montana*.

The business interests in *Arizona Public Service* ignored the pueblos but objected to the inclusion of tribal trust lands as "informal" reservations falling within the ambit of the delegation benefit. They feared gaming tribes might buy isolated lands, press the Department of the Interior to place them in trust status, and then seek Class I redesignations thereby disrupting state expectations for economic development. Somewhat inconsistently, they noted up to this point EPA included only formal reservations within the prevention of significant deterioration program, suggesting the changed approach revealed its arbitrariness.

The court was not troubled by the economic parade of horribles. It found EPA's interpretation of informal reservations reasonable and consistent with the Supreme Court's oft-repeated directive that statutes be construed so as to benefit Indian tribes. Congress had defined the term Indian reservation differently in at least a dozen other statutes, never settling on one rigid formulation. The Clean Air Act did not define the term, though its legislative history showed clear intent for broad coverage in Indian country. EPA's changed approach was well explained and, although the court did not observe it, entirely consistent with the standard administrative law principle that an Agency's initial interpretation of a statute is "not instantly carved in stone."[52] And a number of federal cases, including *HRI*, treated tribal trust lands as indistinguishable from formal reservations. *Arizona v. EPA's* acceptance of the Middle Verde parcel as a reservation also supported that view.

Expanding the delegation interpretation to informal reservations offered an incentive for additional tribes to develop air programs. The primary significance of the delegation approach is avoiding delays occasioned by administrative and legal challenges to tribal applications for air programs that might affect non-Indians. *Montana v. EPA* showed that tribal assertions and EPA determinations of inherent sovereignty based on health and welfare impacts were vulnerable to attack on a case-by-case basis. Delegation precluded such claims because there are rarely disputes over whether particular lands are held in trust for a tribe.

Strangely enough, disputes over the extent of formally designated reservations are increasingly more common. A series of cases in the 1960s and 1970s showed the Supreme Court's willingness to entertain claims that Congress had implicitly diminished the geographic scope of Indian reservations by its sales of tribal lands to non-Indians during the nineteenth century allotment era. The Court's so-called diminishment doctrine effectively redraws established reservation boundaries to exclude those non-Indian lands. The doctrine's unpredictable calculus for divining Congress' turn of the century intent—parsing ambiguous statutory language while taking account of the surrounding circumstances, subsequent demographics and jurisdictional history of the area—is perfectly suited to propagating disputes.

While EPA was developing the Indian air program in the 1990s, two particularly relevant diminishment disputes were percolating in the environmental context. One was in South Dakota over a solid waste landfill proposed by four municipalities on land within the Yankton Sioux Reservation. The other dispute was in New Mexico over Hydro Resources' plan to inject wastes underground within the Eastern Agency of the Navajo Reservation. Both cases featured assertions of state authority over non-Indian facilities on lands ostensibly within reservation boundaries.

EPA's underground injection program attempted to stave off delays incident to diminishment challenges by asserting federal authority over lands whose Indian country status was in dispute. The Agency suggested that same approach in a 1997 proposal for a federal operating permit program under Title V, which governed certain major air pollution sources. EPA would directly implement the permit program in Indian country, including lands where a status dispute existed.[53]

The air rule was finalized in 1999,[54] one year before *Hydro Resources* would uphold the disputed lands approach for underground injection at Navajo, but one year after the Supreme Court held the South Dakota landfill subject to state not federal regulation because an 1894 statute diminished the Yankton Tribe's reservation.[55] The final rule did not mention the case, but it contained an absolute (and unexplained) declaration not appearing in the proposed rule: "EPA will not consider there to be a question about the status of areas that are clearly within the boundaries of an Indian reservation."

The reference to an Indian country status "question" belied another important geographic change in the final rule. The Agency said it now believed the term "dispute" might be misleading. Active litigation or formal administrative contests were not required. The federal permit program would apply whenever EPA felt the Indian country status of particular land was "in question." Although information submitted by states and tribes would be helpful, EPA reserved the final judgment to itself.

Four state agencies from three states and two national industry organizations immediately recognized the risk for those who preferred state regulation. EPA could assume program jurisdiction, and thereby deny state authority, over any facility the Agency thought might be in Indian country without actually making a determination of the land's Indian country status. If an aggrieved party sought judicial review of EPA's action, the issue would be whether the Agency had reasonably concluded the land's status was in question, not whether the land was in fact Indian country. Absent an on-point federal case decisively answering the question, judicial deference to non-arbitrary agency decisions nearly guaranteed challengers would lose.

The state agencies and national organizations filed separate petitions in the D.C. Circuit Court of Appeals seeking invalidation of the rule. The various claims were consolidated into one case captioned *State of Michigan v. Environmental Protection Agency.*[56] The Navajo Nation, who would in 2004 become the first Indian tribe approved to run the federal Title V permit program, intervened on EPA's side. Two years would pass before the case was argued and decided. During that time, the Tenth Circuit issued *HRI* in EPA's favor. The Agency's understandable confidence before the D.C. Circuit, however, evaporated when the court found reason to distinguish the Navajo underground injection program from the national federal operating air permits rule.

The specific legal question before the D.C. Circuit was whether EPA's treatment of "in question" lands exceeded its authority under the Clean Air Act. The court noted the administrative law axiom that as creatures of statute, agencies possess only those powers granted by Congress. Judicial deference to administrative interpretations of a statute comes into play once courts are assured the agency has authority to act in the first instance. The court said EPA faltered on this preliminary point.

The Clean Air Act certainly authorized federal permit programs to fill gaps created when states missed required deadlines for developing programs, submitted inadequate programs, or inadequately administered otherwise acceptable programs. The Tribal Authority Rule determined the Title V operating permit program was appropriate for tribal delegation, so federal authority similarly existed to fill gaps created by tribal program inadequacies. But nowhere in the Act could the court find a delegation of some generic federal power for implementing programs in instances where neither a state nor tribal program had first been found wanting.

The petitioners "happily conceded" that tribes, and potentially EPA acting for tribes, had jurisdiction in Indian country; their interest was in regulating facilities outside Indian country. The problem with the rule was not that EPA might regulate some of those latter facilities during the time their Indian country status was unclear. The problem was that the time might become indefinite. EPA asserted it had no duty to decide a state's jurisdiction over particular facilities, even in the face of a state's program application.

The court's strong adverse reaction to that position was striking in comparison to the typically deferential tone of judicial review of agency action. "EPA must decide and not simply grab jurisdiction for itself on the ground that an area in 'in question.'" Any other conclusion, the court said, would effectively give EPA "a blank check" to expand its jurisdiction by *not* deciding the jurisdictional question. The absence in the rule of any requirement or timeframe for resolving the issue suggested to the court EPA could acquire "permanent" jurisdiction "in perpetuity." That result was at odds with Congress' provision for temporary federal authority while local program inadequacies were remedied.

In point of fact, the court was completely correct. EPA was executing a federal power grab, but not for itself. Its clear intent, as it explained to the court, was protecting tribal sovereignty consistent with the Indian Policy and presidential executive orders. Title V was a complex program requiring significant infrastructure. It would take time for tribes who desired program approval to develop their capacity. The rule proposed EPA fill the regulatory gap in the interim, as it had done in the underground injection program approved by *HRI*. *Montana* and numerous other cases showed courts' tendency to ascribe legal significance to prior and existing assertions of state regulatory authority in Indian country. EPA thus urged the court to construe the Clean Air Act liberally to favor tribes' interests in future program assumptions.

The court was unconvinced. Just as the Ninth Circuit in *Arizona v. EPA* rejected promulgation of the Yavapai-Apache redesignation through a federal implementation plan, the *Michigan v. EPA* court seized on what appeared as a federal preemptory strike to tribal programs. The court said EPA was interpreting the Act to favor itself, not the tribes. The Agency could decline to rule on a tribal application just as it might a state application, thereby depriving tribes of the opportunity Congress explicitly offered in the treatment-as-a-state provision. *HRI* had not approved that approach. It was limited to the Agency's conclusion that one particular parcel was disputed, and the court there remanded the case for a determination on its Indian country status. That, the *Michigan v. EPA* court said, was a far cry from allowing federal jurisdiction in perpetuity over any lands whose status EPA deemed were questioned.

Lacking the Agency's longer and broader experience with the development of tribal environmental programs, the court could not perceive the rule's significance to the Indian program. The statutory state-like roles for tribes were a key step toward environmental justice in Indian country, but realizing them would take time and money neither the tribes nor EPA had in excess. Some functioning program was necessary in the interim, but inviting states in threatened tribal sovereignty on several levels. Avoiding final agency decisions that could be challenged on diminishment and related grounds was thus an important goal. The court's invalidation of the rule thus portended additional diminishment cases in the environmental context in the future.

CHAPTER 6

PROTECTING MOTHER EARTH: SEEKING EFFECTIVE SOLID WASTE MANAGEMENT FOR INDIAN COUNTRY

America's frenetic consumerism is a solid waste juggernaut distinguishing the United States as the world's leader in municipal solid waste production. On average volume, every man, woman and child in this country generates over four pounds of solid waste each day, contributing to an annual waste stream that in 2003 was 236 million tons and is predicted to reach 262 million tons by the year 2010. Paper, paperboard, glass and plastics account for over half of the total municipal waste generated every year by weight, with the remaining balance made up of rubber, textiles, wood, aluminum, ferrous metals, and food and yard wastes.[1] Recent disposal trends show recycling and composting reduce the stream by twenty-four percent, incineration treats about fifteen percent, with the remaining sixty-one percent of municipal solid waste disposed of in landfills.

Unlike recycling, composting and incineration, landfill disposal is not designed as treatment but rather as permanent storage. Waste compaction, liquid extraction and installation of soil and synthetic covers minimize natural degradation of buried constituents. Anaerobic decomposition of organic waste and migration of liquid wastes occur nonetheless, generating combustible methane gas and hazardous leachate potentially threatening air and water quality. Small amounts of household hazardous wastes like paint thinners, pesticides and used batteries as well as industrial non-hazardous wastes can exacerbate risks of water contamination.

The significant public health and environmental risks associated with management of today's landfills pale in comparison to those presented before 1984 when large volumes of all manner of hazardous wastes were routinely deposited in landfills. Concern for those risks and the view that landfill disposal needlessly polluted the nation's valuable land resources contributed to enactment of the Resource Conservation and Recovery Act in 1976, which Congress amended in 1984 specifically banning land disposal of untreated hazardous wastes. The Act's formidable "cradle to grave" provisions governing the generation, treatment, storage and disposal of hazardous wastes—which EPA proposed directly implementing in *Washington Department of Ecology*—were intended to remove those more dangerous constituents from the municipal solid waste stream.

The Act's lesser-known program directed EPA establish minimum national performance standards necessary for ensuring that "no reasonable probability of adverse effects on health or the environment" results from solid waste disposal facilities or practices. States were left to translate the extensive federal requirements governing the construction, operation and closure of municipal solid waste landfills into locally administered permit programs. A new facility that did not comply with the federal standards was classified as an open dump and could not be permitted; permanent closure was required for existing open dumps.

Open Dumping in Indian Country

The predominantly rural nature of Indian country creates a solid waste conundrum. Indian and non-Indian residents are accustomed to local options for free uncontrolled disposal at illegal open dumps while sanitary facilities complying with federal landfill criteria are typically long distances from the Indian country households and businesses generating waste, charge high tipping fees for disposal, and regulate the kinds of waste allowed. Seventy-five percent of tribes responding to a 1986 EPA survey reported solid waste management as either a major problem or growing issue.[2] In 1994, Congress enacted the Indian Lands Open Dump Cleanup Act of 1994 directing the Indian Health Service inventory the estimated 600-plus open dumps in Indian country and propose plans for closing them.[3] The resulting study in 1998 indicated at least 1,100 open dumps being operated in violation of the Resource Conservation and Recovery Act.[4]

The situation in the 1980s at the Pine Ridge Reservation in southwestern South Dakota, home of the Oglala Sioux Tribe, typified the practical solid waste management dilemma posed by undeveloped rural Indian reservations. The reservation's approximately two million acres is relatively expansive by today's Indian country standards, though the Tribe's aboriginal territory was of course much larger. Oglala was one tribe of the Great Sioux Nation that historically claimed lands encompassing nearly the entire Midwest and which reserved much of western South Dakota including the Black Hills in the 1868 Treaty of Fort Laramie with the United States. The federal government's solemn promises for respecting the tribes' reduced homeland were almost immediately dashed as they were in Oklahoma and Arizona and so many other native places by the illegal discovery of valuable minerals. The 1889 General Allotment Act carved the Great Sioux Reservation into five smaller ones including the Pine Ridge Reservation, exposing the lush Black Hills to the environmental impacts of non-Indian gold miners, land developers and monument carvers.

One hundred years later none of the commercialism of western South Dakota had reached Pine Ridge when the issue of solid waste open dumping first drew attention to application of the Resource Conservation and Recovery Act to Indian country. The large scale of the reservation and its dearth of improved roadways made solid waste disposal for the approximately 12,000 residents a practical and financial challenge. The Indian Health Service and the Tribe, believing in all probability that the alternative of random dumping was worse, designated thirteen regional disposal sites across the reservation.

They were quite literally "open" dumps. About half of the sites consisted simply of waste piled on the ground, while the other sites featured a pit or ditch euphemistically termed a "sanitary trench" in which garbage was thrown. Waste was generally left exposed to the elements in both systems. A dirt cover to contain odors and blowing litter was infrequently applied so rain and snowmelt freely migrated through the piles, mixing wastes and carrying contaminants to the soil. No clay or plastic liner captured the liquids that would commingle to become contaminated leachate. Water samples from some sites detected contamination and potentially infectious organisms.

Only one of the sites was fenced and none of them were supervised or secured. Any person could enter at any time and dump any waste there. Children and roaming pets were known to play and scavenge at the dumps. Old lead batteries and used containers of oil, diesel fuel, pesticides, herbicides, paint and other caustic and toxic chemicals randomly joined diapers, paper, food scraps and general household and business trash. Fires had occurred at one time or another at each site.

Federal officials were well aware of the situation. Two health facilities operated by the Indian Health Service routinely burned waste at local dumps. Maintenance employees for the Bureau of Indian Affairs transported solid waste from three schools and a subdivision of government housing to several reservation dumps. Both federal agencies contracted for their other wastes to be hauled and disposed at various reservation dumps by a tribal garbage service.

With their government and the federal trustee unwilling to follow federal law, several Oglala citizens filed suit seeking permanent closure and cleanup of the dumps. A unique feature of many federal environmental laws is the so-called citizen suit provision that supplements the government's enforcement powers by creating private attorneys general. Private citizens affected by environmental law violations are authorized to sue violators directly if the government does not prosecute, and courts generally may order the same kinds of relief available in an EPA prosecution. The provisions typically specify that federal and state governmental bodies can be defendants.

Governmental accountability for environmental degradation is another key feature of American environmental law. The first modern environmental law, the National Environmental Policy Act of 1969, was directed entirely at the federal government. Congress recognized the government's central role in economic and other activity affecting natural environments and imposed on it a duty for analyzing the environmental impacts of proposed federal legislation and major federal actions significantly affecting the environment.[5]

The first reported Indian country environmental law case, decided in 1972 just before EPA's first Indian program action in the water context, applied the National Environmental Policy Act to a federal housing development project proposed in Indian country.[6] Federal propensities for environmental damage are particularly acute in Indian country where the federal government has historically played a major role in all manner of affairs. As a class, federal officials generally have the longest tenure of all non-Indians in Indian country.

So it was at Pine Ridge. The Oglala citizen suit argued the federal agencies' actions amounted to the "disposal of solid waste or hazardous waste which constitutes the open dumping of solid waste" in violation of the Resource Conservation and Recovery Act. The Eighth Circuit Court of Appeals agreed in *Blue Legs v. Bureau of Indian Affairs*,[7] disregarding the agencies' protestations they did not actively manage the tribal dumps. Nor did they get any credit for offering occasional "technical assistance" on solid waste management to the Tribe. The court found the agencies contributed to reservation open dumping by generating solid waste, contracting for its disposal, and in some cases transporting the waste to dumps operated in violation of federal law. Not only did those activities clearly violate the statute, they also breached the federal trust responsibility to the Tribe. The federal agencies could not simply contract away their fiduciary duties and remain indifferent to environmental injustice in Indian country. Neither the Bureau nor Health Service had regulatory responsibility per se for Indian country environmental management, but the court said the federal trust counseled against their direct and knowing contributions to illegal waste management. Tribal self-determination, represented by the Tribe's operation of the dumps, did not absolve the federal government of its duty to protect tribal health and welfare, especially where federal activities presented some of the risks.

That conclusion would seem equally true for EPA although it had no role in generating or disposing solid waste at Pine Ridge. Its 1984 Indian Policy clearly implied Agency responsibilities for discharging the federal trust obligation to protect tribal environments. Two years before *Blue Legs,* the *Washington Department of Ecology* court upheld EPA's direct implementation of the Resource Conservation and Recovery Act's hazardous waste program in Indian country in part on the federal trust responsibility and EPA's Indian policies.

The Oglala citizen suit originally named EPA as the lead defendant, but did not assert the trust responsibility or cite the Agency's policies. The South Dakota district court focused instead on the statute and regulations in dismissing the claim against EPA.[8] The Act's treatment of hazardous waste regulation was fundamentally different from solid waste management. EPA had extensive "cradle to grave" authority over the generation, treatment, storage and disposal of hazardous waste. In contrast, its primary role in the solid waste arena was setting criteria for local governments' management.

The district court did not account for EPA's extensive enforcement powers irrespective of local governments' management prerogatives. EPA could issue administrative orders or sue in federal court any person contributing to solid waste disposal activities presenting "an imminent and substantial endangerment" to health or the environment.[9] EPA also possessed specific authority to enforce the Act's open dumping prohibition where it determined the local government's plan inadequately ensured compliance with federal criteria for managing landfills potentially receiving household hazardous waste or hazardous waste small quantity generators.[10] While not landfill regulation per se, federal enforcement was surely competent to end the illegal open dumping.

Oddly enough, the district court suggested direct action by EPA over reservation dumps would be an "enforcement encroachment ... [in] violation of the inherent sovereignty of the Oglala Sioux Tribe." The premise that the Tribe's independent governmental authority extended over reservation environmental threats was entirely consistent with EPA's Indian policies and Congress' treatment-as-a-state provisions. The court's conclusion of federal infringement on tribal prerogatives was theoretically sound, but had been essentially rejected or severely constrained by the cooperative federalism model, as well as the reasoning in *Phillips Petroleum* and *Washington Department of Ecology* supporting direct federal implementation in Indian country. The court did not address those concerns, and because its dismissal of EPA was not appealed, neither did the Eighth Circuit.

A second aspect of environmental justice in *Blue Legs* was its treatment of tribal liability for environmental violations. The Tribe was not blameless. To the extent any of the dumps were managed at all, it was the Tribe who operated them. And, like the federal agencies, the Tribe generated solid wastes disposed at reservation dumps. The Oglala citizens originally sued only the federal agencies, but later joined the Tribe itself. This was the first time the question whether tribes were themselves bound by federal environmental law was put at issue. The 1984 Indian Policy principle promising compliance assistance to tribes before formal prosecution surely implied EPA's view tribes were subject to federal requirements just as other actors, but the issue had not arisen previously.

Federal Indian law recognizes tribes' inherent immunity from private suits unless they waive its protection similar to other governmental sovereigns, but also posits in Congress a unilateral power to waive tribal sovereign immunity independent of tribal wishes. The Resource Conservation and Recovery Act's citizen suit provision specifically listed federal and state instrumentalities among the "persons" potentially liable for violating the Act, but did not mention tribes. The Act's general definitions section, however, further defined persons by a list including municipalities, which were in turn defined as including Indian tribes.[11] The Eighth Circuit found the logical progression—tribes were municipalities, municipalities were persons, and persons were subject to citizen suits—amounted to a congressional waiver subjecting tribes to the prohibition against open dumping. The Tribe was thus liable for its active role in disposing of federal and tribal waste at the open dumps.

Indian country citizen suits thus offered another tool addressing the regulatory gaps creating environmental injustice. Even where federal programs were not being implemented and/or enforced, individual Indian citizens could sue non-Indians, states and federal entities to enforce the basic duties imposed by the environmental statutes. Tribes themselves were subject to the same duties, but as "persons" tribes were also entitled to bring citizen suits. Tribal citizen suits are sovereign exercises offering a measure of direct control over polluters of the Indian country environment for tribes lacking developed programs, and without putting tribal sovereignty at risk.[12]

The Last Indian Country Regulatory Gap

Many if not most tribes residing on rural reservations like Pine Ridge continue to struggle with open dumping. Indian and non-Indian reservation residents as well as non-Indians living near reservations have historically benefited from the convenience of close, unsupervised sites where all manner of waste can be dumped for free. Better alternatives rarely exist; state of the art municipal landfills are expensive to build and operate. Financial assistance from the Bureau of Indian Affairs and the Indian Health Service is limited and generally directed at planning or specific operations rather than facility construction. EPA has infrequently made available small financial grants typically under $50,000 for planning, program development, public education and the like. The solid waste program has never seen the kind of capital investment Congress appropriated in the early 1980s for building tribal water treatment works that made important strides in addressing injustices created by lack of potable running water.

Outside Indian country waste management is big business. Metropolitan areas burgeoning with American consumers and the businesses they require generate a constant stream of municipal solid waste. Fees are assessed on the generators for the costs of collection, transportation and disposal, presumably at landfills located some distance away. Land in the city is too scarce and therefore too valuable to be used for waste disposal. And, since no one wants a landfill in their backyard, political will is generally more influential with the larger city populations.

For a few tribes proximate to cities facing landfill shortages and/or expanding solid waste needs, constructing and operating a landfill offers the prospect of significant economic opportunity. Annual gross revenues for larger facilities serving major metropolitan areas can easily run into the tens of millions. Dozens of semi-skilled and non-skilled jobs accompany a modern landfill operation. And a reservation landfill meeting federal requirements and its associated infrastructure would provide an alternative to illegal dumping and could assist in the closure of existing open dumps.

The Campo Band of Mission Indians perceived these positive possibilities. The Campo Indian Reservation sits near the Mexico border in Southern California, about 70 miles east of San Diego. Its twenty-three-square mile size is small in comparison to Pine Ridge but huge by Yavapai-Apache standards. The land is arid and undeveloped, with few economic opportunities. Some of the scrublands are leased for small-scale cattle grazing. A minor sand mining operation serves local concrete needs. Unemployment on the reservation in the late 1980s was nearly eighty percent and the poverty rate was higher.

A 1987 San Diego county study predicting increasing waste volumes and decreasing regional disposal capacity helped spur the Band's interest in exploring development of a large-scale commercial municipal solid waste landfill. The Band's partnership with Mid-American Waste Systems, Inc., a national publicly traded company that operated nearly two dozen landfills in more than ten states, made the prospect realistic and thus sparked resistance from non-Indian neighbors, county officials and state representatives. Some commenters saw environmental injustice in their perception of industry targeting Indian country's desperate need for economic opportunity;[13] Dan McGovern's book THE CAMPO INDIAN LANDFILL WAR chronicled the disputes from the seemingly inverted environmental justice context of a tribe sponsoring potentially damaging economic development over the objections of a small non-Indian grassroots organization.

The Band focused on the environmental justice concern of filling Indian country's regulatory gap. It assembled a team of expert legal, financial and solid waste advisors and shrewdly negotiated with Mid-American for advance lease payments helping defray the costs of developing tribal legal and administrative infrastructure for regulating the construction and operation of the landfill. The contract and the Band's capacity building were based on the assumption the Campo environmental agency would seek from EPA a state-like role in permitting and regulating the Mid-American landfill, although no such role had yet been officially proposed.

As Campo was developing its program EPA had proposed new mandatory criteria for municipal waste landfills. The detailed requirements—on location, design, operation and closure—were self-executing in the sense that they applied directly to every landfill operator as written regardless of the status of any local government's permit program. Significant incentive existed for local program development, however, by provisions for local variance from the federal requirements, much like Congress' approval for alternative state oil and gas injection programs. A local government's permit program could vary from the federal requirements, say for example, by allowing a bottom liner constructed of compacted clay rather than more expensive plastic, so long as the alternative standard met EPA's performance expectations for health and environmental protection.

Congress required states develop landfill permit programs, but as with the other early environmental laws, said nothing specific about regulation of Indian country landfills. EPA viewed the congressional omission as falling short of authorizing state implementation for the fifth consecutive time. The Agency's standard fallback on direct federal implementation, which had succeeded for the underground injection program in *Phillips Petroleum* and for the hazardous waste program in *Washington Department of Ecology*, was not a good fit for the solid waste program. As *Blue Legs* noted, the Resource Conservation and Recovery Act's approach to solid waste management was distinct from the hazardous waste regulatory scheme in that EPA possessed no backup authority or obligation to operate municipal landfill permit programs where states fell short of achieving statutory or regulatory compliance. That structure was similar to the 1986 Emergency Planning and Community Right to Know Act that directed the establishment of state emergency response commissions but contained no parallel federal program authority in the event of a state's failure. EPA's solution for closing the Indian country gap there had been authorizing tribal emergency response commissions identical to states.[14]

Tribal implementation of the solid waste program was the natural, and final, option. Partnering with Indian tribes in a government-to-government fashion was the centerpiece of the Agency's 1984 Indian Policy. In the six years following the Policy, Congress had reauthorized four environmental laws and added tribal treatment-as-a-state provisions to each. To EPA, those actions surely sounded a ringing endorsement in spirit if not word. EPA Administrator William Reilly reaffirmed the 1984 Policy without qualification and urged further strengthening of tribal capacity for environmental management in 1991,[15] the same year the Agency finalized the revised landfill criteria.

No treatment-as-a-state provision has yet been added to the Resource Conservation and Recovery Act. Congress has not significantly revisited the Act since its 1984 amendments, coincidentally signed into law by President Reagan on the same day EPA Administrator William Ruckelshaus put his signature on the Indian Policy. During the 102nd Congress in 1991–92, Senators McCain, Inouye and others attempted to surmount that obstacle to Indian country environmental justice through a separate bill entitled the Indian Tribal Government Waste Management Act. Among other things, the bill envisioned a tribal state-like role for solid waste management in Indian country. Although the Senate Committee on Indian Affairs reported the bill out favorably, it died when the Committee on Environment and Public works objected it was an inappropriate way to amend the Resource Conservation and Recovery Act.

Congress' original silence on tribal roles in environmental regulation had not stopped EPA before. Of its first three Indian program actions in the 1970s—direct implementation of water pollution permit programs, tribal redesignation of air quality and tribal certification of pesticide applicators—two created new tribal management roles without congressional direction. Congress had almost immediately ratified those decisions, and *Nance* unequivocally deferred to EPA's judgment in resolving the ambiguity presented by Congress' silence in favor of tribes.

There was a seemingly minor but ultimately crucial difference between the 1970 Clean Air Act at issue in *Nance* and the 1984 Resource Conservation and Recovery Act controlling EPA's decision at Campo. The former was completely silent on Indians and Indian country; the latter was not. Its predecessor, passed in the same year as the early Clean Air Act, defined the term "municipality" by a list of entities that included Indian tribes.[16] Congress adopted the modern version of the Resource Conservation and Recovery Act in 1976, expanding the municipality definition to include "authorized tribal organizations" and Alaska native villages.[17]

No explanation appeared in the legislative history of either act for equating sovereign Indian tribes with state subdivisions. Nor did Congress explain why it repeated the tribe-as-municipality definition in the 1972 Clean Water Act[18] and the 1974 Safe Drinking Water Act.[19] Cooperative federalism posited important regulatory functions in state governments, not municipalities. Municipalities serve program goals only indirectly through environmental planning exercises, demonstration projects, and occasional consultations with the state or EPA on specific initiatives. For tribes, the most direct consequence of being labeled municipalities was making them eligible for federal grants related to regulated activities.

In several water program actions EPA consistently assumed Congress' target was tribal eligibility for federal financial assistance. That conclusion made more sense for an unexplained definitional reference than one inferring Congress intended thereby to limit tribes to planning functions in federal environmental programs. The *Blue Legs* court saw the Resource Conservation and Recovery Act's municipality definition as waiving Oglala's sovereign immunity from citizen suits as regulated actors, but having no effect on tribes' pre-existing inherent sovereignty over solid waste management. The *Washington Department of Ecology* court took note of the Agency's air and pesticides rules treating tribes as states in the absence of clear congressional authorization, and specifically declined to foreclose EPA from following that approach in promoting tribes' hazardous waste management functions notwithstanding the Act's municipality definition.

If the courts were correct, tribes remained well positioned to assist in accomplishing the Act's national objectives by assuming regulatory responsibilities for solid waste landfills and hazardous waste disposal facilities. Much had changed since EPA promulgated the air and pesticides rules in the mid 1970s, but nearly all of the administrative, legislative and judicial developments favored increased tribal roles. And as recently as 1990 EPA had administratively created another tribal program role—in the emergency-planning context—in the face of congressional silence. Some public comments on that proposal suggested tribal response commissions be considered local (that is, municipal) under the auspices of state commissions, which the Agency specifically rejected as contrary to federal Indian law and the 1984 Indian Policy.

In the fall of 1992, EPA made clear its decision to fill the Resource Conservation and Recovery Act's regulatory gap in Indian country by administratively creating tribal state-like roles. The Agency's semiannual regulatory agenda listed proposed rules for an Indian hazardous waste program and for a "State/Tribal" municipal solid waste landfill permit program.

States were part of the solid waste rule because unlike the hazardous waste program, no guidelines yet existed for approving state landfill programs. That gap was suddenly more pressing because the year before EPA had issued criteria all municipal solid waste landfills would have to meet by specified dates or cease operation. The requirements were extensive, expensive and effective without further action. They were also rigid; a landfill operator could avoid them only where a previously approved state program offered alternative means for protecting human health and the environment. But, since no guidelines for state program approval existed in 1991, the criteria offered no flexibility whatsoever.

With the Agency's Indian program gathering steam, the timing of developing state program rules was ripe for including Indian tribes. Several other contemporary events probably contributed to the Agency's decision to start down that road in 1992. The 102nd Congress closed that year without addressing the proposed Indian Tribal Government Waste Management Act and its tribal solid waste management role. Nor had Congress considered EPA's recommendation for adding a treatment-as-a-state provision to the Resource Conservation and Recovery Act Act. It did add a few specific provisions to the Act, including one waiving the government's sovereign immunity where federal facilities violated applicable requirements;[20] in contrast, the amendment made no reference to *Blue Legs'* holding that the Act's municipality definition implicitly waived tribal sovereign immunity for open dumping violations.

Blue Legs, which drew attention to the problems of open dumping in Indian country in 1989, must have been on EPA's mind when it began developing the tribal solid waste management role in 1992. And, no doubt, so was Campo. The Campo landfill was the largest commercial facility then being proposed in Indian country, and the most controversial. Non-Indian sentiment was running high in California, sparking several unsuccessful state legislative attempts in 1990 and 1991 to require reservation landfills obtain state licenses.[21] EPA became intimately familiar with the pending project in 1992 when it commented on the Bureau of Indian Affairs' environmental impact statement prepared under the National Environmental Policy Act because the landfill was proposed on tribal trust land.

It would be four years before a draft of the State/Tribal Implementation Rule for solid waste programs was proposed. In the meantime, states were clamoring for the flexibility not available under the 1991 criteria. The Agency began using the unpublished developing State/Tribal rule as non-binding "guidance" for addressing state program applications. By the time the rule was proposed in 1996, EPA had already approved forty state programs under its terms. The proposed rule's introduction all but admitted that its timing effectively limited the scope of the final rule; the proposal was designed to "minimize disruption of existing state/Tribal [sic] programs."

Only two tribal programs were at risk of disruption. The Cheyenne River Sioux Tribe in South Dakota developed the nation's first tribal solid waste permit program under the federal Act in 1993. Using the developing State/Tribal rule as guidance, EPA issued a tentative determination of its adequacy seven months later.[22] The Campo Band of Mission Indians submitted its program in early 1994, and EPA issued a tentative adequacy determination within three months.[23]

The Cheyenne River and Campo program applications offered the opportunity for EPA to preview its approach for treating tribes as states under the Resource Conservation and Recovery Act before proposing the State/Tribal Implementation Rule. The Agency requested Cheyenne River and Campo demonstrate they met threshold criteria borrowed from the other acts with explicit tribal state-like roles. EPA followed its approach in the Clean Water and Safe Drinking Water Acts requiring a showing of inherent jurisdiction over reservation landfills. EPA would not make the delegation argument under the Clean Air Act for another four years, and it surely made no sense here since Congress had not even authorized a tribal management role.

Also borrowed from the water acts was the process of showing jurisdiction over non-Indians on a case-by-case basis. The "interim operating principle" of the 1991 water quality standards rule, requiring a showing that non-Indian activities pose serious and substantial potential impacts on tribal health and welfare, was adopted. The "generalized findings" under the Clean Water Act were translated into solid waste terms. The statute itself reflected Congress' determination that improper waste disposal threatened public health and welfare interests. Protecting those interests is a core governmental function critical to self-government. While solid waste generally does not move readily, leachate from improper disposal can contaminate groundwater that is highly mobile, making separation of Indian and non-Indian impacts difficult and increasing the chance of tribal exposure to non-Indian contamination. As in the water context, these "generalized findings" would supplement the jurisdictional analysis such that a tribe needed only to assert that non-Indian solid waste disposal activities presented serious and substantial risks to tribal health and welfare.

The jurisdictional requirement appeared first in the Cheyenne River tentative determination, which made sense because non-Indians own almost half of the Tribe's reservation in fee simple. Some 300 miles down the Missouri River, the Yankton Sioux Tribe was at that moment beginning a major legal battle for jurisdiction over a landfill proposed by four counties on fee land within the reservation. The Campo reservation, however, is entirely trust land. So it seemed odd that EPA repeated the jurisdictional requirement in the Campo tentative determination, since by its own terms, the *Montana* test applied only to non-Indian fee land. The Rehnquist Supreme Court would eventually decouple non-Indians from their fee lands, applying the *Montana* test to non-Indians on trust lands, but not until 2001.[24] Regulation of Mid-American's proposed landfill at Campo was thus presumptively within the Band's inherent sovereignty, just as the Crow Tribe's sovereignty included regulation of non-Indian sportsmen on trust lands in *Montana*.

Public comments on EPA's tentative adequacy determination of the Campo program made no mention of the non-Indian jurisdiction issue.[25] Like so many public processes addressing tribal environmental regulation, though, nearly everything else was fair game. Many comments had no legal relevance to the decision at hand—whether the Tribe's regulatory program adequately assured compliance with the federal landfill criteria. Objections over possible impacts of the future Mid-American landfill were premature, and EPA had no direct authority over local permits for particular landfills at any rate. The complaint that the Tribe's program contained no mitigation measures to be taken in the event the aquifer became contaminated was similarly misplaced.

Some comments, ostensibly directed at the Tribe's institutional capacity, demonstrated society's general Indian law illiteracy, at times reflecting the ethnocentric if not racist views too often heard in these contexts. One commenter asked what gave the Tribe the right to form its own environmental agency, and how tribal citizens could still be California residents if they were above state law. Another suggested that importing non-Indian trash to the reservation could "hardly be viewed as self-government." Some commenters apparently perceived the Tribe's proposal as payback for all that had been done to Indians in the past. Still others said the Tribe's inexperience in landfill management meant its regulation would be less than effective.

Noting the Tribe would receive revenue from the landfill's operation, a number of commenters expressed concern over the inherent conflict of interest. One characterized the Tribe's program as "the fox guarding the chicken house." Others brashly attacked the integrity of tribal officials, asserting they had or would accept "gifts" or payments to favor the landfill operator over environmental protection.

EPA addressed the conflict of interest issues in some detail, but only after noting that neither the Act nor the draft rule required such consideration incident to the program approval process. EPA noted the not uncommon situation where one state agency owns and operates a landfill regulated by a sister state agency. The Campo landfill would be operated by Mid-American, a non-Indian company, and Muht-Hei, a tribal business concern separate from the Campo environmental agency responsible for regulating the landfill. Tribal environmental regulations and the Tribe's Environmental Policy Act both contained restrictions on agency officials and judges having financial interests in regulated entities. As to the suggestion the Tribe's program would not be particularly rigorous, EPA observed that in several key respects the Tribe's standards were more stringent than the State's program and the federal criteria.

Comments more directly on target questioned EPA's authority for treating Indian tribes as states under the Act. Not surprisingly, the Agency drew an analogy to *Nance*, which upheld the 1974 tribal air quality redesignation role, giving "great weight" to EPA's interpretation of the silent Clean Air Act. Judicial deference to reasonable agency interpretations of ambiguous statutes was the central holding of *Chevron*,[26] a seminal administrative law case decided three years after *Nance*. EPA explicitly claimed entitlement to *Chevron* deference for resolving the Resource Conservation and Recovery Act's ambiguity in favor of tribes.

An ambiguity existed, EPA asserted, because Congress had not authorized state implementation in Indian country and had not specified a tribal solid waste management role. The Supreme Court had recently rejected California's attempt to regulate Indian gaming, holding once again that state civil regulatory laws do not apply to Indian reservations absent congressional authorization.[27] That decision supported *Washington Department of Ecology's* conclusion that EPA reasonably interpreted the Act as not authorizing state implementation of the hazardous waste program.

As for tribal roles, EPA viewed the tribe-as-municipality definition as fostering rather than clarifying the Act's opacity. Tribes were obviously not "public bodies created pursuant to state law." No other reference to tribes appeared in the Act, and nothing in the legislative record hinted at Congress' intent. Municipalities were entitled to federal financial and technical assistance for solid waste management planning, so EPA concluded Congress' inclusion of tribes was a "definitional expedient" making such assistance available to tribes without having to add the phrase "and Indian tribes or tribal organizations or Alaska Native villages or organizations" wherever the term municipality appeared. It made no sense to EPA that Congress would abrogate tribes' sovereign authority over the Indian country environment through an unexplained definition.

Other considerations buttressed that conclusion. The national policy of tribal self-determination took form in this context through the 1984 Indian Policy recognizing tribes' primary responsibility for environmental management in Indian country. A key Policy goal was the elimination of legal and other barriers to tribal program assumption. EPA's limited role in solid waste management meant direct federal implementation was not an option to fill the Indian country regulatory gap. And, as EPA noted in creating flexibility in the federal underground injection program context years before, it seemed unfair that Indian county landfill operators would not have the same opportunity as their off-reservation counterparts for variance from the federal criteria.

EPA issued its final determination of adequacy for the Campo program in 1995, and was promptly sued by a non-Indian whose land was less than one mile from the proposed landfill site, and the small grassroots group she organized. Undeterred, EPA proposed its State/Tribal Implementation Rule in January 1996 while the case was pending.[28] The rule's approach, requirements and rationale tracked the Campo and Cheyenne River determinations nearly exactly. Six months later, EPA followed those general contours again in a proposed rule for Indian hazardous waste programs under the Act.[29]

That fall, the D.C. Circuit Court of Appeals sided with the opponents of the Campo landfill, effectively ending any administrative treatment of tribes as states under the Act until Congress amends it. In *Backcountry Against Dumps v. Environmental Protection Agency*,[30] the court held that *Chevron* deference, upon which administrative law cases so often turn, was not available to EPA here. Congress' intent, the court said, was perfectly clear: states were required by the Act to submit solid waste management plans to EPA for approval, and tribes were municipalities not states.

> In approving the Campo Band's plan, the EPA essentially removed Indian tribes from their statutory status as "municipalities," creating a new, intermediate status for Indian tribes..., a status equivalent to that of a state. Not only does the agency's interpretation ... conflict with the plain language of [the Resource Conservation and Recovery Act's] definitional provisions, but it also rewrites [the permitting provision] itself. According to the agency, the formerly clear permitting provision now reads: "States must, and Indian tribes may, but other local governments may not" adopt permit programs and submit them to the agency for review and approval. This is not what the statute says.[31]

That analysis seemed straightforward, but it glossed over the distinction between a congressional mandate and agency discretion. Congress' mandate that states develop waste management plans did not necessarily foreclose the possibility of other plans, especially since state plans did not apply in Indian country. For example, courts generally do not interpret Congress' directive that an agency make rules on a particular topic as precluding rules on other topics. Similarly, a congressional list of factors guiding particular administrative decisions is not typically understood as forbidding consideration of other relevant concerns. It would not have been inconsistent with those common administrative law decisions to conclude EPA could accept tribal solid waste management plans.

The court's suspicion that EPA would not allow plans from "other local governments" indirectly addressed this issue. But it did not observe that tribes are the only other "local" government like states in the federalist system. The Act's distinction between state landfill permit programs and municipalities' solid waste management planning activities made clear that local in this sense did not include state subdivisions. Of course that was why Congress' decision to label tribes as municipalities was so troubling.

The municipality label also distinguished the 1970 Clean Air Act, which was completely silent on the question, and *Nance*, which upheld EPA's administratively created tribal air redesignation role. EPA's case would have been stronger had the Resource Conservation and Recovery Act said nothing about tribes. The real problem for EPA, once again, was timing. In 1981, when *Nance* was decided, Congress had not yet begun referring to tribes as states. By 1996, when the *Backcountry Against Dumps* decision was issued, four environmental statutes contained specific treatment-as-a-state provisions, so the court could not help but observe that when Congress wishes to treat Indian tribes as states "it does so in clear and precise language."

The explanation that Congress just had not yet gotten around to amending the outdated municipality definition could not save EPA or the Campo Band. Concerns over the perceived unfairness of the statute's different treatment of tribes were properly addressed to Congress. EPA's prediction for a regulatory gap creating the specter of reservations as "safe havens for all manner of illegal dumping" also did not frighten the court. The Act's citizen suit provisions and EPA's enforcement powers helped ensure compliance with the self-executing landfill criteria.

What's more, the court specifically commented its decision did not "strip the tribe of its sovereign authority to govern its own affairs." The Tribe's environmental agency and court and its regulations remained in force and carried as much legal effect as they had before the case. The court perceived the only loss to the Tribe was its ability to vary the federal landfill criteria for reservation operators. And that loss was mitigated somewhat by EPA's offer during oral argument to accept from the Tribe a request for a "site-specific" regulation providing some of the flexibility lost by the disapproval of the Tribe's program.

The Campo Band has not yet sought a specific variance. As the case was developing, Mid-American missed the contact deadlines for beginning construction of the landfill. Anticipating a national landfill shortage, the Company had accumulated over $600 million of debt in acquiring disposal capacity in addition to Campo and was in severe financial distress. The Tribe terminated the lease but did not immediately seek another partner because of uncertainties in the California waste market. In 2001, the Tribe's General Council reaffirmed its commitment to the landfill project, and secured a new business partner, BLT Enterprises, for construction and operation of the landfill. The Bureau of Indian Affairs began in 2005 preparing a supplemental environmental impact statement for new or changed information, which is expected to be completed in 2007 and to set off a new wave of contention.

Backcountry Against Dumps was the most significant setback EPA's Indian program had encountered in two-plus decades. Though occasioned by one tribe's program in Southern California, the D.C. Circuit's conclusion Congress provided no state-like solid waste management role for tribes directly indicted the premise of EPA's proposed Tribal Implementation Rule. It also threw cold water on the similarly justified Indian hazardous waste program. Those programs—the only major regulatory schemes lacking formal tribal implementation roles—represented the last structural breaks in the circle of Indian country environmental protection. Ironically, EPA's proposals for closing the circle consistent with the complimentary policies of tribal self-determination and cooperative federalism failed precisely because of the Agency's success in securing tribal roles in other environmental programs.

A Different Attack on the Indian Program

Back in South Dakota, another important loss for tribes and Indian country environmental justice was developing, again in the context of landfill regulation. It was not at Cheyenne River, whose tentative program approval received no further attention from EPA once *Backcountry Against Dumps* invalidated the Campo program. The case arose on the Yankton Sioux Indian Reservation in southeastern South Dakota, and this time the environmental justice issues seemed more obvious than those at Campo; non-Indians were proposing a large commercial landfill within the reservation over the Tribe's objection.

When Meriwether Lewis and William Clark pushed their boats up the Missouri River into Sioux territory in 1804, the Yankton Tribe controlled some thirteen million acres in central South Dakota.[32] Between 1815 and 1858 the United States negotiated six treaties with the Tribe,[33] the last one reducing the Tribe's lands to a reservation of just over 400,000 acres, where about 2,000 Yanktons settled. The Treaty promised that "no white person" would ever be allowed to reside on the reservation, but just over twenty years later the government was back seeking Yankton land for non-Indian settlers.

By that time Congress had put an end to treaty making with Indian tribes, so the government sent agents to negotiate an "agreement" with the Tribe that Congress would later ratify into law. An 1892 agreement and an 1894 federal act provided for the sale of just under half of Yankton land soon settled by non-Indians. Other reservation lands were allotted to individual Yankton citizens, but over time much of that land also found its way into non-Indian ownership. Today, the Tribe and individual tribal citizens own less than ten percent of the reservation. Approximately seventy-five percent of the population within the 1858 Treaty boundaries is non-Indian.

Several municipalities incorporated after South Dakota was admitted to the Union in 1889 are located within the reservation, and the boundaries of Charles Mix County nearly parallel those of the reservation. Charles Mix and three adjacent counties—Gregory, Douglas, and Bon Homme—faced a 1995 deadline for closing their non-complying town dumps. In 1992, they formed the Southern Missouri Recycling and Waste Management District to construct and operate a replacement landfill serving their approximately 25,000 residents.

The District selected a site in Charles Mix County. Sitting in the middle of a semi-circle formed by the other counties, Charles Mix seemed a practical location from the perspective of accessibility. Perhaps it was only coincidence, but the site also fell within the exterior boundaries of the Yankton reservation, on land owned by a non-Indian.

The District purchased the property and sought a permit for landfill construction and operation from the State rather than the Tribe. At the time, neither the State nor the Tribe had a solid waste program approved as adequate by EPA. Congress' definition of Indian country, which explicitly included non-Indian fee lands within reservations, surely implied the landfill site was outside the State's jurisdiction. In 1993, EPA effectively came to that conclusion in approving the State's landfill permit program except for Indian country, finding the State's assertions of authority short of showing jurisdiction there.[34]

The State immediately narrowed its original request for program authority from all lands on the State's nine reservations to certain non-Indian lands on three reservations. The State cited two Supreme Court decisions finding turn-of-the-century sales of surplus Indian lands made pursuant to Congress' allotment policies "disestablished" the Lake Traverse Reservation in the northeastern corner of the State[35] and partially diminished the south-central Rosebud Indian Reservation.[36] Similar surplus land sales took place at Yankton in the 1890s, and four South Dakota Supreme Court cases held or implied they diminished the Yankton reservation.[37] Lands owned by non-Indians in diminished or disestablished reservation areas are not Indian country unless they constitute dependent Indian communities. A 1980 Eighth Circuit case held that one town on the Yankton reservation was not a dependent Indian community.[38] South Dakota's amended program sought landfill authority over the surplus lands on the Lake Traverse, Rosebud and Yankton reservations.

After submitting its new request, the State continued processing the District's request for the Yankton landfill permit as if EPA's disapproval had never occurred. The State's Department of Environment and Natural Resources recommended permit approval to the State's Board of Minerals and Environment, which held a lengthy administrative hearing two months after EPA denied the State's authority at Yankton. The Tribe intervened in the hearing, cross-examining the District's witnesses and offering the testimony of two experts in rebuttal.

The Tribe's experts raised six specific concerns on the landfill's location and design. The site was located above major aquifers, which exhibited potential for "mounding" or localized rising that could shorten the distance between the landfill waste and the water table. The Tribe argued the District had not performed adequate test drilling to assess the risk of groundwater contamination from escaping leachate. Geologic features like fissures and sand and gravel "lenses" beneath the site could facilitate leachate migration, and that risk was compounded by an allegedly inadequate leachate collection system. The Tribe's central concern was over the efficacy of the landfill's proposed bottom liner of clay.

The federal landfill criteria required installation of a composite liner—a flexible synthetic (plastic) membrane at least 30 milliliters thick over a minimum of two feet of compacted soil material—unless an approved state program allowed an alternative liner meeting EPA's performance standard for very low hydraulic conductivity. The State's proposed program allowed an alternative liner of compacted clay, but EPA had rejected the program as it applied to the Yankton reservation. The Board of Minerals and Environment applied the State's alternative liner requirement nonetheless, concluding it prevented any significant risk of groundwater contamination.

The Tribe sued on this patent violation of federal law. EPA had tentatively approved the State's amended program for non-Indian lands on the State's assertion the reservation had been disestablished,[39] but had not made a final decision. Nor had a decision been made on the Tribe's competing program application, which had been submitted by this time. In the absence of an approved local program, the Agency's position was that federal regulations required the landfill be constructed with a composite liner. The South Dakota federal district court agreed, noting one of the Tribe's experts testified a composite liner would alleviate his concerns of groundwater contamination, and the District had offered to install one during trial.[40]

The court rejected two arguments that would have preempted EPA's decision on which local program applied to the landfill site. The Tribe claimed its inherent sovereignty over the site under *Montana*. Although the Tribe's experts testified at length about the landfill's possible health and welfare risks, which were entirely consistent with EPA's generalized findings in the Cheyenne River and Campo adequacy determinations, the court somehow missed the connection completely. It literally disposed of the argument in two sentences, saying the Tribe's evidence consisted only of the testimony of the Tribal Chairmen, who inexplicably commented the Tribe desired regulatory authority only over Indians.

For its part, the State iterated the disestablishment and diminishment arguments it made in the amended program application. The district court's detailed consideration of those issues consumed the bulk of its opinion. The century-old evidence was conflicting and confusing, as it typically is for these sorts of claims, so the court fell back on the longstanding and oft-repeated Supreme Court adjuration that "doubtful expressions" are to be resolved in favor of the tribe.[41] The district court concluded Congress had not terminated or reduced the reservation, so the landfill site remained within Indian country. EPA later rejected the State's program application for Yankton on that ground.[42]

The State was undaunted. South Dakota, like Oklahoma, is well known for its strategic and tenacious attacks on tribal sovereignty. It appealed the district court's more vulnerable decision the landfill was in Indian country. The Supreme Court's diminishment jurisprudence is notoriously subjective, and lower courts receive no deference from appellate courts on questions of law, offering the State a third opportunity to argue the same issues. The federal landfill criteria, on the other hand, were quite clear and EPA's position on their application at Yankton entitled to judicial respect. Thus, the State did not appeal the court's composite liner order, even though it no longer wished to honor the installation offer it made at trial.

The State made an end run instead. An EPA regulation allowed an unapproved state to petition for a facility-specific waiver of the composite liner requirement. The option of a similar site-specific regulation altering the federal criteria for the Campo landfill in California was mentioned in oral argument in the *Backcountry Against Dumps* case in early September 1996. Two weeks later, South Dakota's Chief Deputy Attorney General and officials from the Southern Missouri Waste District met in Washington D.C. with EPA's Administrator, Carol Browner, to request she waive the composite liner requirement for the Yankton landfill.

The meeting was arranged by the State's congressional delegation, which attended the meeting and expressed great interest in resolving the issue promptly. The delegates—Representative Tim Johnson, Senator Larry Pressler and Senator Tom Daschle—made clear their support for the waiver at the meeting or in later correspondence. Daschle all but threatened to address the matter legislatively if EPA did not resolve it satisfactorily. Emboldened by the political pushback, the State's attorney went beyond the waiver issue and urged Browner delegate program authority over non-Indian reservation lands to the State since the district court held the Tribe lacked jurisdiction over those lands. Browner walked the political tightrope, professing the Agency's interest in finding a flexible, reasonable solution while acting consistent with applicable regulations. She could not delegate programs to states absent a showing of jurisdiction and needed to determine if EPA could accept a liner waiver request from the Waste District itself.

Back home on the plains, District officials asked the State's Department of Environment and Natural Resources to submit a waiver request on the District's behalf. Although EPA's regional solid waste office had communicated its desire that the request come from the District directly, the State submitted the waiver petition. William Yellowtail, the Agency's first Indian Regional Administrator, returned the request because the State "does not currently have program authority over the Yankton lands." The Department's Secretary, Nettie Meyers, wrote to Yellowtail expressing "great disappointment" that EPA continued to honor "a flawed, outdated Indian jurisdiction policy" to the financial detriment of the District.

The District got its waiver nonetheless, though it had to wait nine months. EPA borrowed the disputed lands approach from the underground injection and air programs, "augmenting" its liner petition process for landfills in Indian country where neither the state nor tribe had approved programs. The landfill operator rather than the state (or tribe) would petition for the waiver, and EPA rather than the state (or tribe) would analyze whether the alternative liner met the applicable performance standard. Here, the District offered to build a three rather than two foot compacted clay liner, and EPA found the groundwater at the site to be of fairly poor quality. EPA ultimately issued the waiver but placed additional construction and monitoring conditions on the District.

When the Tribe first learned EPA was leaning toward a waiver, it objected the Agency was bowing to political pressure. Once the decision allowing the clay liner was finalized, the Tribe sued EPA in the same federal district court that ordered installation of a composite liner a year earlier. Citing the recent *Backcountry Against Dumps* decision, the Tribe argued the waiver regulation was just as clear as the Act's language on state waste management programs: petitions for waivers of liner requirements were authorized from states, not landfill operators. The court misunderstood the analogy, saying *Backcountry Against Dumps* was distinguishable since the Yankton Tribe's authority was not at issue, but it agreed with the Tribe that the regulation did not authorize EPA's acceptance of the District's petition.[43]

On the other hand, the existence of the liner waiver regulation was a testament to the Resource Conservation and Recovery Act's delegation to EPA of broad rulemaking authority for accomplishing the Act's purposes. The court accepted EPA's authority to promulgate the Yankton waiver as a site-specific regulation toward that end, which was probably proper. The court's conclusion that EPA followed proper procedures in doing so, however, was suspect.

The federal Administrative Procedures Act generally requires a proposed legislative rule be announced in the nationally circulated Federal Register, subjected to public comment from interested persons, and finalized with an explanation of the rule's basis and purpose.[44] The Agency did give public notice, take comments and explain its approval of the District's waiver request, but the notice was published in local South Dakota newspapers rather than the Federal Register, and more importantly, sought comment on the specifics of the request, not the threshold question of amending the waiver regulation to allow petitions from operators. EPA's decision to "augment" the liner petition regulation for disputed Indian country lands, made via an internal memorandum that was not published or subjected to public comment, had national implications beyond the Yankton landfill. No opportunity was offered for interested persons outside the region—for example, the residents opposed to the Campo landfill—to comment.

The court's analysis entirely missed these administrative law violations. It upheld the Agency's waiver, handing the State its first win in the expanding legal battle. Two months earlier the had State lost its appeal of the district court's decision that the landfill was in Indian country. The Eighth Circuit Court of Appeals agreed that Congress' turn-of-the-century sales of Yankton land did not evince a clear congressional intent that the reservation be diminished: the landfill site was in Indian country, and the State therefore had no regulatory authority over it.[45]

The U.S. Supreme Court was the State's last chance, but it was also the best one. The Court's 1994 decision in *Hagen v. Utah*[46] signaled a retreat from foundation Indian law principles favoring tribes in the specific context of reservation diminishment. The Court proclaimed it "will not lightly find diminishment," but distanced itself from earlier statements that Congress must "clearly evince" such intent. *Hagen* also recited the longstanding canon of construction resolving ambiguities in favor of tribes, but found no ambiguity in a 1905 allotment act opening the Ute Indian Tribe's reservation lands to non-Indians. The act's silence on a particularly salient point was rendered clear, according to the Court, by a single phrase included in an earlier version of the law that Congress never enacted.

In 1996, the same year the Eighth Circuit held the Yankton reservation had not been diminished, well-known Indian law scholar David Getches criticized the Supreme Court's increasing "subjectivism" in Indian law cases, which he argued focused more on discerning "what the current state of affairs ought to be" than applying the foundation principles.[47] Professor Getches noted *Hagen*, which cited but did not apply the canons of construction, as one of the most recent examples of the Court's unprincipled departure.

Getches' article was clearly intended as an indictment of the Rehnquist Court's perceived activism in dismantling tribal sovereignty, but it incidentally supported South Dakota's continued hope for success. The demographic data at Yankton was incomplete and disputed, but the clear majority of reservation residents were non-Indians, who owned an overwhelming majority of the land. In both prongs of its attack on tribal regulation of non-Indians—diminishing the extent of Indian country and narrowing the scope of *Montana's* health and welfare test—the Supreme Court had pointedly hinted at its desired state of affairs in such situations.

Hagen took note of demographic statistics showing eighty-five percent of the population in the affected area was non-Indian, saying "when an area is predominantly populated by non-Indians with only a few surviving pockets of Indian allotments, finding that the land remains Indian country seriously burdens the administration of state and local governments." The opinions of six Justices in *Brendale* showed the Court's disaffection for claims of tribal sovereignty over reservation areas populated by large numbers of non-Indians, or in the words of Justice Stevens, areas perceived as having lost their "Indian character."

Both *Hagen* and *Brendale* had drawn sharp dissents from Justice Blackmun. In *Hagen*, joined by Justice Souter, he quoted Justice Black's famous statement "[g]reat nations, like great men, should keep their word"[48] in reminding the Court it should not lightly find Congress had broken its solemn promise to the Ute Tribe. He questioned the value of subsequent demographic data and argued previous cases rejected it where compelling evidence of congressional intent to diminish was lacking. In *Brendale*, joined by Justices Brennan and Marshall, Blackmun berated the "stereotyped and almost patronizing view of Indians and reservation life" suggested by Justice Stevens' Indian character reference.

During the 1970s and early 1980s, Brennan, Marshall and Blackmun had formed the core of the Court that respected and protected tribal sovereignty. Brennan and Marshall retired in the early 1990s before *Hagen,* and Blackmun retired at the end of that term. Justice Souter, who joined Blackmun's dissent in *Hagen,* remained. But that same year he joined the majority in a case finding state interests in tax collection justified exercising jurisdiction over Indian-owned on-reservation smokeshops.[49] The Court's changes could only have encouraged South Dakota.

The State sought Supreme Court review of the Eighth Circuit's decision that Congress had not diminished the Yankton reservation in April 1997. Its petition for a writ of certiorari highlighted the conflict between the Eighth Circuit's decision and several South Dakota Supreme Court cases holding or implying diminishment of the Yankton reservation. *Hagen* had granted certiorari to resolve a similar conflict between the Tenth Circuit and the Utah Supreme

Court on the status of the Ute reservation, and the Court granted certiorari in the Yankton case for the same reason.

South Dakota had nothing to lose and something to gain, and its gamble paid off. *South Dakota v. Yankton Sioux Tribe,*[50] like *Hagen,* echoed the state courts' conclusion. Congress had diminished the reservation by the sale of the Tribe's so-called surplus lands in the 1890s. As a result, the Waste District's landfill was not in Indian country, and the State possessed regulatory authority over it no differently than any other landfill covered by the State' approved program. With Brennan, Marshall and Blackmun in retirement, the decision went against the Tribe on a unanimous vote.

The crux of the case—indeed, of the diminishment doctrine itself—was reflected in the two-paragraph introductory recitation of diminishment "rules" derived from applicable precedents. Justice O'Connor wrote for the Court, as she had in *Hagen.* She noted Congress' broad power over Indian affairs included authority to alter established reservation boundaries unilaterally, even in violation of previous treaties requiring tribal consent. Because of the federal government's trust responsibility, the Court would not lightly find diminishment; Congress' intent must be "clear and plain," because ambiguities would be resolved in favor of the Tribe. O'Connor said the "touchstone" judicial inquiry was congressional purpose.

The problem was that Congress' purpose during the allotment era had little or nothing to do with changing the jurisdictional contours of Indian country. Its primary and immediate objective was converting communally owned tribal property into private property. Allotting parcels of tribal land to individual Indian men, it was believed, would help Indians break free of their prior savage and primitive ways.[51] As a Senate report concerning allotment of the Yankton reservation noted, the road to civilization for those unfortunate souls would be facilitated by "bringing them in close contact with the frugal, moral, and industrious [non-Indian] people" who would settle nearby.[52] Non-Indian settlement of reservations was expected to increase through purchases of tribal lands designated as "surplus" or otherwise no longer "needed" by the Tribe once all individual tribal citizens received their private allotments. In only a handful of instances did Congress specifically say as a result of allotment a particular reservation was "discontinued," "vacated" or "abolished;" more often Congress manifested an "almost complete lack of ... concern with the boundary issue."[53]

Given the Court's apparent willingness to ascribe a diminishment motive to Congress, such a lack of concern seems odd. The explanation, as O'Connor noted in both *Hagen* and *Yankton Sioux Tribe,* was two-fold. First, today's common understanding that Indian country includes non-Indian lands was unknown at the turn of the century. Pre-allotment, Indian country consisted almost entirely of tribally owned land. It was not until 1948 that Congress defined Indian country as including fee patented lands and rights of way within reservations.

> Another reason why Congress did not concern itself with the effect of surplus land acts on reservation boundaries was the turn-of-the-century assumption that Indian reservations were a thing of the past. Consistent with prevailing wisdom, members of Congress voting on the surplus land acts believed to a man that within a short time— within a generation at most—the Indian tribes would enter traditional American society and the reservation system would cease to exist. Given this expectation, Congress naturally failed to be meticulous in clarifying whether a particular piece of legislation formally sliced a certain parcel of land off one reservation.[54]

One hundred years later, tribes still existed as semi-autonomous sovereigns, clinging steadfastly to their homelands, and the federal government had rejected the ethnocentric policy of assimilation, replacing it with a somewhat more enlightened vision of tribal self-determination. But in diminishment cases the Court gives effect to Congress' intent at the time the laws that opened Indian country to non-Indian ownership were enacted, and does not, Justice O'Connor added gratuitously, "remake history" in light of hindsight.

The problem still remained: by definition, Congress generally had no specific diminishment intention during the allotment era. Blackmun's dissent in *Hagen* noted the allotment acts presented the Court with questions "their architects could not have foreseen." Faithful adherence to the canon of favoring tribes where intent was unclear thus implied the majority of diminishment cases would fail. Yet, over half succeeded.

So it was at Yankton. The Court said the most probative evidence was the statutory language Congress used. The 1894 act adopted most of the terms of an 1892 agreement wherein the Tribe agreed to "cede, sell, relinquish, and convey to the United States all their claim, right, title, and interest in and to all of the unallotted lands within the limits of the reservation." That language was copied from the 1891 act the Court found disestablished the Sisseton-Wahpeton Tribe's Lake Traverse Reservation. O'Conner cited that case, saying the language was "precisely suited" to terminating reservation status because it reflected "a complete and total surrender" of the tribes' interests in the unallotted lands.

The literal translation of the double four-part refrain masked two troubling issues the Court did not confront directly. One was the pure legal question of the impact of the Tribe selling its "claim, right, title, and interest" in the unallotted lands. At its core, the case was a fight over tribal versus state regulation of the landfill. The Court's conclusion necessarily implied one of the "interests" the Tribe sold was its governmental authority over lands that, at least up to the moment of the sale, were indisputably part of the Tribe's territory. That simply did not square with O'Connor's oblique comment that congressmen of the time did not consider whether lands opened to non-Indian ownership might maintain a reservation status and thus be subject to tribal sovereignty.

Nor did it accord with the common usage then and now of the "claim, right, title, and interest" phrase to denote private property ownership and not governmental power. The phrase appears in literally hundreds of cases involving private property conveyances and transactions like sales, leases, divorce settlements, and lawsuits. A South Dakota case decided in the same year as the Yankton allotment act used the phrase to describe a company's transfer of a mechanic's lien arising from labor and materials used in improving a building to another business.[55] Indian diminishment cases are the only ones where a government's transfer of property interests, a fairly common occurrence, eviscerates its governmental power.

The second troubling aspect of the Court's conclusion the Tribe completely surrendered its governmental interests through a land sale was its abject heartlessness. The land deal was not a sale; it was armed robbery. Federal negotiators appeared on the reservation in the fall of 1982, announcing the "Great Father" wanted more land, again. Opposition was immediate and drew out the talks for two months. As winter closed in on the South Dakota prairie, Commissioner John J. Cole grew weary of the wind and the objections. He threatened to break the 1858 Treaty promises of food, clothing and other resources, leaving the Tribe to starve in the harsh plains winter unless the tribal representatives agreed to the sale.

> I want you to understand that you are absolutely dependent upon the Great Father to-day [sic] for a living. Let the Government send out instructions to your agent to cease to issue these rations, let the Government instruct your agent to cease to issue your clothes.... Let the Government instruct him to cease to issue your supplies, let him take away the money to run your schools with, and I want to know what you would do. Everything you are wearing and eating is gratuity. Take all this away and throw this people wholly upon their own responsibility to take care of themselves, and what would be the result? *Not*

one-fourth of your people could live through the winter, and when the grass grows again it would be nourished by the dust of all the balance of your noble tribe.[56]

Cole's extortion was not redeemed by the fact the United States paid cash for the land taken. The fair market value was at least $1.3 million; the government paid $600,000. Eighty years later the federal court of claims called that price "unconscionable and grossly inadequate," and awarded the Tribe the difference plus interest,[57] but ordered no apology or return of lands from the federal government.

Any credit the *Yankton* Court deserved for admitting these troubling facts was vacated by the manner in which they were treated. The Court said the lump sum payment, in conjunction with the language of cession, raised "an almost insurmountable presumption of diminishment." That the payment was unconscionable and grossly inadequate apparently had no legal relevance; the court of claims' embarrassing finding was reported matter-of-factly in a footnote. Cole's bare knuckle negotiating strategy, which the Court unapologetically quoted extensively, merely reflected the federal negotiators' "tendency to wield the [Treaty] payments as an inducement to sign the agreement."

That "inducement," according to the Court, explained the Act's unique savings clause that expressly preserved the "full force and effect" of the 1858 Treaty. It was not, as the Tribe and the United States argued, intended to preserve the reservation boundaries established by the Treaty. The "most plausible interpretation" of the clause, given Cole's death threat, was to ensure the Tribe's continued receipt of government food rations and clothing. Other plausible interpretations, like saving the Treaty-established reservation boundaries, apparently created no ambiguity since the Court made no reference to resolving them in favor of the Yankton Sioux.

Beyond the statutory language O'Connor found most probative, the historical context and subsequent treatment and settlement of the area also supported diminishment. Again, Commissioner Cole's gift for language came in handy:

> This reservation alone proclaims the old time and the old conditions…. The tide of civilization is as resistless as the tide of the ocean, and you have no choice but to accept it and live according to its methods or be destroyed by it. To accept it requires the sale of these surplus lands and the opening of this reservation to white settlement. You were a great and powerful people when your abilities and energies were directed in harmony with the conditions which surrounded you, but the wave of civilization which swept over you found you un-

prepared for the new conditions and you became weak.... [Y]ou must accept the new life wholly. You must break down the barriers and invite the white man with all the elements of civilization, that your young men may have the same opportunities under the new conditions that your fathers had under the old.[58]

One wonders what the Yankton, who had from time immemorial lived about as far from an ocean as possible on the North American continent, thought of Cole's inapt analogy to tides and waves. But the Court had no trouble seeing a federal intent to alter the reservation boundaries in a single negotiator's reference to breaking down "the barriers" of the old ways. Congress and the Executive branches were no help. Numerous references over the years indicated an understanding the reservation continued to exist, while others talked of a "former" Yankton reservation. But the ambiguity did not favor the Tribe since the Court viewed the statutory language so clearly.

Several other factors influenced the Court's view that the reservation was diminished. Within a year of the Act, non-Indians settled ninety percent of the opened lands. The Tribe's population declined significantly by the turn of the century. The area's current demographics showed a increase in the Tribe's numbers, but still non-Indians comprise over seventy-five percent of the population. Indians now hold less than ten percent of the Treaty lands. And the State of South Dakota had assumed jurisdiction over the opened area soon after the 1984 Act and continued exercising it without challenge until the landfill case.

EPA's waiver of the composite liner requirement for the Southern Missouri Waste District turned out unnecessary in the end. The landfill site, located on surplus land opened to non-Indians one hundred years earlier, was not within the boundaries of the reservation as divined by the Supreme Court in 1998. EPA's 1993 approval of the State's solid waste management program thus encompassed the site. Nether the Tribe nor EPA had any direct regulatory authority over it.

In the specific context of Indian country environmental justice, *Yankton Sioux Tribe* represents both an obstacle and threat to tribal environmental management. EPA's disputed lands rules, which succeeded in *HRI* for the underground injection program but failed in *Michigan v. EPA* for the air program, were primarily aimed at precluding diminishment claims. That would not work here because EPA lacked backup program authority. The modified approach of issuing facility-specific regulations solved the practical problem of providing landfill operators with some flexibility, and it was certainly more consistent with the Indian Policy than approving state programs. But, it was a cumbersome process that still left day-to-day landfill operations unsupervised.

Yankton Sioux Tribe was also troubling on a broader level. The circumstances of the 1894 cessions and subsequent history at Yankton, like so many instances of federal-tribal relations at that time, were fair targets for moral outrage. Under the auspices of "negotiating" a land sale agreement, the Tribe's self-appointed trustee threatened in the middle of winter to cease providing food solemnly promised in an earlier treaty that netted the federal government some eleven million acres. Yet, not one hint of discomfort or unease appeared in the Court's opinion that dispassionately described Cole's cold-blooded threat as an "inducement" to sell and reported the unfair payment and the court of claims' award as if it were a subsequently corrected clerical error. Then, having glossed right over their patent unfairness, attributed to those two facts irrefutable legal significance.

Perhaps that is as it should be. In one of the foundation Indian law cases, Chief Justice John Marshall suggested the rule of law did not allow the Court to indulge its sympathies.[59] One hundred fifty years later, in another important Indian law case, Justice Rehnquist opined it would be "quite unfair to judge by the light of revisionist historians or the mores of another era actions that were taken under pressure of time more than a century ago."[60] Similarly, Justice O'Connor ended the Yankton decision with a half-hearted call for leniency:

> The allotment era has long since ended, and its guiding philosophy has been repudiated. Tribal communities struggled but endured, preserved their cultural roots, and remained, for the most part, near their historic lands. But despite the present-day understanding of a "government-to-government relationship between the United States and each Indian tribe," ... we must give effect to Congress' intent in passing the 1894 Act. Here, as in [the Sisseton-Wahpeton case], we believe that Congress spoke clearly, and although "[s]ome might wish [it] had spoken differently, ... we cannot remake history."[61]

In other words, the Court's modern role is not to seek justice delayed for Indian people, but rather to ensure those who benefit from a nation built on land and natural resources acquired from Tribes by force, threats, artifice and fraud continue to do so. In his recent book LIKE A LOADED WEAPON, Indian law scholar Robert Williams Jr. argues a compelling case for how the Rehnquist Court used the racist language of nineteenth century Indian cases to "justify and defend the privileges and aggressions of the dominant society against Indian tribes" in the modern era.[62] *Yankton Sioux Tribe's* uncritical acceptance of the federal government's contemptible "negotiating" tactics under the auspices of divining a congressional intent acknowledged not to exist similarly suggests a post hoc colonial rationalization directed at preserving states' assertions of Indian country authority.

Viewed from the perspective of tribal sovereignty, the diminishment doctrine is a more pernicious attack than *Montana's* general proposition or its illusory exceptions. The decisions barring the Crow and Yakama Tribes from applying their sovereign authority to non-Indian sportsmen and land developers did not directly affect tribal regulation of other non-Indian activities. For example, under the rationale of *Montana v. EPA*, those Tribes might very well regulate water pollution emanating from non-Indian lands despite lacking regulatory authority over wildlife management and land use.

Yankton Sioux Tribe was different. A regulatory dispute over a five-acre landfill begat a decision directly implicating over 200,000 acres. Those reservation lands were no longer Indian country so the Tribe's sovereign authority could not extend there. Thus, *Yankton Sioux Tribe* precluded in one fell swoop any and all regulatory claims the Tribe might ever assert over non-Indians on nearly half of the reservation, regardless of the threats they presented to tribal health and welfare and Congress' specific authorization for tribal management in the other environmental laws. And while EPA's authority over the surplus lands was not put at issue, the decision also preempted any Indian program exercises of federal environmental authority in furtherance of the trust responsibility.

CHAPTER 7

CONCLUSION:
CLOSING THE CIRCLE

In many respects the homelands of America's indigenous peoples resemble other communities affected by environmental injustice. Relatively large populations of racial and ethnic minorities occupy Indian reservations and other areas of Indian country. Many of these communities are low income or are otherwise of modest means. Although American Indians are national citizens and state residents, they typically enjoy less access to and influence over legislative and administrative decision-making at state and national levels.

Indian country's lack of political power, distance from politically influential communities, and generally rural undeveloped nature make it an attractive target for new development activities sometimes referred to as "locally undesirable land uses" because of their attendant negative impacts on public health and welfare and the quality of the environment. The Indians' federal trustee has also encouraged industry to exploit Indian country's wealth of natural resources, not infrequently over the expressed objections of tribal governments and/or tribal citizens. Intensive and invasive natural resource development activities have caused and continue to present concerns of disproportionately higher health and welfare risks in comparison to the general population.

While Indian communities face similar environmental challenges, their source, and hence, their solution, is fundamentally different. The environmental justice movement spawned in the early 1990s was generally premised on claims that federal and state environmental programs were being unfairly administered in ways that excluded minority and low-income communities from meaningful participation and resulted in higher health and welfare risks for them. Claims were leveled that federal and state agencies had set regulatory standards or permit conditions too lax to ensure protection of specific community interests, sited new polluting facilities without adequately analyzing the cumulative effects presented by existing pollution sources, selectively enforced program violations or enforced them not at all, and remediated unpermitted pollution releases slowly or inadequately. Those situations have also affected Indian tribes, but most commonly their predicate has not been unfair program administration but rather the absence of tribe-specific environmental programs operating in Indian country.

When the environmental justice movement took hold in the early 1990s the cooperative federalist paradigm was over two decades old. EPA's partnership with state governments had matured through development of extensive regulatory infrastructure, but those efforts had not reached Indian country. They ran afoul of historic federal-tribal relations that set tribal territories apart and altered the constitutional balance of federal-state power by constricting state interests over governmental matters typically exercised at the local level like environmental management. The modern environmental laws had not accounted for the anomalous allocation of federal and state interests in Indian country, and lacking express congressional authorization, states' limited powers held little promise for full protection of the Indian country environment.

EPA's substantial powers could theoretically fill the resulting regulatory gap in national environmental protection and ostensibly discharge the federal government's trust responsibility for protecting tribal lands. Yet, unilateral federal implementation of Indian programs had fallen into disfavor in the self-determination era of Indian policy. And Congress had designed EPA's authority for supervisory and backup roles in deference to local governments' site-specific knowledge and long-standing responsibility for balancing environmental quality with economic development and other local priorities.

Those policy principles, however, fit naturally with the crucial attribute distinguishing Indian tribes from all other disaffected groups: governmental status. Tribal homelands are not just the location where tribal citizens live but are the territories of semi-independent sovereign governments that have maintained political relations with the United States for over two hundred years. The solution to the Indian country regulatory gap most consistent with environmental and Indian policy, then, was the creation of state-like implementation roles for tribal governments. And, by definition, tribal-EPA partnerships would address in some measure the environmental justice concerns of ensuring the meaningful involvement of all people in environmental decision-making and protecting unique community interests, ideally in a culturally relevant manner.

A Sense of Place

Indigenous cultures place great emphasis on place. Ironically, the colonizer's federal Indian law also features a primary geographic focus. The areas within the United States known as Indian country demarcate territorial claims and corresponding governmental power spheres. The constitutional balance of retained state powers and limited federal authority shifts perceptibly at the boundaries of Indian country. State interests lose their assumed preeminence; justifications for state intrusions in Indian country are generally required rather than presumed. Federal interests blossom beyond the specific strictures of the constitutional paradigm, invoking a seemingly limitless federal power over Indian affairs that may restrict or expand state and tribal prerogatives. Tribal interests acquire governmental status in Indian country, which combine with federal interests in tribal self-government to shift the balance toward preemption of state laws.

From its inception, EPA's Indian program has necessarily grappled with the geographic aspect of federal Indian law. The Agency's first program action in 1973 announcing direct federal implementation of water pollution permit programs was limited to pollution discharges "from any Indian activity on Indian lands." Focusing on Indians and Indian tribes as regulated entities accorded with contemporary Supreme Court decisions stressing the deeply rooted policy of leaving reservation Indians free from state regulation and the supremacy of federal authority in Indian affairs. But it left unstated whether EPA or states would regulate non-Indian facilities operating in Indian country on either tribal lands or non-Indian fee lands.

The next two Indian program decisions—the 1974 tribal air quality redesignation and the 1975 tribal certification of commercial pesticide applicators regulations—seemed directed at closing the regulatory net around non-Indian facilities and lands. The rules broadened the Agency's geographic scope beyond Indian actions on Indian lands to formal Indian reservations. Congress' definition of Indian country clearly encompassed non-Indian lands within reservations, so the circle of national protection had grown. That program expansion was particularly significant for its context: whereas the earlier water program regulation asserted federal regulatory authority, these latter rules authorized tribal state-like roles. In fact, EPA's explanation for the pesticide rule specifically contemplated direct tribal regulation of non-Indian applicators on reservations.

But in its regulation for the approval of state hazardous waste programs adopted five years later, EPA went back to the Indian lands phrase. Following that rule the Agency denied the State of Washington's application for program delegation over "Indian lands," provoking the lawsuit that would spawn the

Washington Department of Ecology decision upholding EPA's direct implementation authority.

The 1980 Indian Policy was the first effort at an Agency-wide approach transcending particular media programs. The Policy's geographic orientation was a schizophrenic amalgamation of the prior media-specific rules. Throughout the Policy the terms "Indian lands" and "Indian reservation" were used interchangeably without explanation.

> Another consequence of this special legal status of Indian tribes in our Federal system is that the states generally have only limited authority to regulate activities conducted *on Indian reservations*.... As state governments usually lack, *on Indian reservations*, the kind of power and regulatory authority they enjoy off-reservation, they cannot, in these cases fulfill *on Indian lands* the full regulatory role originally designed by Congress for the local implementing government.... Hence, without some modification, our programs, as designed, often fail to function adequately *on Indian lands*.[1]

The 1984 Indian Policy largely tracked the essential elements of the 1980 Policy, but resolved the language inconsistencies in favor of references to reservations rather than Indian lands. Like some prior rules, the 1984 Policy apparently left unprotected informal reservations and other non-reservation areas of Indian country and yet in dropping Indian lands it appeared the Indian program's geographic focus had expanded.

Curiously, EPA argued the contrary conclusion during the *Washington Department of Ecology* litigation in 1985. The State expressed confusion over the Agency's use of the Indian lands phrase in the regulation and in its disapproval of the State's program application. EPA claimed the term was synonymous with Indian country, which of course Congress defined as including Indian reservations but other lands as well. The court found the Indian law term of art a reasonable frame of reference for marking the line between state and federal authority. The dissonance between that view and the Indian Policy's more narrow focus on Indian reservations was left open.

Congress' treatment-as-a-state amendments in the late 1980s and 1990 were not especially helpful in resolving the confusion. The Safe Drinking Water Act provision authorized tribal roles where tribes possessed jurisdiction without specifying the areas eligible, but an earlier amendment preserving tribal rights referred to tribal sovereignty over Indian lands. The Clean Water Act referred to reservations and waters held by an Indian or a tribe. The Clean Air Act cited reservations and other areas within tribal jurisdiction.

EPA's rules implementing the provisions were similarly inconsistent. Its drinking water rules expressed concern over possible litigation arising from tribal program assertions beyond reservations, but did not limit tribal applications to reservations. On the other hand, the Agency read the Clean Water Act's references to waters held by an Indian or a tribe as limited to reservations and did not include other portions of Indian country. It did say, however, that tribal trust lands or so-called informal reservations would qualify. The more recent Tribal Authority Rule took a broader view, reading Congress' references to the "reservation or other areas within a tribe's jurisdiction" as providing tribal roles for all of Indian country, including informal reservations.

Interestingly, EPA's broadest position was staked out under the one statute lacking a treatment-as-a-state provision, the Resource Conservation and Recovery Act. The State/Tribal Implementation Rule, which would have implemented the Act's solid waste program, invoked the Indian lands phrase. Unconstrained by any congressional directive, the rule followed the Agency's position in the *Washington Department of Ecology* case by explicitly defining Indian lands as Indian country. But the rule was never implemented; *Backcountry Against Dumps'* conclusion that EPA could not treat the Campo Band as a state because Congress labeled tribes municipalities effectively invalidated the rule.

Thus, the geographic scope of EPA's Indian program remains inconsistent across the various media programs, which all differ in some respects from the Agency's guiding Policy. Disparate treatment is certainly not unusual in the western model of public administration and may not automatically equate to inefficiency. Yet, time and again EPA has asserted a need for some uniformity in the Indian program. And for tribes who already struggle to reconcile the linear, compartmentalized approach of federal environmental law with a more holistic perspective, the vacillating scope of the territories where they can implement federal programs implicates environmental justice at yet another level.

Stopped at the Border

Congress' development of the cooperative federalism approach in the early 1970s squarely presented but left unresolved the issue of Indian country regulation. Had modern environmental law wholly preempted state management in favor of exclusive federal authority, the Indian program would exist today, if at all, in a dramatically different form. Courts have rarely questioned the extent of federal authority in Indian affairs and in Indian country.

Instead, Congress left intact states' primary responsibilities for public health and welfare but addressed their historically ineffective environmental management by subjecting their programs to an extensive overlay of federal constraints. The federally specified mechanisms and standards established a mandatory floor perceived necessary for comprehensive national protection, yet left states with independent discretion to exceed the federal minimum expectations. Federal-state partnerships theoretically reconciled respect for local value judgments and the need for nationwide protection, with one exception: the representatives states sent to Congress did not consider Indian country.

The federal government's constitutionally authorized power over Indian affairs had historically limited state authority in Indian country. Initially the Supreme Court pronounced absolutely that state law had no effect in Indian country because exercises of state authority could disrupt federal-tribal relations and hinder federal Indian policy goals. Yet, the Court would defer to congressional conclusions that federal interests would be better served by state action; the federal power over Indian affairs could be delegated to states for implementation.

The early federal environmental laws contained no clear state authorization. In fact, they said nothing at all about Indian country implementation. State officials and others viewed that silence as insignificant in light of Congress' specific acknowledgement of states' primary responsibilities in relevant environmental matters and its expressed preference for local over federal implementation. They asserted Congress had implicitly sanctioned state regulation of Indian country. EPA consistently drew a different inference, imposing on states the burden of showing authorization pursuant to a specific treaty or jurisdictional law independent of the environmental statutes. Courts found the Agency's early Indian program premise a reasonable interpretation of congressional intent, and deferred to EPA's choice of federal rather than state environmental programs in *Washington Department of Ecology* and *Phillips Petroleum*. States have not seriously made the argument again since those cases were decided in the mid-1980s.

Instead, states and others have narrowed their regulatory claims by focusing on non-Indians in Indian country. While the modern Supreme Court continues to recite the deeply rooted national policy of leaving Indians in Indian country free from state regulation, it has completely rejected the early Indian law principle that state law may not intrude into Indian country without congressional permission. The Court now says inherent state authority extends to non-Indians in Indian country unless it has been preempted by federal Indian law or would infringe on tribal self-governance.

Like so much of the Court's Indian law jurisprudence, the analytic standards for assessing those exceptions are exceptionally indeterminate. Their lack of predictability combined with the political contentiousness associated with tribal assertions of authority over non-Indians in Indian county offers ripe fodder for widespread litigation. That seems especially true in light of the Court's increasingly narrow view of tribal self-government. And yet, none of the significant Indian country environmental law cases have featured holdings on the preemption of or infringement limitations on inherent state regulatory authority.

There are at least three likely explanations for the dearth of state preemption and infringement cases in the environmental context. One is that states may perceive they can more effectively accomplish their goals by keeping the question of state authority out of court and attacking tribal authority over non-Indians instead. *Montana* rather pointedly demonstrated a state that prevails in challenging tribal authority over non-Indians in Indian country is essentially left to continue exercising any previously asserted authority without the inconvenience of justifying its authority to do so. A second probable explanation is that the passage of the various treatment-as-a-state amendments considerably weakened states' arguments on those issues. Congress clearly expressed in those provisions a preference for tribal regulation and EPA's Indian program is arguably a pervasive regulatory regime reflecting significant federal interests in tribal implementation roles. Those roles directly serve tribal health and welfare interests, which are core self-government interests. Finally, states are cognizant that the preemption and infringement rules put the burden of persuasion on the state, as compared to the *Montana* test that shifted the burden of justification to tribes.

Nonetheless, EPA has acted to limit the opportunities for such claims because of their potentially negative impacts on effective Indian country regulation. Drawn out court battles over state authority invariably delay development and implementation of federal and tribal programs. In some cases, eventual resolution may not completely solve the Indian country regulatory gap and in the event a state ultimately prevailed, the resulting two regulatory regimes running side-by-side on a parcel-by-parcel basis could undermine the goal of effective protection for human health and the environment.

EPA's solution was its anti-checkerboard policy, which stemmed from the unitary management approach raised in the 1983 Discussion Paper and supported by a tribal representative when the State of Washington asserted underground injection control authority over non-Indian lands in 1984. The Agency's 1991 concept paper announced EPA would treat Indian reservations as single administrative units. A state desiring program authority over non-Indians would thus be forced to apply for delegation over the entire reservation, including Indian facilities. EPA would not approve partial program applications, so a state could receive program delegation only where it showed independent jurisdiction over all pollution sources on the reservation. The Supreme Court, of course, has consistently denied state authority over reservation Indians, so the anti-checkerboard policy essentially foreclosed the possibility of state delegations for reservations even where state jurisdiction over non-Indian pollution sources existed.

States have not challenged the policy directly, though they frequently complain about it in their briefs in Indian country environmental law cases. They are particularly provoked that the ostensibly neutral unitary management policy really applies only one way; EPA is willing to approve tribal programs for Indian facilities even where the tribe cannot show jurisdiction over all reservation sources, simply retaining federal program responsibility for non-Indian facilities. The concept paper did not acknowledge or address whether that creates the same potentially ineffective system of dual parcel-by-parcel programs EPA asserted the policy avoided.

For reservations broken apart by surplus land sales during the allotment era, states may have more success in asserting jurisdiction over non-Indians by making diminishment claims. South Dakota's success in *Yankton Sioux Tribe* showed the value to states and the risks to EPA and tribes of the diminishment doctrine. The assertion of federal authority over the proposed landfill was not defeated by preemption and infringement arguments, but by the more direct claim that the site simply was not Indian country. The Supreme Court's agreement went far beyond precluding federal and potentially tribal environmental regulation of the landfill to include every non-Indian activity conducted on Yankton surplus lands sold to non-Indians.

New Mexico and Hydro Resources attacked the federal underground injection program in the Eastern Navajo Agency on essentially the same basis. EPA's disputed lands rule, providing federal authority for Navajo lands whose Indian country status was in dispute, did not avoid litigation, but it did ensure continued federal regulation until such time as EPA or a court rendered a final decision on the actual status of one of the Company's mine sites. *HRI* found that approach a reasonable exercise of the Agency's authority.

The later Title V federal operating permits rule for air pollution sources expanded the approach in two ways. It eschewed the ostensibly more formal requirement of a "dispute" in favor of being triggered any time EPA felt a "question" existed about the status of a particular parcel of land. No formal objection or pending litigation was necessary. The rule also applied to the entire Title V program wherever implemented, whereas the underground injection program in *HRI* had been promulgated for a limited number of specifically identified tribes.

The *Michigan v. EPA* court suspected the Agency was attempting to postpone litigation over the Indian country status for major air pollution sources but did not invalidate the in question lands portion of the rule because of that goal per se. The court agreed with the *HRI* decision that holding state regulation in abeyance until land status could be resolved was an appropriate exercise of federal authority. EPA's fatal mistake was not limiting the time or process for coming to resolution; the court was concerned the postponement could become indefinite. EPA might never make a final decision that could be challenged and reviewed in court, thus creating a perpetual federal program at odds with Congress' preference for local implementation either by states or tribes.

Policy devices like the unitary management and disputed lands approaches to avoid or limit state challenges have become an implicit theme of EPA's Indian program. They can be effective where the Agency's expertise in environmental management is implicated, so that courts' administrative law deference sheaths the action from challengers who assert other plausible options. They fail where the court believes Congress' contrary intent is clear. The *Michigan v. EPA* court's suspicion of a federal power grab invalidated the lands in question device because it appeared inconsistent with the cooperative federalism model. Ironically, EPA's desire to preserve the option for future tribal regulation over all Indian country sources was its real motivating factor. *Montana* and related cases showed the danger to tribal sovereignty claims of prior state regulation of reservation non-Indians.

Filling the Indian Country Regulatory Gap

The timing of EPA's creation is central to understanding how a new federal agency with no experience in Indian country came to develop the most progressive Indian program in the federal administrative bureaucracy. EPA was born in 1970 almost precisely at the origins of modern federal environmental law and modern federal Indian law. Presidential, congressional and judicial directives in both arenas inexorably urged the Agency toward the place it occupies today.

The cooperative federalism paradigm ensconced in the 1970 Clean Air Act and every major regulatory statute enacted thereafter surely preserved states' primary public health and welfare responsibilities. The statutory programs largely assumed local implementation and paid significant deference to local value judgments. However, the major new feature was a dramatic increase in the importance and preeminence of federal interests affected by local control. National environmental protection would be assured through federal supervision and approval of local programs designed in compliance with federal strictures so they formed a cohesive and reinforcing whole.

Federal interests and control have always been key factors in federal Indian law and policy. Only once in the history of the county has Congress dabbled with terminating the historic federal-tribal relationship and subjecting Indian country to state regulation. The policy of termination was short-lived, due in part to Richard Nixon's urging just before he created EPA, and no hint of Indian country regulatory roles for states appeared in the new federal environmental programs. Courts' consistent references to states' limited Indian country authority suggested the impotence of the cooperative federalism approach in view of Congress' failure, creating an apparent regulatory void. Such a gap frustrated Congress' intention for national environmental quality and implicated the federal government's trust responsibility for the general welfare of Indians and protection of their lands.

EPA's initial solution was straightforward: the Agency would close the circle of national environmental management itself. Rather than utilize the cooperative federalism model that could not work absent congressional amendment, EPA fell back on the strong federal authority and interests evident in both Indian law and environmental law. Its first Indian program action, the 1973 Clean Water Act rule, announced an intention for directly implementing the pollution discharge permit program rather than delegating it to states. No state or regulated entity challenged the Agency's asserted direct implementation authority when the rule was promulgated, and no reported court decision since that time has questioned the validity of federally issued discharge permits in Indian country.

EPA survived two legal attacks a decade later when it again claimed direct implementation authority in the face of statutes silent on Indian county management. *Washington Department of Ecology* upheld the Agency's interpretation of the Resource Conservation and Recovery Act as providing federal and not state authority for administering the hazardous waste program on Indian reservations and *Phillips Petroleum* validated federal implementation in the Safe Drinking Water Act's underground injection control program. Both courts found federal program administration consistent with federal Indian law and policy and thus deferred to the Agency's interpretation of the ambiguous acts.

EPA's Indian Policies explicitly posited direct implementation only as an interim solution to the Indian country regulatory gap. The modern Indian policy of tribal self-determination, soon to be realized through Congress' treatment-as-a-state amendments, envisioned tribes assuming full program administration responsibilities and leaving EPA in the supervisory role it typically played for state implementation. Yet, a complicated combination of factors has revealed that the road to comprehensive tribal environmental management is long and rocky. A number of tribes have made impressive forward progress, but full local protection of Indian country is still far from reality some thirty years after the Indian program began. EPA's direct implementation thus remains the most prevalent form of environmental regulation of the quality of the Indian county environment for the health and welfare of American Indians.

EPA's primary focus has necessarily been on federal permit programs because activities regulated under the environmental laws are typically prohibited unless conducted pursuant to a valid permit. The federal permit programs are for the most part generic and generally differ little if at all from the federal requirements applied outside Indian country where adequate state programs do not exist. The reason is partly the administrative convenience of national uniformity among federal programs and partly the lack of adequate federal resources for promulgating reservation-specific programs. In a few instances, most notably the underground injection control program, EPA has honored its policy commitment for tailoring direct implementation activities to fit local needs and priorities communicated by tribal governments. Most current Indian country environmental law and regulatory programs, however, reflect only basic federal expectations rather than site-specific tribal value judgments on the level of desired environmental quality.

Albuquerque's challenge to the Pueblo of Isleta's water quality standards starkly illustrated that different governments' values on common subjects can vary dramatically. Tolerance for such difference is a fundamental underpinning of cooperative federalism. The Isleta case also showed how the treatment-as-a-state approach translates tribal value judgments into federally enforceable permit conditions. Indeed, EPA admits, "without applicable standards, the Clean Water Act's mechanisms for protecting water quality in Indian country are limited."

EPA has twice taken the position its authority under the Clean Water Act includes setting federal standards for Indian country where necessary to meet the Act's requirements. In fact, Indian country's first water quality standards were promulgated by EPA in the late 1980s at the request of the Confederated Tribes of the Colville Indian Reservation in Washington. As it did with several tribes who showed particular interest in the underground injection control program, EPA tailored its effort toward incorporating Colville priorities and interests, in that instance by modeling the final federal requirements largely on standards previously developed by the Tribes. The collaborative process took three years during which Congress enacted section 518 authorizing tribal water quality standards for Indian reservations. EPA's notice of final adoption of the Colville standards emphasized the "very deliberate process" and its unique timing in disavowing any interest in future federal promulgations and directing other tribes toward section 518:

> EPA notes that today's rule does not establish a precedent for future EPA promulgations.... This process is not intended as a model for other reservations. Where other Indian Tribes wish to establish standards under the [Clean Water Act], EPA would expect such Tribes to apply, under the [Act's] section 518 regulation, to be treated as States for purposes of water quality standards. Once recognized by EPA as qualified to be treated as States, such Tribes would be responsible for developing their own water quality standards under the Act and making ongoing refinements to suit particular Tribal needs.
>
> Indian Tribes should not conclude from today's action that Federal promulgation is EPA's preferred method of establishing water quality standards on reservations. Historically, EPA's preference has been to work cooperatively with States on water quality standards issues and to initiate Federal promulgation actions only where absolutely necessary. EPA believes that this preference is consistent with the intent of the Act to provide States, and Tribes qualifying for treatment as States, with the first opportunity to set standards.[2]

The Agency's position seemed fully consistent with the Indian Policy as well. Direct implementation was designed as a temporary gap-filler until the legal and administrative barriers to tribal implementation were addressed. Once the treatment-as-a-state provisions were enacted, self-determination counseled that federal control would yield to tribal operation, at least for those tribes that decided to seek program responsibility. EPA's hesitance over developing federal standards before tribes had the opportunity to try their newly authorized powers under the Act anticipated by some ten years *Arizona v. EPA's* invalidation of EPA's federal implementation plan for the Yavapai-Apache air quality redesignation and *Michigan v. EPA's* rejection of the federal air operating permits program over in question lands. Both courts saw those federal initiatives as improperly pretermitting tribes' options for administering the federal programs contrary to Congress' expressed preferences.

By the same token, congressional authorization did not ensure immediate Indian country protection. EPA's expectation that tribes would not fill the Indian country gap for some time was revealed by its misguided decision in the 1991 tribal water quality standards rule to "assume without deciding" that state water quality standards applied to reservation waters in the interim. That was one of two instances where the Agency abandoned law and policy in treating state programs not approved for Indian country as if they were. Unapproved state programs could have no legal effect and the Indian Policy clearly promised federal implementation in such a context, but the three-year Colville experience drove home for EPA its resource limitations. The Agency was simply not equipped to develop water quality standards for every Indian tribe on a reservation-by-reservation basis.

By 1998, ten years after EPA urged tribes toward self-development, only twenty-two tribes or about three percent of eligible tribes had approved standards.[3] The Agency set a modest goal of increasing that number to fifteen percent by 2005[4] and began reconsidering the idea of federally promulgated Indian country water quality standards, this time in the context of a uniform national program much like the generic federal permit programs. The concept followed the underground injection control program model set in the late 1980s; EPA would apply a set of "core" standards across-the-board to all reservations lacking tribal standards unless a tribe opted out of the program to work with EPA on specific standards or develop its own standards.

EPA initiated a series of conversations with tribal representatives that led to preparation of a draft approved by the Administrator for publication as a proposed rule three days before the end of Bill Clinton's presidential term.[5] Incoming President George W. Bush issued a temporary moratorium on unreleased non-final administrative rules that tripped up several significant environmental regulations in progress including the core standards rule. Bush's first administrator, Christine Todd Whitman, reviewed the draft rule in 2001 and declared additional consultation with tribes and states was necessary before making any proposal, but to date the proposal has not resurfaced. Indian country waters thus remain largely unprotected; EPA reports only thirty approved tribal standards programs as of May 2007, leaving approximately 300 reservations lacking the primary anchor for Clean Water Act implementation.[6]

The newest programmatic development on the direct implementation front is a creative blend of federal authority and tribal governance modeled generally on the concept of self-determination contracts for tribal administration of federal human services programs in Indian country.[7] In 2001, Congress for the first time authorized formal arrangements whereby tribes would assist EPA or act on its behalf in undertaking direct implementation activities.[8] These Direct Implementation Tribal Cooperative Agreements recognize tribes as governmental partners but do not require treatment-as-a-state status, thus obviating the practical and legal barriers associated with showing full tribal capability and jurisdiction over non-Indian lands and pollution sources. EPA lists a wide variety of possible tribally operated federal implementation activities including setting water quality standards, issuing water pollution discharge permits, developing air quality implementation plans, issuing Title V air pollution permits, regulating public water systems and underground injections, and certifying pesticide applicators, as well as implementing hazardous waste disposal and underground storage tanks programs under the Resource Conservation and Recovery Act, the only major regulatory statute lacking a treatment-as-a-state provision.[9]

Tribes do not receive the same extent of authority provided by state-like status, but still possess significant discretion for incorporating tribal values and priorities into the federal implementation activities and get a valuable opportunity for developing tribal capacity and experience that may facilitate later state-like program assumptions. In that sense the cooperative agreements approach mediates the tension between the two central themes of the current Indian program: direct federal implementation and EPA's policy commitment to tribal self-determination. EPA's judgments are influenced by a local partner with better knowledge of and closer ties to the environments and activities implicated. At the same time, Indian country health and protection need not wait for full tribal program development, and the existence of an operating program helps minimize unauthorized state incursions thus strengthening tribal arguments in the face of *Montana* test challenges based on pre-existing state regulation. The only major legal risk not avoided by the cooperative agreements model is the diminishment threat demonstrated by *Yankton Sioux Tribe;* whether conducted by EPA or tribes, direct federal implementation in the context of the Indian program can only take place in Indian country.

Tribal Solutions for Indian Country Environmental Justice

An underlying premise of environmental injustice is that certain communities within the larger society lack an adequate voice to ensure their interests in health and welfare are respected on par with others' desires, contributing to the creation of inequitable environmental risks. Nearly two decades before those concerns coalesced into a social movement, EPA anticipated their unique application to Indian country where the new cooperative federalism paradigm faltered in providing no local implementation mechanism. The Agency's potent solution for filling the regulatory void would by definition improve American Indians' influence over the administration of federal programs and distinguish Indian country environmental justice from all other areas of the nation.

EPA's 1974 decision treating tribes in the same manner as states for the air quality redesignation program despite Congress' complete silence on the matter capitalized on the fundamental difference between Indian tribes and other minority communities—their legal status as sovereigns with independent public health and welfare responsibilities to their citizens and government-to-government relations with the United States. Tribes' independent sovereign status, the Supreme Court had said, was an adequate base upon which Congress could locate the administration of federal programs. Congress' rejection of the nation's termination policy in favor of tribal self-determination at about the same time it adopted the cooperative federalism model implied tribal operation rather than direct federal implementation was the appropriate vehicle for achieving environmental protection. Tribal programs accorded with the assumption that local implementation was better attuned to local needs and priorities, and tribes were obviously more familiar with the cultural needs of the community than the federal government. Presumably they could also facilitate more meaningful public participation in the affected communities.

EPA's first Indian country environmental law success in *Nance* upholding the tribal air quality redesignation role validated those convictions and just as importantly established the key Indian program theme of judicial deference to EPA's alternative creative solutions to the Indian country regulatory gap and the most effective way of achieving national environmental protection. An equally important boost to the program and its imminent expansion was Congress' prompt codification of the Agency's first bold treatment-as-a-state experiments respecting tribal value judgments and governmental administration. Those express authorizations were followed with similar amendments squarely incorporating tribal self-determination in one form or another into nearly every significant environmental statute.

Congress' decision to equate Indian tribes with states rather than create a new body of environmental law specific to Indian country held significant potential perhaps not fully realized at the time. The compromise inherent in the cooperative federalism paradigm was the preservation of states' powers to exceed federal requirements and/or meet them through alternative means, and the obligation of federal permitting agencies and adjacent states to honor such individual state value judgments. Limiting the scope of EPA's approval authority when confronted with stronger local commitments to environmental protection actualized congressional respect for state prerogatives. Industry complaints of excessive compliance costs and fears of undue burdens on economic profitability thus fell on deaf ears since the Agency generally lacked discretion to second guess local political decisions balancing social and economic interests with public health and welfare.

Tribal environmental programs cast in the federal mold similarly benefit from EPA's focus on the bottom line of compliance with federal procedure and substantive minimum requirements. Tribes treated as states could, for example, promulgate water quality standards more stringent than necessary for protecting the minimum federal fishable/swimmable goals, redesignate their airsheds from the federally established Class II to the more exacting Class I, and establish underground injection programs stronger than the generic federal one. Reflexive objections by non-Indian residents, businesses and adjacent jurisdictions over higher standards impacting their economic development hopes are simply inapt comments on the determination of program adequacy. In that same vein EPA has consistently rejected interpreting statutory tribe-state dispute resolution provisions as implicit authorization for rejecting varying tribal standards in the face of state protests.

Tribal program standards approved by EPA as consistent with federal parameters then constrain pollution permits issued by EPA and other federal agencies in tribal territories. Animating the federal regulatory machinery with tribal value judgments arguably enhances federal trust accountability for protecting tribal interests and helps curb inadvertent state incursions through EPA reliance on state standards. It can also influence environmental programs developed and pollution permits issued in adjacent states and tribal territories through statutory mechanisms for limiting transboundary contamination. Indeed, as the Isleta Pueblo's water quality standards downstream from Albuquerque and the Northern Cheyenne air quality redesignation downwind from the Colstrip power plant demonstrated, the potential for federally enforceable influence over environmentally harmful activities outside Indian country—a result that simply cannot occur through reliance on tribal sovereignty alone—is a potent consequence of the treatment-as-a-state opportunity.

Perhaps the most valuable benefit, however, is the measure of insulation partnerships with EPA may offer from activist courts bent on restricting tribal governmental power over non-Indians within Indian country. The Rehnquist court's multiple departures from settled Indian law principles—claiming an authority and ability to divine when the dependent status of tribes is inconsistent with governmental power, expanding and legitimizing states' claims in Indian country, rewriting the geographic boundaries of Indian country, and discarding the historic distinctions between Indian and non-Indian lands within it, to name just a few—have been well documented. Professor Getches has reported in the ten years preceding 2001 Indian tribes lost eighty-two percent of their cases in the Supreme Court, a record worse than convicted criminal defendants over the same time in the same court.[10] Since the Supreme Court announced the *Montana* health and welfare test in 1981, no tribe has yet convinced a majority of Justices that its self-government interests are sufficiently impacted to justify tribal regulation of non-Indian activities.

In contrast, the Salish and Kootenai Tribes' claim of inherent sovereignty over non-Indians fairly sailed through the *Montana v. EPA* case in the Ninth Circuit Court of Appeals. The courts were different of course, and that difference cannot be overstated; *Oliphant, Montana* and *Brendale* are poignant reminders that the Supreme Court often overturns Ninth Circuit Indian law decisions. There was a second key difference, however, that typifies nearly every significant Indian country environmental case and distinguishes them from Supreme Court decisions where tribes had stood alone. The State of Montana's suit challenged EPA's approval of the Tribes' water quality standards rather than any direct assertion of regulatory authority by the Tribes over non-Indians. The posture of the State's claim channeled the court's Indian law analysis to a confluence with environmental and administrative law that triggered the respect courts routinely pay to federal agencies but rarely accord Indian tribes.

EPA could not and did not garner administrative law deference for its reading of the *Montana* test because Congress has not committed implementation of federal Indian law to the Agency's discretion. Application of the test in the context of federal environmental program delegation, on the other hand, fell squarely within EPA's expertise. EPA's interim operating rule requiring tribal showings of serious and substantial health and welfare impacts from non-Indian pollution translated the *Montana* test into the language of environmental law, and the Agency's generalized findings—on the seriousness of water quality impairment, the mobility of water pollution increasing the chance of Indian exposure and the difficulty of separating Indian and non-Indian pollution, as well as Congress' preference for federal-tribal partnerships—buttressed tribes' already legitimate claims that environmental management implicated core self-government interests. Such acknowledgement by the expert agency was a reasonable exercise of EPA's congressionally authorized discretion entitled to the court's deference and clearly tipped the balance in the Tribes' favor.

Judicial acquiescence to the Agency's statutory interpretations has been key to keeping opportunities for environmental program roles open to tribes. The most dramatic example was EPA's success in *Arizona Public Service*, which upheld its interpretation of the ambiguous Clean Air Act as a federal delegation to tribes of jurisdiction over non-Indian air polluters on reservations, foreclosing in one fell swoop individual jurisdictional challenges to future tribal program delegations. Administrative law deference also validated EPA's views that tribes could redesignate the federal classification of their airsheds despite the early Clean Air Act's silence on the matter, and adopt water quality standards more stringent than the federal minimum even though the Clean Water Act's treatment-as-a-state provision did not specifically preserve tribes' inherent powers to do so as the Act did for states. EPA's unwillingness to appease states who invoke statutory dispute resolutions processes by rejecting more stringent tribal standards or insisting on more detailed tribal analyses also prevailed on standard administrative law analyses.

Multiple courts have also respected EPA's assertion of broad direct implementation powers for Indian country across the entire spectrum of federal environmental programs. While direct implementation posits federal rather than tribal value judgments and control, it can indirectly benefit tribal sovereignty in several ways. It serves tribal governments' fundamental public health and welfare interests by closing the regulatory gap for Indian country environmental protection. More specific tribal priorities have on occasion influenced federal program design and implementation since at least the late 1980s when EPA began tailoring underground injection control programs consistent with the Indian Policy principle for tribal consultation. The recent Indian program development of Direct Implementation Tribal Cooperative Agreements has added further opportunities for developing tribes' experience and capacity through operation of federal programs in Indian country. Finally, an active federal program presence in Indian country preempts state regulatory intrusions in Indian country, thus strengthening future tribal self-government claims.

Interestingly, even in the few losses the Indian program has suffered there were threads of support for tribal sovereignty. The *Arizona v. EPA* court rejected the Agency's federal implementation plan as a means for effectuating the Yavapai-Apache's air quality redesignation out of concern that it would preclude the Tribe from developing its own plan as authorized by the 1990 Clean Air Act amendments. Similarly, *Michigan v. EPA* voided EPA's rule providing direct implementation of the Title V air permits program for lands whose Indian country status was in question because the court saw it as creating perpetual federal jurisdiction contrary to Congress' intent for tribal implementation. Even *Backcountry Against Dumps*, the Indian program's only true loss, offered some solace. But for EPA's and tribes' tremendous successes in obtaining explicit tribal treatment-as-a-state provisions in the other laws, the court likely would have deferred to the Agency's creation of state-like roles for the solid and hazardous waste programs under the Resource Conversation and Recovery Act despite its definition of tribes as municipalities. And even in deciding against the Agency and the Campo Band, the court specifically commented that its ruling did not undermine the Band's inherent sovereignty over environmental management for solid waste disposal activities on the reservation.

Conclusion

EPA's Indian program has come a long way since the Agency first confronted the Indian country regulatory gap Congress inadvertently created when it adopted the cooperative federalism paradigm for national environmental protection. The Indian program's maturation could be characterized as a progression through five distinct phases building toward effective Indian country environmental protection. Much work remains, however, for achieving environmental justice in Indian country.

The first phase in the mid-1970s was perhaps the boldest. EPA first announced it would retain regulatory responsibilities for Indian facilities rather than delegate them to states, despite Congress' expressed preference for general state implementation of federal programs. Then, stretching its administrative discretion to the limit and driving home the point it would not partner with states in Indian country, EPA created two state-like implementation roles for Indian tribes notwithstanding the complete absence of congressional authorization. Those administratively derived solutions to program-specific regulatory gaps in Indian country, taken without clear congressional direction and before the Supreme Court's 1984 *Chevron* decision calling for judicial deference to agency interpretations of ambiguous statutes, set EPA on a path to becoming the most progressive federal agency in conforming its work to the new self-determination era of federal Indian policy.

Legislative, judicial and executive reactions—following the Agency's lead rather than invalidating it—marked the second phase of the Indian program. Congress codified EPA's unilateral experiments with the tribal air and pesticide management roles almost immediately, encouraging EPA to develop its first agency-wide Indian Policy in 1980. The Agency's victory in defending the Northern Cheyenne air quality redesignation in 1981 and President Reagan's 1983 call for a renewed federal commitment to government-to-government relations spurred development of the 1984 Indian Policy unequivocally declaring tribal self-determination as EPA's guiding principle. Congress similarly affirmed EPA's Indian policy direction with broad treatment-as-a-state amendments to each regulatory statute revised between 1986 and 1990. In word and spirit, tribal self-determination had become a feature of the cooperative federalism era of environmental management.

The Indian program's third phase overlapped the second chronologically and conceptually. EPA needed a temporary bridge over the practical chasm between policy aspirations for tribal management, which would take time to realize, and the environmental laws' immediate prohibition of unpermitted pollution releases. Direct federal implementation ensured an entity with clear authority for issuing pollution permits needed by new and existing facilities in Indian country, although federal control seemed at odds with tribal self-determination. Courts nonetheless deferred to EPA's hazardous waste and underground injection control programs in Washington and Oklahoma in the mid-1980s. The federal programs were consistent with the Indian Policies' reconciliation of environmental and Indian law because they necessarily reduced the incidence of unauthorized regulatory incursions by states and could act as precursors to eventual tribal management. EPA's efforts to tailor some generic federal programs to tribal wishes, as it did for the Osage underground injection control program and the Colville water quality standards, were slightly more tangible steps toward honoring its Indian Policy goal of empowering tribes in a government-to-government fashion.

Somewhat ironically, about the same time the environmental justice movement outside Indian country was drawing attention to unfairness in the administration of existing state and federal media-specific programs, the Indian program's fourth phase was just beginning its focus on building the administrative foundations necessary for the initial development of tribal media-specific programs. EPA activated Congress' treatment-as-a-state amendments through a series of regulations promulgated between 1988 and 1998 that opened the door to primary tribal roles in the groundwater, surface water and air quality programs, as well as in the solid and hazardous waste programs not yet addressed by Congress. The regulations envisioned full tribal regulatory partnerships, respected tribal governments' more stringent value judgments, and strengthened tribal claims of jurisdiction over non-Indians.

Dozens of Indian tribes took the predicate steps of obtaining federal grants for assessing reservation environmental quality and planning programmatic responses. A number of tribes developed federally enforceable water quality standards and several redesignated their airshed classifications. EPA's regulations and tribal program approvals drew a predictable spate of lawsuits, but administrative law deference for the Agency's statutory interpretations and program decisions turned back nearly every state and non-Indian legal claim with the notable exception of *Backcountry Against Dumps*, which indirectly invalidated EPA's proposed treatment-as-a-state regulations for the Resource Conservation and Recovery Act's solid and hazardous waste programs.

The foundation set by the remaining treatment-as-a-state regulations issued in the 1990s could not, however, instantly fill the regulatory void in Indian country. William Ruckelshaus, EPA's first administrator who later signed the 1984 Indian Policy when he returned to the Agency for a second term, noted it took nearly fifteen years for states to develop effective programs and working relations with EPA just in the air and water context,[11] notwithstanding the benefit of the states' prior experience, existing administrative infrastructure, and a significant outlay of federal financial and technical resources.

Tribes, on the other hand, were just coming off the Termination era's attack on their governmental status when the cooperative federalism model developed, and have seen comparatively little assistance since then. In 1988, Senator Inouye disgustedly observed the Indian program had historically garnered less than one tenth of one percent of the Agency's annual budget. Twenty years later that number has grown only to about one half of one percent of EPA's over $7 billion annual budget, a pitifully small allocation given the number of tribes, the infancy of their programs, and the comparative maturity of state programs. The Tribal Caucus of the Agency's national Tribal Operations Committee, created by Administrator Carol Browner in 1994 to convey tribal governments' views directly to Agency leadership, has repeatedly noted during annual budget processes that continuing resource limitations further delay realizing the goals of the 1984 Indian Policy.

Increased apprehension of tribes and the Agency over recent judicial developments has also contributed to the slow growth of tribally developed environmental programs. In 2001, the Supreme Court demonstrated its increasingly narrow view of the *Montana* health and welfare test by twice finding tribal self-government interests insufficient justification for jurisdiction over non-Indians. One decision applied the test to protect a state fish and game officer who allegedly damaged a tribal member's personal property on tribal trust land, drawing an objection from three Justices that doing so was not faithful to *Montana's* result that was explicitly limited to non-Indian land.[12] The other case insulated an on-reservation non-Indian hotel from a tribal occupancy tax by dismissing as dicta repeated prior Court statements that taxation of commercial activities is a fundamental attribute of tribal self-government.[13] In 2004, the Court upheld Congress' affirmation of tribal sovereignty over non-member Indian criminals, but pointedly hinted that future congressional "fixes" to the Court's Indian common law might receive less deferential treatment if they affected state sovereignty. It is unclear whether or how such federal affirmation might relate to the concept of federally delegated power over non-Indians that prevailed in the D.C. Circuit's *Arizona Public Service* decision upholding the Agency's interpretation of the Clean Air Act.

EPA's bold win in *Arizona Public Service* may have been largely academic at any rate. As the Agency anticipated, only a few tribes have attempted the expense and commitment of time and human resources necessary for developing the Clean Air Act's more complex programs. Just this last February, nine years after the Tribal Authority Rule went into effect, the Gila River Indian Community in Arizona submitted to EPA the nation's first tribal implementation plan for ensuring reservation air pollution sources comply with national ambient air quality standards. Four others are said to be in development. No tribe has yet sought approval for implementing a tribal Title V operating permits program for major air pollution sources.

So while the groundwork was set in the fourth phase of the Indian program for a significant increase in the number of tribally developed programs, the fifth and current phase has been marked more by retrenchment in the form of increased direct federal implementation, although with an interesting new twist. EPA's direct implementation in the third phase acknowledged the Indian Policy in a few instances by incorporating particular tribes' interests into generic permit programs developed and administered by EPA for managing groundwater, surface water and hazardous waste in Indian country. The current phase, which has focused largely on air pollution regulation, features several experiments with the more active tribal role envisioned by Congress' 2001 authorization for federal direct implementation conducted by tribes: tribal administration of programs developed in the first instance by EPA.

In addition to treatment-as-a-state provisions, the 1998 Tribal Authority Rule authorized federal implementation plans for Indian country until tribes developed reservation-specific plans to replace them. In 2005, EPA issued an omnibus federal implementation plan covering all thirty-nine Indian reservations in Idaho, Oregon and Washington[14] and later announced it was delegating responsibility for administering the plan to the Nez Perce Tribe for its reservation in Idaho and to the Confederated Umatilla Tribes for their reservation in Oregon.[15] EPA has also proposed a federal plan regulating two specific facilities on the Navajo reservation,[16] another to implement a pending redesignation by the Forest County Potawatomi Community in Wisconsin,[17] and another omnibus federal plan for the nation's remaining Indian country.[18]

EPA's 1999 rule applied the generic federal Title V operating permits program to Indian country in the absence of approved tribal (or state) programs. *Michigan v. EPA* circumscribed the Agency's Title V authority over lands whose Indian country status was in question, but left unaffected EPA's general power to issue permits for the approximately 100 major sources subject to Title V in Indian country. In 2005, the Navajo Nation became the first tribe delegated responsibility for administering EPA's federal operating permits program over twelve existing facilities and all new ones constructed on the Navajo reservation.

The so-called partial delegations to the Nez Perce, Umatilla and Navajo may signal the next phase of the Indian program. With its long experience and ability to draw on pre-existing requirements for state programs and generic federal backup programs, EPA is in most cases probably better suited to address Indian country's practical need for functioning programs in a timely manner than most Indian tribes who face the complex and costly task of environmental infrastructure building with relatively little experience and few resources. Tribal operation of federal programs offers a pertinent opportunity for building management experience and capacity, but without the risks of non-Indian *Montana* test challenges inherent in most tribally developed programs.

Federally developed programs, of course, do not necessarily reflect tribal value judgments, although the Agency has shown some willingness to account for expressed tribal priorities in their development. That approach is consistent with commitments in both the Indian Policy and the Office of Environmental Justice strategy for seeking tribal governments' contributions on how cultural uses and values can be incorporated into federal program activities. Tribal operation of federal programs, which intrinsically carries significant administrative discretion for deciding when and how program activities will occur, provides another opportunity to serve cultural values in particular instances. One example might be conducting federally required procedures for public participation in culturally relevant and appropriate ways. As the traditional law of the Diné provides, "[i]t is the right and freedom of the Diné to choose leaders ... who will communicate with the people for guidance."[19]

A 2004 report of the Indigenous Peoples Subcommittee of EPA's National Environmental Justice Advisory Council urged federal assistance to tribes in providing and enhancing "meaningful [public] involvement and fair treatment" when running federal programs, and understanding the perspectives of tribal members and community-based organizations on public involvement.[20] In that spirit, EPA's Office of Environmental Justice sponsored a unique pilot project on the Navajo reservation in 2006 and 2007, holding workshops on alternative dispute resolution and environmental law attended by representatives from the Navajo Tribal Council, the Navajo Environmental Protection Agency, and half a dozen Navajo environmental justice organizations. Participants developed written protocols and ground rules for enhancing communication and collaboration between the Navajo agency and the environmental organizations, drawing heavily on the Fundamental Laws of the Diné and traditional methods of dispute resolution facilitated by Navajo Peacemakers. The workshops and protocols may serve as models for future environmental justice efforts in other tribes' territories.

More effective public participation processes in tribal operation of federally developed programs might also improve communication and trust between non-Indians and tribes over the long term. With *Montana* test challenges off the table, non-Indians could focus their energies on contributing to fair and effective tribal program actions rather than jurisdictional complaints. Mike Connolly, the Campo Band's environmental director, noted during the landfill dispute that his non-Indian opponents routinely skipped opportunities for influencing the content of tribal decisions in favor of making collateral attacks on the Band's right to decide in the first instance.

Even more sophisticated and experienced environmental organizations can succumb to the temptation, making for uneasy relations between parties that seem like natural allies. An article in the national magazine of the Sierra Club criticized its San Diego chapter for potentially "jeopardizing long-term chances for a healthy alliance" with tribes by following the ragtag organization Backcountry Against Dumps in challenging Campo sovereignty even though the Band's landfill standards were more stringent than California's requirements.[21] Dean Suagee, a long time advocate for tribal environmental programs, notes a certain level of distrust between environmental groups and Indian tribes exists in part because some groups have challenged tribes' governmental status in pursuit of a particular agenda, but also simply because environmentalists like most Americans know little of the nuances of federal Indian law and the doctrine of retained tribal sovereignty.[22]

EPA's Office of Environmental Justice's initial steps toward improving public participation procedures for implementing federal environmental programs in Indian country are positive developments that should be expanded. But as the National Tribal Environmental Council, a national organization representing some seventy-five Indian tribes, reminded EPA's leadership in 2004, focusing on public involvement processes may distract the Agency from the more pressing environmental justice concerns of eliminating inequities in program funding and building tribal environmental capacity for protecting Indian country.[23] That claim was not prophetic; despite its 1995 strategy commitment to tribal program capacity development, the Office of Environmental Justice's few Indian initiatives since then have emphasized public involvement issues, leaving to the Agency's American Indian Environmental Office the harder work of getting tribal management programs online.

There remains the related question whether tribal interests are truly served by following the federal government's linear, compartmentalized model of environmental regulation. The model offers concrete practical benefits, in particular the prospect of limiting tribal health risks and environmental damage caused by harmful activities outside Indian country, as the Northern Cheyenne and Isleta cases demonstrated. But obtaining those benefits requires tribes act within procedural and substantive constraints imposed by the western model, which may distance tribes from traditional approaches and thus constitute just another form of colonialism and federal paternalism.[24]

Yet, tribal self-determination in the cooperative federalist environmental system must of course be understood in context; that is, as a construct of United States Indian law and policy rather than an anthropological description of an existing state of affairs. To be sure, the racist and logically indefensible origins of federal Indian law cast indisputable questions on its contemporary legitimacy. Nonetheless, today, American Indian tribes self-determine their destinies only to the extent of and within confines established by federal tolerance or indifference.

So it is with the treatment-as-a-state approach that requires tribal environmental regulatory programs conform to the parameters and language of federal environmental law. But presumably tribes who elect that path have either found it consistent with their traditional values or have developed means for making it consistent. Navajo traditional law explicitly envisions the people and the tribal government will "incorporate those practices, principles and values of other societies that are not contrary to the values and principles of Diné Bi Beenahaz'aanii [Navajo traditional, customary, natural and common law] and that they deem is in their best interest and is necessary to provide for the physical and mental well-being of every individual."[25] Dean Suagee notes "when tribal governments become engaged in environmental federalism, they do not act exactly like state governments [because their] policy decisions tend to reflect tribal cultural values."[26]

The Pueblo of Isleta, for example, respected the Rio Grande as the source of life and believed upstream sewage discharges from the City of Albuquerque threatened it. Isleta saw in the treatment-as-a-state approach a powerful opportunity for translating its cultural value into the language of a regulatory regime that could protect the river even from insults outside the Pueblo. EPA accepted the Pueblo's cultural value and respected its sovereign decision to protect the river through water quality standards exceeding the federal minima and those established by the State of New Mexico. The Tenth Circuit Court of Appeals respected EPA's discretionary imposition of additional permit conditions on the City as fully consistent with Congress' decision animating the federal Clean Water Act with tribal value judgments.

True environmental justice for Native America cannot be achieved through mechanisms that are culturally irrelevant, insensitive, or worse, culturally destructive. We might hope the time comes when the preservation of American indigenous culture needs no federal agency, court or legislative body. Until that day, tribal primacy for federal environmental programs may well be the most effective means for addressing environmental injustice in Indian country because it can be conducted in a culturally relevant manner, as defined by the culture itself.

ENDNOTES

Preface

1. Richard A. DuBey, Mervyn T. Tano, & Grant D. Parker, *Protection of the Reservation Environment: Hazardous Waste Management on Indian Land*, 18 Environmental Law 449 (1988).

Chapter 1

1. *See, e.g.,* THE LAW OF ENVIRONMENTAL JUSTICE: THEORIES AND PROCEDURES TO ADDRESS DISPROPORTIONATE RISKS xxix (Michael B. Gerrard ed., 1999).

2. *See generally* LUKE COLE & SHEILA FOSTER, FROM THE GROUND UP: ENVIRONMENTAL RACISM AND THE RISE OF THE ENVIRONMENTAL JUSTICE MOVEMENT (2001).

3. *See, e.g.,* CLIFFORD RECHTSCHAFFEN & EILEEN GAUNA, ENVIRONMENTAL JUSTICE: LAW, POLICY AND REGULATION 3–4 (2003).

4. *See* Judith V. Royster, *Native American Law, in* THE LAW OF ENVIRONMENTAL JUSTICE: THEORIES AND PROCEDURES TO ADDRESS DISPROPORTIONATE RISKS xxix (Michael B. Gerrard ed., 1999); Jace Weaver, *Triangulated Power and the Environment: Tribes, the Federal Government, and the States, in* DEFENDING MOTHER EARTH: NATIVE AMERICAN PERSPECTIVES ON ENVIRONMENTAL JUSTICE (Jace Weaver ed., 1996); Dean B. Suagee, *Turtle's War Party: An Indian Allegory on Environmental Justice*, 9 Journal of Environmental Law and Litigation 461 (1994).

5. COMMISSION FOR RACIAL JUSTICE (UNITED CHURCH OF CHRIST), TOXIC WASTES AND RACE IN THE UNITED STATES: A NATIONAL REPORT ON THE RACIAL AND SOCIO-ECONOMIC CHARACTERISTICS OF COMMUNITIES WITH HAZARDOUS WASTE SITES (1987).

6. Robert R. Kuehn, *A Taxonomy of Environmental Justice*, 30 Environmental Law Reporter 10,681 (2000).

7. ENVIRONMENTAL EQUITY: REDUCING RISK FOR ALL COMMUNITIES (1992).

8. BENJAMIN A. GOLDMAN ET AL., TOXIC WASTES AND RACE REVISITED: AN UPDATE ON THE 1987 REPORT ON THE RACIAL AND SOCIO-ECONOMIC CHARACTERISTICS OF COMMUNITIES WITH HAZARDOUS WASTE SITES 13–14 (1994).

9. Exec. Order No. 12,898, 59 Fed. Reg. 2679 (Feb. 11, 1994).

10. EPA Environmental Justice Strategy: Executive Order 12898 (1995).

11. U.S. EPA Office of Environmental Justice, Background, http://www.epa.gov/compliance/basics/ejbackground.html (last visited July 27, 2007).

12. *See generally* Charles F. Wilkinson, American Indians, Time and the Law (1988).

13. James M. Grijalva, *The Origins of EPA's Indian Program*, 15 Kansas Journal of Law & Public Policy 191, 205–222 (2006).

14. EPA Policy for Program Implementation on Indian Lands 1 (Dec. 19, 1980).

15. Council of Energy Resource Tribes, Inventory of Hazardous Waste Generators and Sites on Selected Indian Reservations (1985).

16. EPA Survey of American Indian Environmental Protection Needs on Reservation Lands: 1986 (1986).

17. Federal, Tribal and State Roles in the Protection and Regulation of Reservation Environments 1 (July 10, 1991).

18. Principles of Environmental Justice, Proceedings, First National People of Color Environmental Leadership Summit xiii (1991).

19. Rebecca Tsosie, *Tribal Environmental Policy in an Era of Self-Determination: The Role of Ethics, Economics and Traditional Ecological Knowledge*, 21 Vermont Law Review 225 (1996).

20. Dean B. Suagee, *The Indian Country Environmental Justice Clinic: From Vision to Reality*, 23 Vermont Law Review 567 (1999).

21. Title I, ch. 1, §5, Navajo Nation Code (2002).

22. Robert Williams, Jr., *Large Binocular Telescopes, Red Squirrel Piñatas, and Apache Sacred Mountains: Decolonizing Environmental Law in a Multicultural World*, 96 West Virginia Law Review 1133 (1994).

23. Tribes At Risk: The Wisconsin Tribes Comparative Risk Project (1992).

Chapter 2

1. EPA Memorandum, Draft Policy on Federal Oversight of Environmental Programs Delegated to States (Nov. 25, 1983), 14 Environmental Reporter. 1449,1449–50 (Dec. 16, 1983).

2. 18 U.S.C. §1151 (2007).

3. DeCoteau v. District County Court, 420 U.S. 425, 427 n.2 (1975).

4. Federal Power Commission v. Tuscarora Indian Nation, 362 U.S. 99 (1960).

5. Davis v. Morton, 469 F.2d 593 (10th Cir. 1972).

6. 31 U.S. (6 Pet.) 515 (1832).

7. *Id.* at 561.

8. McClanahan v. Arizona State Tax Commission, 411 U.S. 164, 170–71 (1973).

9. National Pollutant Discharge Elimination System, 38 Fed. Reg. 13,528, 13,530 (May 22, 1973) (codified at 40 C.F.R. §125.2(b)).

10. Cherokee Nation v. Georgia, 30 U.S. (5 Pet.) 1, 2 (1831).

11. Environmental Quality: The First Annual Report of the Council on Environmental Quality 165 (1970).

12. *Iron Eyes Cody*, http://www.snopes.com/movies/actors/ironeyes.htm (click movie camera icon to view PSA).

13. Jerry L. Clark, *Thus Spoke Chief Seattle: The Story of an Undocumented Speech*, 18 Prologue Mag. 58 (Spring 1985).

14. Indian Self-Determination and Education Assistance Act of 1975, Pub. L. No. 93-638, 88 Stat. 2203 (1975); Indian Education Act of 1972, Pub. L. No. 92-318, 86 Stat. 235 (1972).

15. Prevention of Significant Air Quality Deterioration, 39 Fed. Reg. 42,510, 42,515 (Dec. 5, 1974) (codified at 40 C.F.R. §52.21(c)(3)(i)).

16. Certification of Pesticide Applicators, 40 Fed. Reg. 11,698, 11,704 (Mar. 12, 1975) (codified at 40 C.F.R. §171.10(a)).

17. S. Rep. No. 95-127 at 34–35 (1977), *as reprinted in* 1977 U.S.C.C.A.N. 1077, 1112–1113.

18. Arnold Reitze, Jr., Air Pollution Law 233–34 (1995)

19. Marjane Ambler, Breaking the Iron Bonds 84, 184 (1990).

20. EPA Policy for Program Implementation on Indian Lands (Dec. 19, 1980).

21. Seminole Nation v. United States, 316 U.S. 286, 297 (1942).

22. Delaware Tribal Business Committee v. Weeks, 430 U.S. 73 (1977).

23. Morton v. Ruiz, 415 U.S. 199 (1974).

24. Gros Ventre Tribe v. United States, 469 F.3d 801 (9th Cir. 2006).

25. EPA Policy for Program Implementation on Indian Lands 4 (Dec. 19, 1980).

26. Fisher v. District Court, 424 U.S. 382 (1976).

27. Santa Clara Pueblo v. Martinez, 436 U.S. 49 (1978).

28. United States v. Wheeler, 435 U.S. 313 (1978).

29. Bryan v. Itasca County, 426 U.S. 373 (1976).

30. Wheeler, 435 U.S. at 323 (emphasis added).

31. Oliphant v. Suquamish Indian Tribe, 435 U.S. 191 (1978).

32. White Mountain Apache Tribe v. Bracker, 448 U.S. 136 (1980).

33. *Nominations of Anne M. Gorsuch and John W. Hernandez, Jr.: Hearing to consider the nominations of Anne M. Gorsuch to be Administrator, EPA, and John W. Hernandez to be Deputy Administrator, Before the S. Comm. on Envtl. & Pub. Works*, 97th Cong. 246, 248 (1981).

34. Americans for Indian Opportunity, Handbook of Federal Responsibility to Indian Communities in Areas of Environmental Protection and Individual Health and Safety (1981).

35. Council of Energy Resource Tribes Resolution No. 81-7, Appropriate Recognition of Tribal Governments (October 28, 1981).

36. 645 F.2d 701 (9th Cir. 1981).

37. Administration of Environmental Programs on Indian Lands, EPA Indian Work Group Discussion Paper, Office of Federal Activities 10 (July 1983).

38. Exec. Order No. 12,401, 48 Fed. Reg. 2309 (Jan. 18, 1983).

39. Report on Reservation and Resource Development and Protection, Task Force Seven: Reservation and Resource Development and Protection, Final Report to the American Indian Policy Review Commission 12, 25 (G.P.O. 1976).

40. Statement on Indian Policy, 1 Pub. Papers 91 (January 24, 1983) (President Ronald Reagan).

41. Merrion v. Jicarilla Apache Tribe, 455 U.S. 130, 137 (1982) (*quoting* Washington v. Confederated Tribes of Colville Indian Reservation, 447 U.S. 134, 152 (1980)).

42. Montana v. United States, 450 U.S. 544, 566 (1981).

43. *William D. Ruckelshaus: Oral History Interview,* at www.epa.gov/history/publications/print/ruck/index.htm (Jan. 1983) (follow hyperlink for *Press, White House and Congress*).

44. *Nomination of William D. Ruckelshaus; Hearing on S. 278 and S. 280, Pub. L. 98-124, Before the Comm. on Envtl. & Pub. Works,* 98th Cong. 1, 280 (1983).

45. Memorandum from Josephine Cooper, Asst. Administrator, Office of External Affairs, to Asst. Administrators and General Counsel (April 12, 1984) (reporting the comments of Jack Ravan, Director, Office of Water).

46. Memorandum from Alvin L. Alm, Deputy Administrator, to Josephine Cooper, Director, Office of External Affairs (Jan. 4, 1984).

47. EPA Policy for the Administration of Environmental Programs on Indian Reservations 2–4 (Nov. 8, 1984).

48. 752 F.2d 1465 (9th Cir. 1985).

49. Permit Regulations for [the Resource Conservation and Recovery Act, the Safe Drinking Water Act, the Clean Water Act and the Clean Air Act], 45 Fed. Reg. 33,290 (May 19, 1980) (codified at 40 C.F.R. pts. 122–125).

50. 42 U.S.C. § 6903(13) (2007).

51. Washington; Phase I and Phase II, Components A and B, Interim Authorization of the State Hazardous Waste Management Program, 48 Fed. Reg. 34,954 (Aug. 2, 1983) (codified at 40 C.F.R. pt. 271).

52. Williams v. Lee, 358 U.S. 217, 220 (1959).

53. William C. Canby, Nutshell on American Indian Law (first ed. 1981).

54. 467 U.S. 837 (1984).

55. Letter from F. Henry Habicht II, Assistant Attorney General, Land and Natural Resources Division, Department of Justice, to Josephine S. Cooper, Assistant Administrator, Office of External Affairs (Sept. 11, 1984).

56. Letter from Frank K. Richardson, Solicitor, U.S. Department of the Interior, to Josephine S. Cooper, Assistant Administrator for External Affairs (Sept. 6, 1984).

57. State of Washington, Department of Ecology v. United States Environmental Protection Agency, 752 F.2d 1465, 1467–68 (9th Cir. 1985) (citations omitted).

58. Washington; Final Authorization of State Hazardous Waste Management Program, 51 Fed. Reg. 3782 (Jan. 30, 1986) (codified at 40 C.F.R. pt. 271).

59. Washington Department of Ecology; Underground Injection Control Program for Indian Lands, 53 Fed. Reg. 43,080 (October 25, 1988) (codified at 40 C.F.R. pt. 147).

60. *Id.* at 43,082 (Testimony by Alan Moomaw, Environmental Coordinator, Confederated Tribes of the Colville Reservation, EPA Public Hearing, July 11, 1984) (emphases added).

61. Moe v. Confederated Salish and Kootenai Tribes of the Flathead Reservation, 425 U.S. 463 (1976); Seymour v. Superintendent of Washington State Penitentiary, 368 U.S. 351 (1961).

62. DeCoteau v. District County Court, 420 U.S. 425, 467 (1975).

63. Federal, Tribal and State Roles in the Protection and Regulation of Reservation Environments 3–4 (July 10, 1991).

Chapter 3

1. *See* THE POISONED WELL: NEW STRATEGIES FOR GROUNDWATER PROTECTION 29 (Eric P. Jorgensen ed. 1989).

2. H.R. REP. No. 1185, 93rd Cong., 2nd Sess. at 1 (1974), *as reprinted in* 1974 U.S.C.C.A.N. 6454.

3. Phillips Petroleum Company v. United States Environmental Protection Agency, 803 F.2d 545, 553 (10th Cir. 1986).

4. H.R. REP. No. 1185, at 9 (1974), *as reprinted in* 1974 U.S.C.C.A.N. 6462.

5. Pub. L. No. 93-523, 88 Stat. 1660 (Dec. 16, 1974) (codified at 42 U.S.C. §300f(10) (emphasis added).

6. State of Washington, Department of Ecology v. United States Environmental Protection Agency, 752 F.2d 1465, 1469 (9th Cir. 1985).

7. McClanahan v. Arizona State Tax Commission, 411 U.S. 164 (1973).

8. National Pollutant Discharge Elimination System, 38 Fed. Reg. 13,528, 13,530 (May 22, 1973) (codified at 40 C.F.R. §125.2(b)).

9. Permit Regulations for [the Resource Conservation and Recovery Act, the Safe Drinking Water Act, the Clean Water Act and the Clean Air Act], 45 Fed. Reg. 33,290, 33,378 (May 19, 1980) (codified at 40 C.F.R. pts. 122–125).

10. Pub. L. No. 101-41, §9, 103 Stat. 88 (June 21, 1989) (codified at 25 U.S.C. §1773g).

11. Pub. L. No. 96-420, §6, 94 Stat. 1793 (Oct. 10, 1980) (codified at 25 U.S.C. §1725(a)).

12. H.R. Con. Res. 108, 83rd Cong., 1st Sess., 67 Stat. B132 (1953).

13. Act of Aug. 15, 1953, Pub. L. No. 280, sec. 4, 67 Stat. 589 (Aug. 15, 1953) (codified at 28 U.S.C. §1360(a)).

14. Bryan v. Itasca County, 426 U.S. 373 (1976).

15. Pub. L. No. 95-190, §8(d), 91 Stat. 1393 (Nov. 16, 1977) (codified at 42 U.S.C. §300j-6(d)).

16. EPA POLICY FOR PROGRAM IMPLEMENTATION ON INDIAN LANDS (Dec. 19, 1980).

17. 42 U.S.C. §300h-4 (2006).

18. Underground Injection Control Program; Federally Administered Programs, 49 Fed. Reg. 20,138, 20,140 (May 11, 1984) (codified at 40 C.F.R. pts. 122, 144, 146–47) (for wells other than Class II); Underground Injection Control Program, 48 Fed. Reg. 2938, 2938 (Jan. 21, 1983) (codified at 40 C.F.R. §122.46) (for Class II wells).

19. Pub. L. No. 99-339, Title III, §302(c), 100 Stat. 42 (June 19, 1986) (codified at 42 U.S.C. §300h-1(e)). ·

20. Underground Injection Control Programs on Indian Lands, 53 Fed. Reg. 43,084 (Oct. 25, 1988) (codified at 40 C.F.R. pt. 147).

21. Montana v. United States, 450 U.S. 544 (1981).

22. Water Pollution Control; Underground Injection Control Programs on Indian Lands, 52 Fed. Reg. 17,684, 17,684 (proposed May 11, 1987).

23. *See generally* GRANT FOREMAN, INDIAN REMOVAL: THE EMIGRATION OF THE FIVE CIVILIZED TRIBES OF INDIANS (1972).

24. CARL COKE RISTER, OIL! TITAN OF THE SOUTHWEST 12–24 (1949).

25. Underground Injection Control, List of States Requiring Programs, 43 Fed. Reg. 43,420 (Sept. 25, 1978).

26. Oklahoma Corporation Commission Underground Injection Control Program Approval, 46 Fed. Reg. 58,488 (Dec. 2, 1981).

27. Act of June 28, 1906, Ch. 3572, §3, 34 Stat. 540, 543 (1906).

28. RISTER, at 199.

29. JOHN JOSEPH MATTHEWS, THE OSAGES: CHILDREN OF THE MIDDLE WATERS 771–84 (1961).

30. Leasing of Osage Reservation Lands for Oil and Gas Mining, 25 C.F.R. pt. 226 (1983).

31. Underground Injection Control Program; Federally-Administered Programs, 49 Fed. Reg. 20,238 (proposed May 11, 1984).

32. Underground Injection Control Program; Federally-Administered Programs, 49 Fed. Reg. 45,292 (Nov. 15, 1984) (codified at 40 C.F.R. pt. 147, subpt. GGG).

33. 803 F.2d 545 (10th Cir. 1986).

34. State of Washington, Department of Ecology v. United States Environmental Protection Agency, 752 F.2d 1465 (9th Cir. 1985).

35. Pub. L. No. 95-190, §8(d), 91 Stat. 1396–97 (Nov. 16, 1977) (codified at 42 U.S.C. §300j-6(c), later changed to §300j-6(d)).

36. Federal Insecticide, Fungicide and Rodenticide Act, Pub. L. No. 95-396, 92 Stat. 834 (1978) (codified at 7 U.S.C. §136u(a)).

37. Superfund Amendments and Reauthorization Act of 1986, Pub. L. No. 99-499, Title II, §207(e), 100 Stat. 1706 (Oct. 17, 1986) (codified at 42 U.S.C. §9626).

38. Pub. L. No. 99-339, Title III, §302(a), 100 Stat. 665 (June 19, 1986) (codified at 42 U.S.C. §300j-11(a)).

39. Pub. L. No. 99-339, Title III, §302(c), 100 Stat. 42 (June 19, 1986) (codified at 42 U.S.C. §300h-1(e)).

40. Safe Drinking Water Act—National Drinking Water Regulations, Underground Injection Control Program; Indian Lands, 53 Fed. Reg. 37,395, 37,400 (Sept. 26, 1988) (codified at 40 C.F.R. pts. 35, 124, 141, 143–146).

41. Underground Injection Control Programs for Certain Indian Lands, 53 Fed. Reg. 43,096 (Oct. 25, 1988) (codified at 40 C.F.R. pt. 147).

42. Exec. Order No. 709 (1907) (reprinted in 3 C. KAPPLER, INDIAN AFFAIRS: LAWS AND TREATIES 669 (1913)).

43. Pittsburg & Midway Coal Company v. Yazzie, 909 F.2d 1387 (10th Cir.), cert. denied, 498 U.S. 1012 (1990).

44. Hagen v. Utah, 510 U.S. 399, 413 (1994).

45. 198 F.3d 1224 (10th Cir. 2000).

46. Oklahoma Tax Commission v. Sac & Fox Nation, 508 U.S. 114 (1993).

47. Oklahoma Tax Commission v. Citizen Band of Potawatomi Indian Tribe, 498 U.S. 505 (1991).

48. 52 F.3d 1531 (10th Cir. 1995).

49. 522 U.S. 520 (1998).

50. United States v. Arrieta, 436 F.3d 1246 (10Th Cir.), cert. denied, 126 S.Ct. 2368 (2006); United States v. M.C., 311 F. Supp.2d 1281 (D. N.M. 2004).

Chapter 4

1. 1987 Clean Water Act Amendments, P.L. No. 100-4, Title V, §506, 101 Stat. 76 (Feb. 4, 1987) (codified at 33 U.S.C. §1377(e)).

2. 33 U.S.C. §1377(e) (2007).

3. 42 U.S.C. §300j-11(b)(1)(B) (2007) (emphasis added).

4. Amendments to the Water Quality Standards Regulations that Pertain to Standards on Indian Reservations, 54 Fed. Reg. 39,098, 39,101 (proposed Sept. 22, 1989).

5. Oversight Hearing Before the Senate Select Committee on Indian Affairs on the Administration of Indian Programs by the EPA, June 23, 1989.

6. Cherokee Nation v. Georgia, 30 U.S. (5 Pet.) 1, 16 (1831).

7. Johnson v. McIntosh, 21 U.S. (8 Wheat.) 543 (1823).

8. McClanahan v. Arizona Tax Commission, 411 U.S. 164, 172 (1980).

9. United States v. Wheeler, 435 U.S. 313 (1978).

10. Washington v. Confederated Tribes of the Colville Indian Reservation, 447 U.S. 134, 152 (1980).

11. Merrion v. Jicarilla Apache Tribe, 455 U.S. 130, 137 (1982) (citations omitted).

12. 435 U.S. 191 (1978).

13. *Id.* at 210–11 (quoting Ex parte Crow Dog, 109 U.S. 556, 571 (1883)).

14. 450 U.S. 544 (1981).

15. Second Treaty of Fort Laramie, 15 Stat. 649 (1868).

16. Report on Federal, State, and Tribal Jurisdiction, Task Force Four: Federal, State, and Tribal Jurisdiction, Final Report to the American Indian Policy Review Commission 93 (GPO 1976).

17. 450 U.S. at 565–66 (citations omitted).

18. Geer v. Connecticut, 161 U.S. 519 (1896).

19. Administration of Environmental Programs on Indian Lands, EPA Indian Work Group Discussion Paper, Office of Federal Activities 91 (July 1983).

20. 492 U.S. 408 (1989).

21. At the time of the case, the name of the Tribe and its reservation was spelled Yakima. The Tribe later changed the spelling to Yakama.

22. Amendments to the Water Quality Standards Regulations that Pertain to Standards on Indian Reservations, 56 Fed. Reg. 64,876, 64,878 (Dec. 12, 1991) (codified at 40 C.F.R. pt. 131).

23. *Id.* at 64,879.

24. 1855 Treaty of Hell Gate, 12 Stat. 975, Art. 2 (1855–1863).

25. Burton M. Smith, The Politics of Allotment on the Flathead Indian Reservation 5, 13–24 (1995).

26. Letter from Penny and Tom Parsons, residents of Ronan, Montana, to John Wardell, Director, EPA Montana Office 1–2 (Sept. 8, 1993).

27. EPA Decision Document: Approval of Confederated Salish and Kootenai Tribes Application for Treatment as a State under Section 303 of the Clean Water Act 10–11 (Feb. 27, 1995).

28. *Id.* at 8 (citations omitted).

29. Treatment of Indian Tribes as States for Purposes of Sections 308, 309, 401, 402, and 405 of the Clean Water Act, 58 Fed. Reg. 67,966 (Dec. 22, 1993) (codified at 40 C.F.R. pts. 122, 123, 124 and 501).

30. James M. Grijalva, *Where are the Tribal Water Quality Standards and TMDLs?*, 18 NATURAL RESOURCES & ENVIRONMENT 63 (Fall 2003).

31. Letter from Lawrence Jensen, EPA General Counsel, to Dave Frohnmayer, Attorney General, State of Oregon (Sept. 9, 1988).

32. State of Montana v. United States Environmental Protection Agency, 941 F. Supp. 945 (D. Mont. 1996), *aff'd*, 137 F.3d 1135 (9th Cir.), *cert. denied*, 525 U.S. 921 (1998).

33. Lakewood v. Plain Dealer Pub. Co. 486 U.S. 750 (1988).

34. 137 F.3d 1135 (9th Cir.), *cert. denied*, 525 U.S. 921 (1998).

35. 520 U.S. 438 (1997).

36. City of Albuquerque v. Browner, 97 F.3d 415 (10th Cir. 1996), *cert. denied*, 522 U.S. 965 (1997).

37. Colville Confederated Tribes v. Walton, 647 F.2d 42 (9th Cir. 1981).

38. Brief of Amici Curiae States of Arizona, California, Colorado, Florida, Idaho, Michigan, Nebraska, Nevada, South Dakota, Utah, and Wisconsin, in Support of Petition for Writ of Certiorari, State of Montana v. United States Environmental Protection Agency 10–11 (1998) (No. 97-1929).

39. 33 U.S.C. § 1341(a) (2007).

40. Arkansas v. Oklahoma, 503 U.S. 91 (1992).

41. 97 F.3d 415 (10th Cir. 1996), *cert. denied*, 522 U.S. 965 (1997).

42. 133 Cong. Rec. S1003 (daily ed. Jan. 21, 1987) (statement of Sen. Burdick).

43. City of Albuquerque v. Browner, 865 F. Supp. 733, 741–42 (D. N.M. 1993), *aff'd*, 97 F.3d 415 (10th Cir. 1996), *cert. denied*, 522 U.S. 965 (1997).

44. American Indian Religious Freedom Act, 42 U.S.C. § 1996 (2007).

Chapter 5

1. Sierra Club v. Ruckelshaus, 344 F. Supp. 253 (D. D.C. 1972), *aff'd per curiam*, 4 ERC 1815 (D.C. Cir 1972), *aff'd by an equally divided Court, sub nom.* Fri v. Sierra Club, 412 U.S. 541 (1973).

2. Approval and Promulgation of Implementation Plans; Prevention of Significant Air Quality Deterioration, 38 Fed. Reg. 18,986, 18,986 (proposed July 16, 1973).

3. Prevention of Significant Air Quality Deterioration, 39 Fed. Reg. 31,000 (proposed Aug. 27, 1974).

4. Brief of Amici Curiae, the Jicarilla Apache Tribe of Indians, the Committee to Save Black Mesa, Inc., the Oljato Chapter of the Navajo Tribe, Paul Goodman, Mary Gillis, Jackson Gillis, Della Marie G. Black, & Begay Bitsinnie v. Sierra Club 4–5 (No. 72–804) (citations omitted).

5. William R. Baldassin & John T. McDermott, *Jurisdiction Over Non-Indians: An Opinion of the Opinion*, 1 AMERICAN INDIAN LAW REVIEW 13, 13 (1973).

6. Report on Federal, State, and Tribal Jurisdiction, Task Force Four: Federal, State, and Tribal Jurisdiction, Final Report To The American Indian Policy Review Commission 88, 100 (GPO 1976).

7. Prevention of Significant Air Quality Deterioration, 39 Fed. Reg. 42,510 (Dec. 5, 1974) (codified at 40 C.F.R. pt. 52).

8. Sierra Club v. United States Environmental Protection Agency, 540 F.2d 1114 (D.C. Cir. 1976), *vacated and remanded sub nom*, Montana Power Company v. United States Environmental Protection Agency, 434 U.S. 809 (1977).

9. EPA Survey of American Indian Environmental Protection Needs on Reservation Lands: 1986 at 6 (1986).

10. Marjane Ambler, Breaking The Iron Bonds 183 (1990).

11. *Suggested Language for Inclusion in Proposed Amendments to the Clean Air Act: Hearing on S. 252 Before the S. Comm. on the Environment and Public Works*, 95th Congress 862 (1977) (letter from Lonnie C. Von Renner for the Northern Cheyenne Tribal Council).

12. Clean Air Act Amendments of 1977, Pub. L. No. 95-95, title I, § 127(a), 91 Stat. 733 (Aug. 7, 1977) (codified at 42 U.S.C. § 7474(c)) (emphasis added).

13. S. Rpt. No. 95-127 at 35 (1977), *as reprinted in* 1977 U.S.C.C.A.N. 1077, 1113.

14. 645 F.2d 701 (9th Cir.). *cert. denied sub nom.*, Crow Tribe of Indians v. United States Environmental Protection Agency, 454 U.S. 1081 (1981).

15. 42 U.S.C. § 7474(e) (2007).

16. S. Rpt. No. 95-127 at 36 (1977), *as reprinted in* 1977 U.S.C.C.A.N. 1077, 1114.

17. 123 Cong. Rec. H8665 (1977) (statement of Rep. Rogers).

18. Timothy J. Sullivan, *The Difficulties of Mandatory Negotiation (the Colstrip Power Plant Case), in* Lawrence Susskind, Lawrence Backow, and Michael Wheeler, Eds., Resolving Environmental Regulatory Disputes 68 (1983).

19. Redesignation of the Yavapai-Apache Reservation to a PSD Class I Area; State of Arizona; Dispute Resolution, 61 Fed. Reg. 56,450, 56,460 (Nov. 1, 1996) (quoting letter from Fife Symington, Governor of Arizona, to Carol Browner, EPA Administrator (Oct. 3, 1995)).

20. H.R. Rep. No. 95-294 at 147 (1977).

21. 151 F.3d 1205 (9th Cir. 1998).

22. 42 U.S.C. § 7474(b)(2) (2007) (emphasis added).

23. 1977 Clean Air Act Amendments to Prevent Significant Deterioration, 43 Fed. Reg. 26,388 (June 19, 1978) (codified at 40 C.F.R. § 52.21(g)(1)).

24. Approval and Promulgation of State Implementation Plans: Washington, 56 Fed. Reg. 14,861 (April 12, 1991) (codified at 40 C.F.R. § 52.2497(c)) (Spokane Tribe); Approval and Promulgation of State Implementation Plans; PSD Redesignation—Fort Peck Reservation, 49 Fed. Reg. 4734 (Feb. 8, 1984) (codified at 40 C.F.R. § 52.1382(c)(4)); Approval and Promulgation of State Implementation Plans, PSD Redesignation; Flathead Reservation, 47 Fed. Reg. 23,927 (June 2, 1982) (codified at 40 C.F.R. § 52.1382(c)(3)).

25. Indian Tribes: Air Quality Planning and Management, 63 Fed. Reg. 7254 (Feb. 12, 1998) (codified at 40 C.F.R. pts. 9, 35, 49, 50, and 81).

26. 42 U.S.C. § 7601(d)(4) (2007) (emphasis added).

27. Indian Tribes: Air Quality Planning and Management, 63 Fed. Reg. at 7264–65 (codified at 40 C.F.R. § 49.11).

28. Federal Implementation Plan Under the Clean Air Act for Certain Trust Lands of the Forest County Potawatomi Community Reservation if Designated as a PSD Class I Area; State of Wisconsin, 71 Fed. Reg. 75,694 (proposed Dec. 18, 2006).

29. Source-Specific Federal Implementation Plan for Navajo Generating Station; Navajo Nation, 71 Fed. Reg. 53,639 (proposed Sept. 12, 2006); Source-Specific Federal Implementation Plan for Four Corners Power Plant; Navajo Nation, 71 Fed. Reg. 53,631 (proposed Sept. 12, 2006); Review of New Sources and Modifications in Indian Country, 71 Fed. Reg. 48,696 (proposed Aug. 21, 2006); Federal Implementation Plans Under the Clean Air Act for Indian Reservations in Idaho, Oregon and Washington, 70 Fed. Reg. 18,074 (April 8, 2005) (codified at 40 C.F.R. pts. 9 and 49).

30. Nance v. United States Environmental Protection Agency, 645 F.2d 701, 715 (9th Cir.), *cert. denied sub nom.*, Crow Tribe of Indians v. United States Environmental Protection Agency, 454 U.S. 1081 (1981) (citations omitted) (emphasis added).

31. 419 U.S. 544 (1975).

32. United States v. Mazurie, 487 F.2d 14, 19 (10th Cir. 1973), *rev'd,* 419 U.S. 544 (1975).

33. *See generally* ROBERT A. WILLIAMS, JR., LIKE A LOADED WEAPON: THE REHNQUIST COURT, INDIAN RIGHTS, AND THE LEGAL HISTORY OF RACISM IN AMERICA (2005).

34. 42 U.S.C. §7601(d)(2)(B) (2007) (emphasis added).

35. 520 U.S. 438 (1997).

36. Montana v. United States Environmental Protection Agency, 941 F.Supp. 945, 951 (D. Mont. 1996), *aff'd,* 137 F.3d 1135 (9th Cir.), *cert. denied,* 525 U.S. 921 (1998).

37. S. REP. No. 101–228 at 79 (1989).

38. 211 F.3d 1280 (D.C. Cir. 2000), *cert. denied sub nom,* Michigan v. United States Environmental Protection Agency, 532 U.S. 970 (2001).

39. S. 1630, 101st Cong. §113(a) (1990); H.R. 2323, 101st Cong. §604 (1989).

40. 42 U.S.C. §7410(o) (2007).

41. Rice v. Rehner, 463 U.S. 713 (1983).

42. S. 1630, 101st Cong., §111 (1990); H.R. 2323, 101st Cong., §604 (1989).

43. Bugenig v. Hoopa Valley Tribe, 229 F.3d 1210 (9th Cir. 2000), *rev'd,* 266 F.3d 1201 (9th Cir. 2001) (en banc), *cert. denied,* 535 U.S. 927 (2002).

44. 266 F.3d 1201 (9th Cir. 2001) (en banc), *cert. denied,* 535 U.S. 927 (2002).

45. Duro v. Reina, 495 U.S. 676 (1990).

46. Act of Nov. 5, 1990, §8077(b), 104 Stat. 1892 (temporary); Act of Oct 28, 1991, 105 Stat. 646.

47. 25 U.S.C. §1301(2) (2007) (emphasis added).

48. 137 Cong. Rec. S9446 (daily ed. April 25, 1991) (statement of Sen. Inouye).

49. 541 U.S. 193 (2004).

50. United States v. Sandoval, 231 U.S. 28 (1913).

51. Oklahoma Tax Commission v. Citizen Band Potawatomi Indian Tribe of Oklahoma, 498 U.S. 505 (1991).

52. Chevron U.S.A., Inc. v. Natural Resources Defense Council, Inc., 467 U.S. 837, 863 (1984).

53. Federal Operating Permits Program, 62 Fed. Reg. 13,748 (proposed March 21, 1997).

54. Federal Operating Permits Program, 64 Fed. Reg. 8247 (Feb. 19, 1999) (codified at 40 C.F.R. pt. 71).

55. South Dakota v. Yankton Sioux Tribe, 522 U.S. 329 (1998).

56. 268 F.3d 1075 (D.C. Cir. 2001).

Chapter 6

1. EPA MUNICIPAL SOLID WASTE IN THE UNITED STATES: 2005 FACTS AND FIGURES 6 (2005).

2. EPA SURVEY OF AMERICAN INDIAN ENVIRONMENTAL PROTECTION NEEDS ON RESERVATION LANDS: 1986 vii (1986).

3. Pub. L. No. 103-399, § 4, 101 Stat. 4166 (Oct. 22, 1994) (codified at 25 U.S.C. § 3903).

4. INDIAN HEALTH SERVICE AND EPA REPORT ON THE STATUS OF OPEN DUMPS ON INDIAN LANDS 1 (1988).

5. 42 U.S.C. § 4332(C) (2007).

6. Davis v. Morton, 469 F.2d 593 (10th Cir. 1972).

7. 867 F.2d 1094 (8th Cir. 1989).

8. Blue Legs v. United States Environmental Protection Agency, 668 F. Supp. 1328 (D. S.D. 1987).

9. 42 U.S.C. § 6973(a) (2007).

10. 42 U.S.C. § 6945(c)(2)(a) (2007).

11. 42 U.S.C. § 6903(15), (13) (2007).

12. *See* James M. Grijalva, *The Tribal Sovereign as Citizen: Protecting Indian Country Health and Welfare Through Federal Environmental Citizen Suits*, 12 MICHIGAN JOURNAL OF RACE AND LAW 33 (2006).

13. *See, e.g.,* Thomas Daschle, *Dances with Garbage*, CHRISTIAN SCIENCE MONITOR, Feb. 14, 1991, at 36; Conger Beasley, Jr., *Dances With Garbage*, 2 E MAG., Nov./ Dec. 1991; Mary Hager & Bill Harlan, *Dances With Garbage*, NEWSWEEK, Apr. 29, 1991, at 36.

14. Community Right to Know Reporting Requirements, 55 Fed. Reg. 30,632, 60,641 (July 26, 1990) (codified at 40 C.F.R. §§ 350.1, 356.20, 370.2, 372.3).

15. Memorandum from William K. Reilly, EPA Administrator, to Assistant Administrators et al. (July 10, 1991).

16. Resource Recovery Act of 1970, Pub. L. No. 89-272, title II, § 1004, amended by Pub. L. No. 94-580, § 2, 90 Stat. 2798 (Oct 21, 1976) (codified at 42 U.S.C. § 6903(13)).

17. Resource Conservation and Recovery Act of 1976, Pub. L. No. 94-580, Title II, § 1004, 90 Stat. 2795, 2800 (Oct. 21, 1976) (codified at 42 U.S.C. § 6903(13)).

18. Federal Water Pollution Control Act of 1972, Pub. L. No. 92-500, § 2, 86 Stat. 880 (Oct. 18, 1972) (codified at 33 U.S.C. § 1362(4)).

19. Safe Drinking Water Act of 1974, Pub. L. No. 93-523, § 2(a)(10), 88 Stat.1660 (Dec. 16, 1974) (codified at 42 U.S.C. § 300f(10)).

20. Federal Facility Compliance Act of 1992, Pub. L. No. 102-386, Title I, § 102(a), (b), 106 Stat.1505, 1506 (Oct. 6, 1992) (codified at 42 U.S.C. § 6961(a)).

21. Dan McGovern, The Campo Indian Landfill War: The Fight for Gold in California's Garbage, chaps. 7, 8 (1995).

22. Cheyenne River Sioux Tribe; Tentative Adequacy Determination of Tribal Municipal Solid Waste Permit Program, 59 Fed. Reg. 16,642 (April 7, 1994).

23. Campo Band of Mission Indians; Tentative Determination of Adequacy of Tribal Municipal Solid Waste Permit Program, 59 Fed. Reg. 24,422 (May 11, 1994).

24. Nevada v. Hicks, 533 U.S. 353 (2001).

25. Campo Band of Mission Indians; Final Determination of Adequacy of Tribal Municipal Solid Waste Permit Program, 60 Fed. Reg. 21,191 (May 1, 1995).

26. 467 U.S. 837 (1984).

27. California v. Cabazon Band of Mission Indians, 480 U.S. 202 (1987).

28. Subtitle D Regulated Facilities; State/Tribal Permit Program Determination of Adequacy; State/Tribal Implementation Rule (STIR), 61 Fed. Reg. 2584 (proposed Jan. 26, 1996).

29. Authorization of Indian Tribes' Hazardous Waste Program Under RCRA Subtitle C, 61 Fed. Reg. 30,472 (proposed June 14, 1996).

30. 100 F.3d 147 (D.C. Cir. 1996).

31. *Id.* at 150.

32. H. Hoover, A Yankton Sioux Tribal Land History 1 (1995).

33. H. Hoover, A History of Yankton Tribal Governance 1 (1995).

34. South Dakota; Final Determination of Adequacy of State/Tribal Municipal Solid Waste Permit Program, 58 Fed. Reg. 52,486 (Oct. 8, 1993).

35. DeCoteau v. District County Court, 420 U.S. 425 (1975).

36. Rosebud Sioux Tribe v. Kneip, 430 U.S. 584 (1977).

37. State v. Greger, 559 N.W.2d 854 (S.D. 1977); State v. Thompson, 355 N.W.2d 349 (S.D. 1984); State v. Williamson, 211 N.W.2d 182 (S.D. 1973); Wood v. Jameson, 130 N.W.2d 95 (S.D. 1964).

38. Weddell v. Meierhenry, 636 F.2d 211 (8th Cir. 1980).

39. South Dakota; Tentative Determination of Adequacy of State's Municipal Solid Waste Permit Program over Non-Indian Lands for the Former Lands of the Yankton Sioux, Lake Traverse (Sisseton-Wahpeton) and Parts of the Rosebud Indian Reservations, 59 Fed. Reg. 16,647 (April 7, 1994).

40. Yankton Sioux Tribe v. Southern Missouri Waste Management District, 890 F. Supp. 878 (D. S.D. 1995), *aff'd*, 99 F.3d 1439 (8th Cir. 1996), *rev'd sub nom*, South Dakota v. Yankton Sioux Tribe, 522 U.S. 329 (1998).

41. Choate v. Trapp, 224 U.S. 665, 675 (1912).

42. South Dakota; Final Determination of Adequacy of State's Municipal Solid Waste Permit Program Over Non-Indian Lands for the Former Lands of the Yankton Sioux, Lake Traverse (Sisseton-Wahpeton) and Parts of the Rosebud Indian Reservation, 61 Fed. Reg. 48,683 (Sept. 16, 1996).

43. Yankton Sioux Tribe v. United States Environmental Protection Agency, 950 F. Supp. 1471 (D. S.D. 1996).

44. 5 U.S.C. § 553 (2007).

45. Yankton Sioux Tribe v. Southern Missouri Waste Management District. 99 F.3d 1439 (8th Cir. 1996), *rev'd sub nom*, South Dakota v. Yankton Sioux Tribe, 522 U.S. 329 (1998).

46. 510 U.S. 399 (1994).

47. David H. Getches, *Conquering The Cultural Frontier: The New Subjectivism of the Supreme Court in Indian Law*, 84 CALIFORNIA LAW REVIEW 1573, 1642 (1996) (quoting Justice Antonin Scalia).

48. Federal Power Commission v. Tuscarora Indian Nation, 362 U.S. 99, 142 (1960) (Black, J., dissenting).

49. Department of Taxation and Finance of New York v. Milhelm Attea & Brothers, Inc., 512 U.S. 61 (1994).

50. 522 U.S. 329 (1998).

51. FELIX COHEN, HANDBOOK OF FEDERAL INDIAN LAW 77 (2005).

52. S. REP. accompanying S. 1538 from the Committee on Indian Affairs (Feb. 1, 1894), *quoted in* Yankton Sioux Tribe v. Southern Missouri Waste Management District, 890 F. Supp. at 884.

53. Rosebud Sioux Tribe v. Kneip, 430 U.S. 584, 618, 629 (1977) (Marshall, J. dissenting).

54. Solem v. Bartlett, 465 U.S. 463, 468 (1984) (footnote omitted).

55. Hill v. Alliance Building Company, 60 N.W. 752 (S.D. 1894).

56. Council of the Yankton Indians (Dec. 10, 1892) (emphasis added), *quoted in* South Dakota v. Yankton Sioux Tribe, 522 U.S. at 346–47.

57. Yankton Sioux Tribe v. United States, 224 Ct. Cl. 62 (1980).

58. Council of the Yankton Indians (Dec. 17, 1892), *quoted in* South Dakota v. Yankton Sioux Tribe, 522 U.S. at 342–43.

59. Cherokee Nation v. Georgia, 30 U.S. (5 Pet.) 1 (1931).

60. United States v. Sioux Nation of Indians, 448 U.S. 371, 435 (1980) (Rehnquist, J., dissenting).

61. South Dakota v. Yankton Sioux Tribe, 522 U.S. at 357 (quoting DeCoteau, 420 U.S. at 449).

62. ROBERT A. WILLIAMS, JR., LIKE A LOADED WEAPON: THE REHNQUIST COURT, INDIAN RIGHTS, AND THE LEGAL HISTORY OF RACISM IN AMERICA 122 (2005).

Chapter 7

1. EPA POLICY FOR PROGRAM IMPLEMENTATION ON INDIAN LANDS 1–2 (Dec. 19, 1980) (emphases added).

2. Water Quality Standards for the Colville Indian Reservation in the State of Washington, 54 Fed. Reg. 28,622, 28,622 (July 6, 1989) (codified at 40 C.F.R. § 131.35).

3. U.S. EPA, Treatment in the Same Manner as States/Program Approval Matrix (1998).

4. PROTECTING PUBLIC HEALTH AND WATER RESOURCES IN INDIAN COUNTRY: A STRATEGY FOR EPA/TRIBAL PARTNERSHIP 11 (1998).

5. Federal Water Quality Standards for Waters in Indian Country, http://www.epa.gov/waterscience/standards/tribal/ (last visited July 31, 2007).

6. State, Tribal & Territorial Standards; Tribal Water Quality Standards approved by EPA, http://www.epa.gov/waterscience/standards/wqslibrary/tribes.html (last visited July 31, 2007).

7. 25 U.S.C. § 450f (2007) ("638 contracts").

8. 2001 Appropriation Act, Pub. L. No. 107–73, 115 Stat. 686 (2001).

9. Notice of Guidance Issuance; Direct Implementation Tribal Cooperative Agreements (DITCAs) Guidance, 70 Fed. Reg. 1440 (Jan. 7, 2005).

10. David H. Getches, *Beyond Indian Law: The Rehnquist Court's Pursuit of States' Rights, Color-Blind Justice and Mainstream Values*, 86 Minnesota Law Review 267 (2001).

11. *William D. Ruckelshaus: Oral History Interview*, at http://www.epa.gov/history/publications/ruck/13.htm (Jan. 1983).

12. Nevada v. Hicks, 533 U.S. 353 (2001).

13. Atkinson Trading Company v. Shirley, 532 U.S. 645 (2001).

14. Federal Implementation Plans Under the Clean Air Act for Indian Reservations in Idaho, Oregon and Washington, 70 Fed. Reg. 18,074 (April 8, 2005) (codified at 40 C.F.R. pts. 9 and 49).

15. Announcement of the Delegation of Partial Administrative Authority for Implementation of Federal Implementation Plan for the Nez Perce Reservation to the Nez Perce Tribe, 70 Fed. Reg. 54,638 (Sept. 16, 2005) (codified at 40 C.F.R. pt 49); Announcement of the Delegation of Partial Administrative Authority for Implementation of Federal Implementation Plan for the Umatilla Indian Reservation to the Confederated Tribes of the Umatilla Indian Reservation, 71 Fed. Reg. 60,852 (Oct. 17, 2006) (codified at 40 C.F.R. pt 49).

16. Source-Specific Federal Implementation Plan for Navajo Generating Station; Navajo Nation, 71 Fed. Reg. 53,639 (proposed Sept. 12, 2006); Source-Specific Federal Implementation Plan for Four Corners Power Plant; Navajo Nation, 71 Fed. Reg. 53,631 (proposed Sept. 12, 2006).

17. Federal Implementation Plan Under the Clean Air Act for Certain Trust Lands of the Forest County Potawatomi Community Reservation if Designated as a PSD Class I Area; State of Wisconsin, 71 Fed. Reg. 75,694 (proposed Dec. 18, 2006).

18. Review of New Sources and Modifications in Indian Country, 71 Fed. Reg. 48,696 (proposed Aug. 21, 2006).

19. Title I, ch. 1, §3.A., Navajo Nation Code (2002).

20. National Environmental Justice Advisory Council Report on Meaningful Involvement and Fair Treatment by Tribal Programs (2004).

21. Margaret Knox, *Their Mother's Keeper*, Sierra, March/April 1993, at 83.

22. Dean B. Suagee, *Turtle's War Party: An Indian Allegory on Environmental Justice*, 9 Journal of Environmental Law and Litigation 461 (1994).

23. Agenda, National Tribal Environmental Council Executive Committee Meeting with United States Environmental Protection Agency Administrator Michael O. Leavitt 12 (Jan. 20, 2004).

24. Anna Fleder & Darren J. Ranco, *Tribal Environmental Sovereignty: Culturally Appropriate Protection or Paternalism?*, 19 Journal of Natural Resources & Environmental Law 25 (2004–05); Robert Williams, Jr., *Large Binocular Telescopes, Red Squirrel Piñatas, and Apache Sacred Mountains: Decolonizing Environmental Law in a Multicultural World*, 96 West Virginia Law Review 1133 (1994).

25. Title I, ch. 1, sec. §3.J., Navajo Nation Code (2002).

26. Dean B. Suagee, *Tribal Self-Determination and Environmental Federalism: Cultural Values as a Force for Sustainability*, 3 Widener Law Symposium Journal 229, 233–34 (1998).

INDEX